CRACKING THE EGYPTIAN CODE

D1355066

CRACKING THE EGYPTIAN CODE

THE REVOLUTIONARY LIFE OF JEAN-FRANÇOIS CHAMPOLLION

ANDREW ROBINSON

With 66 illustrations, 16 in colour

Thames & Hudson

On the cover

Front:
Leon Cogniet, *Portrait of Jean-Paul Champollion*,
1831 (oil on canvas). Louvre, Paris, France/
Bridgeman Images.

Back:
Page from Champollion's Egyptian notebooks.
Bibliothèque Nationale de France, Paris.

Background:
Last line of the Rosetta Stone (in hieroglyphic,
demotic and Greek), drawing by Thomas Young,
1819. Photo Andrew Robinson. (Image shown in
reflection on back cover.)

First published in the United Kingdom in 2012
by Thames & Hudson Ltd, 181A High Holborn,
London WC1V 7QX

This compact paperback edition first published
in 2018

Cracking the Egyptian Code © 2012 and 2018
Andrew Robinson

All Rights Reserved. No part of this publication
may be reproduced or transmitted in any form
or by any means, electronic or mechanical,
including photocopy, recording or any other
information storage and retrieval system, without
prior permission in writing from the publisher.

British Library Cataloguing-in-Publication Data
A catalogue record for this book is available from
the British Library

ISBN 978-0-500-29417-8

Printed and bound at MBM Print SCS Ltd, Glasgow

To find out about all our publications, please visit
www.thamesandhudson.com. There you can
subscribe to our e-newsletter, browse or download
our current catalogue, and buy any titles that are
in print.

CONTENT

For my wife Dipli
'moromere'

ACKNOWLEDGMENTS

Jean-François Champollion has intrigued me for over two decades, as I wrote books on ancient and modern scripts, on archaeological decipherment, on genius, and on two remarkable individuals. The first of these was Michael Ventris – the 20th-century decipherer of Minoan Linear B, Europe's earliest readable script. Ventris not only admired Champollion: he too became obsessed with an undeciphered writing system as a schoolboy. The second figure was the scientist Thomas Young, a polymath who was Champollion's leading rival in the decipherment of the Egyptian hieroglyphs.

Many scholars helped me generously in my research for those books. With this biography of Champollion, John Baines, professor of Egyptology at the University of Oxford, went to considerable trouble to locate an inaccessible publication about Champollion and to answer various queries. John Ray, professor of Egyptology at the University of Cambridge, has, over the years and through his writings, been a source of stimulating ideas. The London Library proved invaluable for its collection of 19th-century books by and about Champollion. The library of the Egypt Exploration Society was also useful. I should also like to thank Des McTernan, curator of early printed books in French at the British Library, for his sustained attempt to locate the library's missing copy of Champollion's rarest publication, printed in Grenoble in 1821. Sadly, he did not succeed in finding it – thereby, perhaps, inadvertently fulfilling its author's desire to suppress this controversial work.*

I am grateful to my long-time editor at Thames & Hudson, Colin Ridler, for sharing my enthusiasm for a book about Champollion. Its production was expertly overseen by Sam Wythe, Sally Nicholls, Alice Reid, Phil Cleaver, Rachel Heley and Ed Pearce.

*Note added to the paperback edition
Happily, the missing copy turned up in 2014 and has been restored to the library's shelves.

PROLOGUE: EGYPTOMANIA

In 1821 a pioneering exhibition about ancient Egypt opened in Piccadilly, in the heart of fashionable London. Egyptomania, encouraged by Napoleon Bonaparte's dramatic invasion of Egypt two decades earlier, was catching on in Britain as it had in Paris. The exhibition's venue, known as the Egyptian Hall, was a private museum of natural history. It had been built on Piccadilly in 1812, in an exotic 'Egyptian style', and featured an exterior decorated with Egyptian motifs, two statues of Isis and Osiris, and mysterious hieroglyphs. On display to the public, for the first time in Europe, was a magnificently carved and painted ancient Egyptian tomb, which had been discovered and opened three years earlier in the area of ancient Thebes (modern Luxor) that would later be known as the Valley of the Kings. At the inauguration ceremony, held on 1 May 1821, the tomb's Italian discoverer, Giovanni Belzoni – a former circus strongman turned flamboyant excavator of Egypt, who was about to become one of the most famous figures in London – appeared wrapped in mummy bandages before a huge crowd. Some 2,000 visitors

Egyptian Hall, in Piccadilly, London, as seen in the 1820s. An early example of British Egyptomania, its facade was decorated with supposedly Egyptian statues and hieroglyphs.

paid half a crown to see the tomb on the opening day; a reviewer in *The Times* newspaper called the exhibition a 'singular combination and skilful arrangement of objects so new and in themselves so striking'.

Of course, what was on view was not the tomb itself, but rather a one-sixth scale model, which measured over 15 metres (50 feet) in length, complemented by a full-sized reproduction of two of the tomb's most impressive chambers. The bas-reliefs and polychrome wall decoration, showing gods, goddesses, animals, the life of the pharaoh and manifold coloured hieroglyphs, had been re-created from wax moulds taken of the original reliefs, and from paintings made on the spot by Belzoni and his compatriot Alessandro Ricci, a physician turned artist. However, some of the objects on display were originals, such as two mummies and a piece of rope used by the last party of ancient Egyptians to enter the tomb. The *pièce de résistance* – indeed, one of the finest Egyptian works of art ever discovered – was an empty, lidless, white alabaster sarcophagus, almost 3 metres (10 feet) in length, which arrived by boat from Egypt in August, well after the exhibition's inauguration. Translucent when a lamp was placed inside it, with a full-length portrait of a goddess on the bottom, where the royal mummy would once have lain, the sarcophagus had sides carved, inside and out, with hieroglyphs, exquisitely inlaid with a greenish-blue compound made from copper sulphate.

When the exhibition closed, the sarcophagus was deposited in the British Museum. After the museum's trustees prevaricated about purchase and eventually refused the object in 1824, it was sold for £2,000 to the architect Sir John Soane, who added it to the celebrated and curious art collection he kept in his private house not far from the British Museum. There, almost two centuries later, one can still see the sarcophagus as the centrepiece of the unique 'Egyptian crypt' in the labyrinthine basement of what is now Sir John Soane's Museum.

To honour and publicize his new acquisition, and also to assist the widow of Belzoni (who had died in 1823) Soane arranged three separate evening receptions in 1825, specially illuminated by a manufacturer of stained glass and lighting appliances. A visiting artist, Benjamin Robert Haydon, described one of these social occasions in a vivid letter to a female friend that captures the London public's growing fascination with ancient Egypt:

The first person I met ... was Coleridge ... [then] I was pushed up against Turner, the landscape painter with his red face and white waistcoat, and ... was carried off my legs, and irretrievably bustled to where the sarcophagus lay ... It was the finest fun imaginable to see the people come into the Library after wandering about below, amidst tombs and capitals, and shafts, and noseless heads, with a sort of expression of delighted relief at finding themselves among the living, and with coffee and cake. Fancy delicate ladies of fashion dipping their pretty heads into an old mouldy, fusty hierogliphicked coffin, blessing their stars at its age, wondering whom it contained ... Just as I was beginning to meditate, the Duke of Sussex, with a star on his breast, and asthma inside it, came squeezing and wheezing along the narrow passage, driving all the women before him like a Blue-Beard, and putting his royal head into the coffin, added his wonder to the wonder of the rest.

Whose tomb was it that Belzoni had opened in 1817, and how old was the sarcophagus of its erstwhile occupant? No one had more than the vaguest idea, because no one could read the hieroglyphs. Accurate knowledge of hieroglyphic script had vanished since its last usage by Egyptian priests in the 4th century AD, a millennium and a half before Napoleon's invasion.

To begin with, Belzoni described it as the tomb of the sacred bull Apis, because he had discovered in one chamber the embalmed carcass of a bull. But by the time of his 1821 exhibition he had changed his mind: he advertised it as 'Presumed to be The Tomb of Psammis', a hypothetical pharaoh.

This name, Psammis, had come from Dr Thomas Young, a professional physician, a leading physicist and mathematician (who served as foreign secretary of the Royal Society), and a gifted linguist. In the period 1814–19, Young had taken the first correct steps towards deciphering the Egyptian hieroglyphs, guided by the Rosetta Stone discovered by Napoleon's army in 1799. Young studied Belzoni's and Ricci's paintings, and observed a similarity between a prominent hieroglyphic cartouche – i.e. a small group of hieroglyphs inscribed within an oval ring – in the

tomb, and similar cartouches carved on obelisks in Rome and Egypt. These he had already identified, very tentatively, with the name of an Egyptian ruler mentioned in the writings of Herodotus, Manetho and Pliny – three celebrated ancient historians of Egypt, who were Greek, Egyptian and Roman, respectively. They gave the ruler's name as Psammis, or Psammuthis, or perhaps even Psammetichus. 'It is the first time that

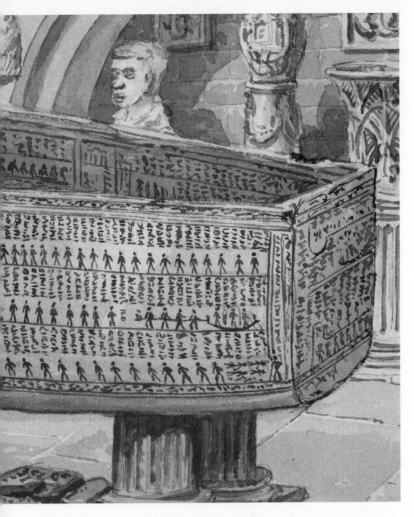

Alabaster sarcophagus of the pharaoh Seti I, discovered in the Valley of the Kings by Giovanni Belzoni, and now in the basement of Sir John Soane's Museum, London.

hieroglyphics have been explained with such accuracy,' enthused Belzoni in his great book of Egyptian travels published in 1820, ignoring Young's own diffident uncertainty. It 'proves the doctor's system beyond doubt to be the right key for reading the unknown language; and it is to be hoped, that he will succeed in completing his arduous and difficult undertaking, as it would give to the world the history of one of the most primitive nations, of which we are now totally ignorant.'

A century later Howard Carter, the English archaeologist who discovered the tomb of the 18th-dynasty pharaoh Tutankhamun in 1922, paid tribute to Belzoni as the first serious excavator of ancient Egypt, whose memoirs had inspired Carter's own determined search for a lost tomb in the Valley of the Kings. Belzoni's *Narrative of the Operations and Recent Discoveries within the Pyramids, Temples, Tombs and Excavations in Egypt and Nubia* was 'one of the most fascinating books in the whole of Egyptian literature', Carter wrote in *The Tomb of Tut.Ankh.Amen.* By 1922, of course, Egyptologists could to a large extent read the hieroglyphs of the newly discovered tomb confidently. Carter and his co-workers were able to identify the name of the virtually unknown young pharaoh immediately and with certainty.

As for Belzoni's sarcophagus, during the course of the 19th century it turned out to have nothing to do with Young's supposed pharaoh 'Psammis' (although Young had correctly identified the pharaoh's cartouche). It was in fact made for the ruler Sethos, now generally known as Seti I, a militarily successful and artistically important pharaoh of the 19th dynasty. Seti I had succeeded his father, Ramesses I, in 1291 BC, and on his death in 1278 BC was in turn succeeded by his son Ramesses II, 'the Great' – Egypt's most famous pharaoh. The goddess portrayed on the bottom of the sarcophagus is now known to be Nut, a deity whose body symbolized the vault of the sky, into whose keeping the corpse of Seti had been committed. The hieroglyphic inscriptions on the sides record, in addition to Seti's royal titles, passages from the so-called Book of the Gates, a magical guide to the journey of a dead man's soul through the Underworld. They describe the route taken by Osiris's solar barque as it navigates an infernal river populated by demons in order to cross the twelve regions of night; magic formulas allow the boat to pass through twelve gates guarded by genies and serpents. Excavations in the floor of the original tomb conducted in 2008–10 revealed a hieroglyphically inscribed fragment of the sarcophagus's missing lid. It was found in a stairwell descending into the base rock, leading to what was presumably intended to be the secret burial chamber of Seti I; the construction was never completed, however, probably on account of the pharaoh's premature death.

We owe this reliable modern knowledge in the first instance to a penurious, brilliant and arrogant young Frenchman, inspired by Napoleon and obsessed with Egypt: Jean-François Champollion, the founder of Egyptology. Champollion's polymathic English rival, Thomas Young, had started the decipherment of hieroglyphs in 1814–19 but had failed to develop it. In mid-September 1822, in Paris, Champollion made a breakthrough and read the 'lost' hieroglyphic spellings of many Egyptian rulers, including Alexander, Berenice, Cleopatra, Ptolemy and Ramesses, for the first time since the late Roman Empire. Shortly afterwards he wrote a sort of catalogue, at the request of Belzoni, for the Paris exhibition of his Egyptian tomb, though under a precautionary pseudonym. As yet, Champollion could not translate the name of the tomb's pharaoh. Six years later, however, after intensive study of Egyptian monuments and papyri brought to Europe, he was able to sail to Egypt and become the first person since antiquity to give true voice to the inscriptions in the Valley of the Kings. Less than four years later, in 1832, he was dead, at the age of just 41. What follows is the life story of this genius, who revolutionized the world's understanding of ancient Egyptian civilization over more than three millennia by cracking the hieroglyphic code.

I

HIEROGLYPHIC 'DELIRIUM' BEFORE CHAMPOLLION

*Hieroglyphic writing, hitherto regarded as formed
purely of signs that represent ideas and not sounds or pronunciations,
was, on the contrary, formed of signs of which the
vast majority express the sounds of words in the spoken
Egyptian language, that is to say phonetic characters.*

(Jean-François Champollion, *Précis du système hiéroglyphique
des anciens Égyptiens*, 1824)

Ancient Egypt was as celebrated in ancient Athens and ancient Rome as it was in 19th-century Paris and London. It had exerted a powerful influence on the world of learning for well over two millennia, ever since the historian Herodotus travelled in Egypt around 450 BC, perhaps reaching as far south as Aswan. In his *Histories*, written in Greek, Herodotus shrewdly identified the pyramids at Giza as places of royal burial, and provided important information about the process of mummification. Yet the works of Herodotus were of little or no help to modern scholars such as Champollion in understanding ancient Egyptian writing.

Hieroglyphic writing fell into disuse in classical antiquity: the latest surviving hieroglyphic inscription was carved by a priest on the Gate of Hadrian, on the island of Philae, in AD 394. Although this date comes at the end of the period of Greek and Roman rule in Egypt, in reality accurate knowledge of the language and script of the pharaohs had already dwindled. Even Julius Caesar and Cleopatra, who took a Nile cruise together on board a royal barge in 47 BC and no doubt stopped to visit the Pyramids, viewed ancient Egypt essentially as 'tourists', the present-day Egyptologist John Ray aptly reminds us, 'since more years stand between Cleopatra and Djoser, the king for whom the Step Pyramid was built' – in about 2650 BC – 'than separate Cleopatra from ourselves'.

The reason for the hieroglyphic script's growing disuse was, of course, that the ancient civilization it described went into eclipse when Egypt was conquered first by Persians, in 525 BC, then by Macedonian Greeks, in 332 BC. (Alexander the Great, who led the campaign, founded the city of Alexandria a year later.) After Alexander, for three centuries Egypt was ruled by the Greek-speaking Ptolemaic dynasty, named after Alexander's general, Ptolemy I; that period ended with the death of Cleopatra VII in 30 BC and the Roman occupation, which lasted until AD 395. The 4th century AD saw the rise of Christianity and Coptic Christian rule. The Library of Alexandria was destroyed by Christian edict at the end of that century, and subsequently many ancient Egyptian temples, such as the temple of Isis at Philae, were converted into Coptic churches. The word 'Copt' was derived from the Arabic *qubti*, which itself came from the Greek *Aiguptos* (Egypt). Spoken Coptic, the Coptic language, was descended from the language of ancient Egypt, but written Coptic, the Coptic script, was not in any way hieroglyphic; instead it was entirely alphabetic, like Greek and Latin. Invented around the end of the 1st century AD, the Coptic script's standard form consisted of twenty-four Greek letters plus six signs borrowed from ancient Egypt – not from the older hieroglyphic script, but from the much more recent demotic (the middle of the three scripts that appear on the Rosetta Stone, as we shall see).

However, such were ancient Egypt's historic customs and architectural magnificence, even if it lay in ruins, that the Greeks and Romans – especially the Greeks – regarded Egypt with a paradoxical mixture of reverence for its wisdom and antiquity, and contempt for its latter-day 'barbarism'. Their attitude somewhat resembled the way British imperialists viewed ancient India's vanished Buddhist civilization during the period of colonial rule. The very word 'hieroglyph' derives from the Greek for 'sacred carving'. Herodotus calculated that 11,340 years had elapsed between the first Egyptian king and his own day on the basis of information provided to him by priests – giving Egyptian civilization a fabulous antiquity that Herodotus apparently accepted as the truth. Egyptian obelisks were taken to ancient Rome and became symbols of prestige; today, thirteen obelisks stand in Rome, while only four remain in Egypt.

Greek and Roman authors generally credited Egypt with the invention of writing, as a gift from the gods (Pliny the Elder, however, attributed it to the Mesopotamian creators of cuneiform). But no ancient Greeks or Romans seem to have learned how to speak or write the contemporary Egyptian language – surprisingly, given the cosmopolitanism of ancient Alexandria. Certainly they did not know how to read hieroglyphs, despite their claims to the contrary. Although their surviving accounts of Egyptian writing vary, they agree in dismissing any phonetic component of hieroglyphic script, while seeming to allow phoneticism in other, non-hieroglyphic, Egyptian scripts. According to the Greek historian Diodorus Siculus, writing in the 1st century BC, Egyptian writing was 'not built up from syllables to express the underlying meaning, but from the appearance of the things drawn and by their metaphorical meaning learned by heart'. In other words, the hieroglyphs were thought to be conceptual or symbolic, not alphabetic like the Greek and Latin (or Coptic) scripts – a crucial distinction in the story of their decipherment. Thus a hieroglyphic picture of a hawk was said to represent the concept of swiftness, a crocodile to symbolize all that was evil. In this firm belief, the Greek and Roman writers were encouraged by Egyptian scribes' natural tendency to emphasize a connection between the pictorial shape of a hieroglyph and its meaning, especially during the Greco-Roman period.

By far the most important classical authority on Egyptian writing was an Egyptian magus named Horapollo (Horus Apollo), who supposedly hailed from Nilopolis in Upper Egypt. Horapollo's treatise *Hieroglyphika* was probably composed in Greek during the 4th century AD or later, and then sank from view until a manuscript was discovered by an intrepid Florentine traveller and archaeologist on a Greek island in about 1419 and became known in Renaissance Italy. Published in 1505, the *Hieroglyphika* was hugely influential: it went through thirty editions, one of which was illustrated by Albrecht Dürer, was studied by Champollion in France in 1806, and even remains in print.

Horapollo's readings of the hieroglyphs were a combination of the (mainly) fictitious and the genuine. Thomas Young called them 'puerile … more like a collection of conceits and enigmas than an explanation of a real system of serious literature'. For instance, according to the esteemed *Hieroglyphika*,

When they wish to indicate a sacred scribe, or a prophet, or an embalmer, or the spleen, or odour, or laughter, or sneezing, or rule, or judge, they draw a dog. A scribe, since he who wishes to become an accomplished scribe must study many things and must bark continually and be fierce and show favours to none, just like dogs. And a prophet, because the dog looks intently beyond all other beasts upon the images of the gods, like a prophet.

– and so on. As we now know, thanks to Champollion, there are elements of truth in this, mixed with absurdity: the jackal ('dog') hieroglyph writes the name of the god Anubis, who is the ancient Egyptian god of embalming, a smelly business (hence Horapollo's meaning 'odour'?). A recumbent jackal writes the title of a special type of priest, the 'master of secrets', who would have been a sacred scribe and considered something of a prophet. A striding jackal can also stand for an official, and hence perhaps for a judge.

The Arab invaders who occupied Christian Egypt in 642 and introduced Islam came to have a marginally more accurate understanding of the hieroglyphs because they at least believed that the signs were partly phonetic, not purely symbolic. (Arab scholars who attempted to read individual hieroglyphs made little progress, however.) But this belief did not pass from the medieval Islamic world to the European. Instead, stimulated by Horapollo's writings, scholars of the Italian Renaissance came to accept the Greek and Roman view of hieroglyphs as symbols of wisdom. The first of many in the modern world to write a whole book on the subject was a Venetian with the Latin name Pierius Valerianus. He published his work in 1556, and illustrated it with delightfully fantastic 'Renaissance' hieroglyphs.

The most famous of these interpreters was the German Jesuit priest Athanasius Kircher, whose works were thoroughly studied by

Champollion. In the mid-17th century Kircher became Rome's accepted pundit on ancient Egypt. But his voluminous writings took him far beyond 'Egyptology'. He is 'sometimes called the last renaissance man' (notes the *Encyclopaedia Britannica*), and was even dubbed 'the last man who knew everything' in the subtitle of a recent academic study of Kircher, because he attempted to encompass the totality of human knowledge. The result was a mixture of folly and brilliance – with the former easily predominant – from which his intellectual reputation never recovered, fascinating though his polymathy may be to modern eyes.

In 1666, Kircher was entrusted with the publication of a hieroglyphic inscription that appears on a small ancient Egyptian obelisk in the Piazza della Minerva, Rome. The monument was erected on the orders of Pope Alexander VII and follows a design by the sculptor Bernini, in which the Egyptian inscription is mounted on a stone elephant, the whole supposedly encapsulating the concept of 'wisdom supported by strength'. Kircher gave his (entirely conceptual) reading of a cartouche on the obelisk as follows: 'The protection of Osiris against the violence of Typho must be elicited according to the proper rites and ceremonies by sacrifices and by appeal to the tutelary Genii of the triple world in order to ensure the enjoyment of the prosperity customarily given by the Nile against the violence of the enemy Typho.' The accepted modern reading of this cartouche is simply the name of a late pharaoh, Wahibre (Greek name Apries), of the 26th dynasty!

By contrast, Kircher genuinely assisted in the rescue of Coptic when he published the language's first European grammar and vocabulary in 1636. From the 4th to the 10th centuries, the Coptic language had flourished throughout Egypt, where it was the official language of the Christian Church. It had then been replaced by Arabic, except within the Coptic Church. By the time of Kircher, in the mid-17th century, it was headed for extinction, though it was still used in the liturgy (as Champollion would delightedly hear for himself from a Coptic priest in a Paris church in 1807). Curiously, Kircher failed to perceive a link between the spoken Coptic of Egyptian Christians and the pagan language of ancient Egypt. However, in the 18th century several European

Athanasius Kircher, Jesuit priest and polymath, in a 1678 portrait based on an engraving by Cornelis Bloemart II made in 1664, when Kircher was about 62 years old.

scholars came to acquire a knowledge of Coptic and its alphabet. Their learning – absorbed and deepened by Champollion – would prove essential in reconstructing the probable ancient Egyptian language during the decipherment of the hieroglyphs.

In the meantime, Kircher's fantastic interpretations of the hieroglyphs licensed many other wrong-headed theories. For example, a Swedish diplomat, Count Palin, suggested in three publications during 1802–4 that parts of the biblical Old Testament were a Hebrew translation of an Egyptian text. It was a reasonable conjecture, given the importance of Egypt in the Bible – until, that is, Palin tried to reconstruct the Egyptian text by translating the Hebrew into Chinese. This was not quite as crazy as it sounds, given that both Egyptian hieroglyphs and Chinese characters have a very strong conceptual and symbolic component, originating from the pictorial nature of many of their earliest signs. But Palin went much too far with his hieroglyphic extravaganza. As Young coolly noted:

The peculiar nature of the Chinese characters ... has contributed very materially to assist us in tracing the gradual progress of the Egyptian symbols through their various forms; although the resemblance is certainly far less complete than has been supposed by Mr Palin, who tells us, that we have only to translate the Psalms of David into Chinese, and to write them in the ancient character of that language, in order to reproduce the Egyptian papyri, that are found with the mummies.

Nevertheless, the existence of a conceptual component of the Chinese script – and, moreover, a particular element in common between Chinese characters and Egyptian hieroglyphs, discovered later – would offer important clues towards deciphering the hieroglyphs in the more cautious hands of Champollion, Young and others.

The first 'scientific' step in the right direction came from an English clergyman. In 1740 William Warburton, the future bishop of Gloucester, suggested that the origin of all writing, hieroglyphic included, might have been pictorial rather than divine. A French admirer of Warburton, Abbé J.-J. Barthélemy, then made a sensible guess in 1762 that obelisk cartouches might contain the names of kings or gods. (Ironically, he arrived at this conclusion on the basis of two false observations, one being that the hieroglyphs enclosed in the oval rings differed from all other hieroglyphs.) Finally, near the end of the 18th century, a Danish scholar, Georg Zoëga, hazarded another useful, though unproven, conjecture: that some hieroglyphs might, at least in some measure, be what he called 'notae phoneticae' – Latin for 'phonetic signs' – representing sounds rather than concepts in the Egyptian language. The path towards decipherment was gradually being cleared of ancient debris at last.

And now we reach a turning point: the arrival of Napoleon Bonaparte's invasion force in Egypt in 1798, and the discovery of the Rosetta Stone. The word 'cartouche', as applied to Egyptian hieroglyphs, dates from this fateful encounter between Occident and Orient. For the oval rings around some hieroglyphs, so easily visible to the soldiers on temple walls and other monuments in Egypt (even on the walls of mosques constructed out of ancient Egyptian inscribed stones), reminded the French soldiers of the *cartouches* (cartridges) in their guns.

Fortunately, the military force was almost as interested in culture as in conquest. A large party of French scholars and scientists – savants who included the mathematician Jean-Baptiste Joseph Fourier, Champollion's later mentor – accompanied the army; there were also many artists, such as the dashing Dominique Vivant Denon, who was shortly to be appointed director of the Louvre Museum in Paris by Napoleon. The artists provided illustrations for the nine elephantine volumes of the *Description de l'Égypte*, the astonishing French government record of the savants' Egyptian studies that would be published between 1809 and 1828, and whose hieroglyphic reproductions would dominate Champollion's apprentice years.

Yet the great expedition did not lead to immediate progress in decipherment. In the cautionary words of Denon's highly influential and still very readable *Travels in Upper and Lower Egypt, during the Campaigns of General Bonaparte*, first published in Paris in 1802 and constantly reprinted during the 19th century:

Every relic of antiquity that is discovered, furnishes ground for an assertion, but often for one that is made in support of error ... each [scholar] has endeavoured to

see in the first fragment of the Egyptian documents brought into Europe the proofs
of a system prematurely adopted; impatient, each has endeavoured to find an
explanation of the heavens, of the earth, of the principles of the government of this
people, and a picture of its manners, and the ceremonies of its worship, of its arts,
of its sciences, and of its labours: the hieroglyphical forms have contributed
to the delirium of the imagination; and, leaning on hypotheses, each has proceeded,
with equal authority, in different directions, all alike obscure and hazardous.

When a demolition squad of military engineers discovered the Rosetta Stone in July 1799 while rebuilding an old fort in the village of Rashid (Rosetta), in the Nile Delta, the officer in charge quickly recognized the importance of its three parallel inscriptions and sent it to the savants in Cairo. That October Napoleon himself, recently returned from Egypt, told the National Institute in Paris: 'There appears no doubt that the column which bears the hieroglyphs contains the same inscription as the other two. Thus, here is a means of acquiring certain information of this, until now, unintelligible language.' Copies of the inscriptions were made and sent to Paris in 1800. But the stone itself was captured by the British army after its victory over the French in 1801 and shipped to London. Plaster casts were made by the Society of Antiquaries for the universities at Cambridge, Dublin, Edinburgh and Oxford, and facsimiles were sent to various institutions in Europe and America, including the National Library in Paris. In 1802 the stone entered the collections of the British Museum. The left edge was inscribed: 'Captured in Egypt by the British Army in 1801', and the right edge: 'Presented by King George III'. Immediately, the stone became an enduring symbol of Anglo-French rivalry: for example, in 1991, during the bicentenary of Champollion's birth, Jean Leclant, a leading French Egyptologist and permanent secretary of the Academy of Inscriptions and Belles-Lettres in Paris, misremembered the left-edge inscription as: 'Taken from the French army, Alexandria 1801'!

From the moment of discovery, it was clear that the inscription on the stone was written in three different scripts, the bottom one being the Greek alphabet, and the top one – unfortunately the most damaged – Egyptian hieroglyphs with visible cartouches. Sandwiched between them was a script about which little was known. It plainly did not resemble the Greek script, but it seemed to bear at least a fugitive resemblance to the hieroglyphic script above it, though without having any cartouches. Today we know this script as 'demotic', which developed (*c.* 650 BC) from a cursive form of Egyptian writing known as 'hieratic' – a 'running hand' used in parallel with the hieroglyphic script from as early as 3000 BC. (Hieratic itself does not appear on the Rosetta Stone.) The term 'demotic' derives from Greek *demotikos*, meaning 'in common use', in contrast to the sacred hieroglyphic, which was essentially a monumental script. 'Demotic' was first used by Champollion, who refused to employ Young's earlier equivalent, 'enchorial', which the English scholar had coined from the designation of the middle script given in the Greek inscription: *enchoria grammata*, or 'letters of the country' – that is to say, a native script.

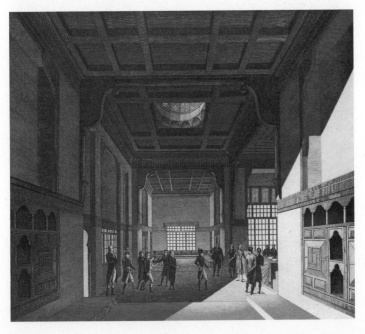

Visit by Napoleon Bonaparte to the headquarters – in a former Mamluk harem – of the recently founded Institut d'Égypte in Cairo, 1798, published in the *Description de l'Égypte*.

The earliest copy of the Rosetta Stone, made by French savants in Cairo in 1800, the year after its discovery at Rosetta. The hieroglyphic section is the most damaged.

The obvious first step towards decipherment was to translate the Greek inscription. It turned out to be a legal decree issued at Memphis, the principal city of ancient Egypt (not far from modern Cairo), by a general council of priests from every part of the kingdom, assembled on the first anniversary of the coronation of the young Ptolemy V Epiphanes, king of all Egypt, on 27 March 196 BC. Greek was used because it was the language of court and government during the Ptolemaic dynasty. The names Ptolemy, Alexander and Alexandria, among others, occurred in the Greek inscription.

The eye of would-be decipherers was caught by the very last sentence of the Greek section. It read: 'This decree shall be inscribed on a stela of hard stone in sacred [i.e. hieroglyphic] and native [i.e. demotic] and Greek characters and set up in each of the first, second and third [-rank] temples beside the image of the ever-living king.' In other words, the three inscriptions – hieroglyphic, demotic and Greek – were equivalent in meaning, though not necessarily word-for-word translations of each other. This Greek sentence was what first told scholars that the Rosetta Stone bore a bilingual inscription – the kind most sought after by decipherers, a sort of Holy Grail of decipherment. The two languages represented on the stone were Greek and (presumably) ancient Egyptian, the language of the priests, which was written in two different scripts – unless the 'sacred' and 'native' characters concealed *two* different languages, which seemed unlikely from the context. (In fact, the Egyptian languages written in hieroglyphic and demotic are not identical but closely related, like Latin and Renaissance Italian.)

Since the hieroglyphic section was very damaged, it was at first ignored in favour of the demotic section, which was almost complete. In 1802 two scholars – a famous French Orientalist, Silvestre de Sacy, and a student of his, Johann Åkerblad, a Swedish diplomat (like Palin) – independently adopted similar techniques. They searched for a name, in particular Ptolemy, by isolating repeated groups of demotic symbols located in roughly the same position as the eleven known occurrences of the name in the Greek inscription. Having found these groups, they noticed that the names in demotic seemed to be written alphabetically, as in the Greek inscription – that is, the demotic spelling of a name apparently contained more or less the same number of signs as the number of alphabetic letters in its assumed Greek equivalent. By matching demotic sign with Greek letter, they were able to draw up a tentative alphabet of demotic signs. By applying this tentative alphabet, certain other demotic words, such as 'Greek', 'Egypt' and 'temple', could be identified. It looked as though the entire demotic script might be alphabetic like the Greek inscription.

But in fact it was not an alphabet *in toto*, unluckily for de Sacy and Åkerblad – even if some elements of the script, such as the names, were very likely written alphabetically. Young was sympathetic to his predecessors: '[They] proceeded upon the erroneous, or, at least imperfect, evidence of the Greek authors, who have pretended to explain the different modes of writing among the ancient Egyptians, and who have asserted very distinctly that they employed, on many occasions, an alphabetical system, composed of 25 letters only.' Taking their cue from classical authority, neither de Sacy nor Åkerblad could cast off the preconception that the demotic inscription was written in an alphabetic script – as against the hieroglyphic inscription, which both scholars took to be wholly *non*-phonetic, its symbols expressing concepts, not sounds, along the lines suggested by Horapollo's *Hieroglyphika*. The apparent disparity in appearance between the hieroglyphic and demotic signs, combined with the suffocating weight of European tradition, dating from antiquity, that Egyptian hieroglyphic was a conceptual or symbolic script, convinced both de Sacy and Åkerblad that the invisible principles of hieroglyphic and demotic were wholly different. They decided that the hieroglyphic had to be a conceptual/symbolic script (like Chinese, supposedly), whereas the demotic was a phonetic/alphabetic script (like Greek).

Except for one element. De Sacy deserves credit for making an original suggestion: that the foreign (i.e. non-Egyptian) names inside hieroglyphic cartouches, which he naturally assumed were those of rulers like Ptolemy, Alexander and so on, might possibly be written in an alphabet, as they almost certainly were in the demotic inscription. De Sacy was led to this suggestion by some information given to him by one of his pupils, a student of Chinese, in 1811. The Chinese script was at this time widely (if wrongly) thought in Europe to be primarily conceptual, like the hieroglyphs – as we know from Palin's attempted decipherment – with only a vanishingly small phonetic component. Yet, as this student pointed out to de Sacy, native writers of the Chinese script were compelled by unfamiliar foreign words and names (for instance, Buddhist names and terms borrowed into Chinese from ancient Indian texts) to resort to phonetic spellings. To highlight the phoneticism, they would add a special sign to a Chinese character or group of characters indicating that these particular characters were reduced to a phonetic value and did not have their normal conceptual meaning. (To make a relevant, if inexact, comparison with English, some foreign words in printed English have their own 'special sign': italicization.) Were not Ptolemy, Alexander and some other Greek proper names foreign to the Egyptian language, speculated de Sacy, and might not the cartouche be the ancient Egyptian hieroglyphic equivalent of the special sign in Chinese characters? But as for the rest of the hieroglyphs – that is, the vast majority that were *not* enclosed in cartouches – this distinguished Orientalist (and the teacher of Champollion in Paris) was sure that these signs must undoubtedly be non-phonetic, as stated by the ancient Greek and Roman authorities.

Such was the extent of understanding of ancient Egyptian writing inherited by Champollion in 1814, when he – and, independently, Young – began to concentrate on decipherment. We shall refer to many of these ideas again more fully later on. But now it is time to turn to the beginnings of Champollion's interest in Egypt, which had its origin in provincial France during the decade following the French Revolution and prior to Napoleon's invasion of Egypt.

II

A REVOLUTIONARY CHILDHOOD

Fortunately, I was given a beak and claws.

(Jean-François Champollion's oft-repeated
comment about his childhood)

Of the many hundreds, if not thousands, of replicas of the Rosetta Stone
that have been made since 1800, ranging from the lithographic copy
taken directly from the newly excavated artefact by French scholars in
Cairo to today's Rosetta Stone mouse mat sold at the British Museum, the
grandest example is an inscribed slab of black granite from Zimbabwe.
It measures 11 metres (36 feet) long and 8.5 metres (28 feet) wide – about
100 times the area of the original. Forming a pavement that fills most
of a small Romanesque courtyard in France, appropriately known as the
Place des Écritures, it is sculpted with three steps – one per script – so
that a pedestrian can step up and walk over the Greek alphabetic section,
step up again onto the demotic section, and finally reach the hieroglyphic
section, with its badly broken corner. Created by the American conceptual
artist Joseph Kosuth to commemorate the bicentenary of Champollion's
birth, the replica is located next to the Musée Champollion in Figeac,
the town where Champollion was born in 1790.

Figeac lies in a river valley among rolling green foothills at the very
edge of the Massif Central, in south-western France. It now falls in the
département of Lot, but in the 18th century it formed part of the old
province of Quercy and in Roman times belonged to Aquitania Prima.
The town may be built on a Roman site; not far away is the disputed site
of Uxellodunum, the hill fort where Julius Caesar's legions finally defeated
the Gauls in 59 BC – a site that Champollion tried to locate and excavate

with his brother in 1816. During the 9th century AD the province was part of the Frankish kingdom of Aquitaine. Figeac was also a stopping point on one of the pilgrimage routes to the shrine of Santiago de Compostela in Spain. By the 12th century it had become an important trading town, as can be seen from its former merchants' houses with sandstone façades, medieval arcades of *boutiques* (small shops), and *soleilhos* – columned attics open to the sun where, for example, fruits were dried. In the 13th century Figeac's Benedictine monastery traded woollen cloth, wine and honey as far afield as England, Cyprus and the Middle East.

When one of King Louis XVI's inspectors of taxes and finances arrived in Figeac in 1781, he noted in his travel journal that the population was a little more than 6,000 inhabitants, out of a total of about 100,000 people in the province of Quercy. Significant local products were wine, wheat, rye, hemp, hay, walnuts and chestnuts. Oils were imported from Lower Languedoc, and cheeses from the Auvergne, while other items came from Bordeaux, away to the west, by riverboat, vehicle or on mule-back. Intellectually, though, not a lot seemed to be happening in the area. What is the genius of the *Quercynois*? the royal inspector enquired, presumably of some notables in Figeac. 'No genius,' came the reply. 'Generally, the spread of ideas is very slow and the mental faculties are difficult to rouse for the grasping of any new method. In general, [there is] much activity especially in the countryside but little in the culture.'

Jacques Champollion, the father of Jean-François, arrived in Figeac in 1770 and set up a bookselling business that prospered for many years. He was not a *Quercynois*, and had travelled a long way from his native place, an Alpine valley in the province then known as Dauphiné, quite close to Grenoble, some 300 kilometres (185 miles) to the east of Figeac. Despite attempts by various biographers and Champollion family members to find a noble line in the Champollions, Jacques's ancestry was relatively humble, either peasant or petit bourgeois. It may have included Italian blood, and the family name may perhaps have descended from the name Campoleone – a connection with a neighbouring land that would appeal strongly to Jean-François when he visited Italy as a scholar in the 1820s. Born in 1744, Jacques was the youngest of five sons, three of whom lived out their lives in the area of their birth, while the fourth, André, became a military officer and in 1798 went to Egypt with Napoleon's army.

As with most aspects of the life of Champollion *père*, his motives in moving from Dauphiné to Figeac are murky, since there is little or no direct evidence. Until 1770 he is known to have made his income as an itinerant pedlar of books. The border region near Grenoble between France, the Savoy, Switzerland and Italy was surely a more promising territory for such a bookseller than the purely French-speaking, commercially oriented Figeac, whatever the town's trading connections with other parts of France might have been. However, itinerant merchants in Dauphiné were forced to travel far from their home regions to make ends meet during the long Alpine winter months. Certainly Jacques Champollion made a point of spending time at the annual Beaucaire Fair, near Avignon, which was famous throughout the south of France for centuries until the arrival of the railways and attracted as many as 300,000 visitors at its height. Conceivably, he may have visited Figeac on business, liked it, and decided to abandon his wandering life and settle down in favour of a softer, more sedentary existence. But it is also possible that he was exiled from his home for his opinions (as his sons would later be exiled from Grenoble), perhaps because he was found to be selling forbidden books. In the 16th century, the religious authorities had burned travelling booksellers for offering heretical publications, and in the 17th and 18th centuries, the government had imprisoned them for selling pamphlets hostile to royal power. Jacques Champollion's future role during the French Revolution might lend support to such a 'republican' interpretation of his move to Figeac in 1770 – as might the fact that he never once returned to his place of birth.

After two years in Figeac Jacques bought a house with the customary open *soleilho*, in a dark and narrow lane in the town centre, the Rue de la Boudousquerie (today renamed as the Impasse Champollion). Seven years later he purchased a *boutique*: a small shop with a window overlooking the town's main marketplace. In the meantime he had married a local woman, Jeanne-Françoise Gualieu – a bond that undoubtedly provided him with an entrée into commerce and society. She was the daughter

Jean-François Champollion's place of birth (at top right) in the Rue de la Boudousquerie, now called the Impasse Champollion, Figeac. He lived here from 1790 to 1801.

of an established local manufacturer; her father and grandfather had been weavers, and her mother belonged to a well-known local family that included a former mayor. Jeanne-Françoise's two younger sisters were married to a dyer and a tanner. The name Gualieu is frequently cited in the archives of Figeac, with reference either to simple artisans or to town worthies. Surprisingly, though, Jeanne-Françoise appears to have been illiterate, since the marriage register of Figeac's church,

Notre-Dame-du-Puy, notes that she was unable to sign her name during her wedding in 1773.

The couple's first child, a son, died within hours of his birth in 1773. A daughter was born a year later, and a second daughter two years after the first; she was followed by a son in 1778; a third son, who died prematurely; and another daughter in 1782, when Jeanne-Françoise was probably 40 years old. At this point there was a long gap before the arrival of the youngest child, Jean-François, in 1790.

Although he would be close to two of his sisters, who tended to spoil him, it was Jean-François's brother Jacques-Joseph, twelve years his elder, who would have by far the greatest influence on Jean-François's life, both as a child and as a man – his parents not excluded. Indeed, without the worldly Jacques-Joseph's lifelong support and *savoir faire*, it is highly unlikely that the world would ever have heard of Jean-François Champollion. In later life, the elder brother called himself Champollion-Figeac, partly to distinguish himself from his more famous sibling, who was known as Champollion *le jeune*. Sufficiently well known to merit an entry in today's *Encyclopaedia Britannica*, Champollion-Figeac became a palaeographer and librarian, first as curator of manuscripts at the National Library in Paris, then at the palace of Fontainebleau. He also edited his brother's posthumous works. The Champollion biographer Jean Lacouture even compares Jean-François and his mentor Jacques-Joseph with Vincent van Gogh and his devoted art-dealer brother Theo, with considerable validity (although Theo was, of course, younger than Vincent). To help us understand the younger Champollion, it is therefore worth considering, briefly, the early years of the older Jacques-Joseph.

Ironically, Jacques-Joseph was a sickly child who would live into his late eighties, whereas his younger brother was a healthy boy who would die of a stroke in his early forties. There was some doubt whether Jacques-Joseph would survive his infancy, but as soon as he was able to say a few words his parents – perhaps unable to cope with his fragility – handed him over to the charge of an old and saintly woman, 'la Catinou', who kept him in her house until he was 7 and gave him some elementary education.

Once back in his family's home Jacques-Joseph received some schooling of undistinguished quality, but in 1791, when he turned 13, his school closed its doors as a result of the Revolution, putting an end to his formal education altogether. Several years of turbulence followed, culminating in the Terror of 1793–94, during which the town's Tree of Liberty and its guillotine were located in a small square within earshot of the Champollion house. During this period, it is claimed by Champollion's first biographer, Hermine Hartleben, that the head of the family, Jacques Champollion, became chief of the police in Figeac along with two fellow citizens; and that he used his official position, surprisingly, to give asylum in his house to two threatened Benedictine priests, Canon Seycy and Dom Calmels. If the claim is true, which seems doubtful, this was dangerously risky behaviour. In the early years of the Revolution, 'Those who had most grounds for fear were the ones who sheltered priests who refused to cooperate with the Revolution,' writes the historian Richard Ballard in *The Unseen Terror*, his study of provincial France in the 1790s. There are no town records or written evidence to support Hartleben's claim, which relied on Champollion family testimony; but, according to Jacques-Joseph himself, during this time Calmels agreed to take charge of Jacques-Joseph's education on a friendly basis. That his father, Jacques, certainly had local influence is proved by the fact that during the Terror the 15-year-old Jacques-Joseph was given a paid position in the secretariat of the municipality, where he quickly became a trusted archivist and assistant to the chief secretary. It was his first step into officialdom in what would become a convoluted career exposed to the vagaries of post-revolutionary French politics over half a century.

This information derives from an unpublished autobiography written by Jacques-Joseph in 1799, at the age of 21, a year after he had moved from Figeac to take a job in Grenoble. In his detailed manuscript he makes no reference at all to the birth of his brother Jean-François on 23 December 1790, even though he was godfather to the infant, according to the baptismal register. This astounding omission, along with other evidence we shall come to, suggests that the truth of the birth may have been rather different from the legend handed down by the Champollion family and reported by Hartleben without comment in her biography.

First, the legend. The source is a report on Champollion made after his death, written in 1833 by a Dr Janin, a physician who had known and examined him personally. According to this document, Champollion's mother was so badly affected by rheumatism in her forties that she became almost paralysed. Doctors could do nothing for her, and so a local healer, a peasant known as Jacquou the Magician, was called. He made her lie on a bed of herbs and massaged her with hot wine containing specially prepared decoctions, which he also required her to drink. Not only did Jacquou promise her a complete and rapid recovery, he also made a prediction: that she would give birth to a son 'who would be a light of centuries to come'. And on the third day she arose from her bed, and was able to climb and descend the stairs in the family house. Less than a year later, she gave birth to Jean-François.

Although Champollion himself apparently did not disavow the miraculous story, which he said his mother had told him frequently in his early years, it is definitely hard to credit. First and foremost, Champollion's mother was 48 years old in 1790, according to Janin – a very advanced age for childbearing in the late 18th century. Moreover, she had not given birth for eight years. Almost as telling is the fact that Jean-François himself, both as a boy and as an adult, would never refer to his mother in his prolific correspondence. By contrast, he did make a number of allusions, right up to his death – twenty-five years after the death of Jeanne-Françoise Champollion – to the existence of an unnamed woman in Figeac who was very dear to him and whom he continued to visit. Finally, there is the fact, referred to by himself and many others (and mentioned in his passport), that unlike his brother he was unusually dark-skinned – so much so that he could easily pass for an Arab in Egypt.

Some Champollion biographers, such as Hartleben and, today, Michel Dewachter, prefer to read no significance into the facts mentioned above. Others, such as Alain Faure and Lacouture, speculate, reasonably enough, that Jeanne-Françoise was not the real mother of Jean-François. Births outside of marriage were by no means unheard of in the parish registers of Figeac in this period, as Faure points out. Lacouture goes further. His view is that it is quite likely Jacques Champollion had a liaison with a woman, perhaps a gypsy – or even an 'Egyptian' – whom he may have met at the annual Beaucaire Fair, and that this liaison produced a son. There are strong hints from his contemporaries that Jacques enjoyed the bohemian life, and he unquestionably took to the bottle in his later years, which destroyed his bookselling business and poisoned relations with his children. To prove such a liaison is by its very nature impossible, but if the theory were true, it might help to explain not only Jean-François's puzzlingly distant relationship with his father (and mother), but also the exceptional difference in temperament between Jean-François and his siblings, including Jacques-Joseph.

Champollion *le jeune*, unlike his generally cautious and calculating elder brother, was a hot-blooded southerner, subject to mercurial mood swings. From an early age, the lion was his favourite animal, which he liked to associate with the 'lion' in his surname. 'Outbursts, renunciations, enthusiasm, dejection – such was and would always be the way with Jean-François,' observes Lacouture. He had a 'volcanic temperament' and 'a furious impatience – his principal fault,' admits Hartleben. These emotions would give him the passion and dedication to succeed in Egyptology, yet at the same time they would undermine both his health and many of his relationships with other scholars.

The revolutionary temper of the times probably exacerbated his natural tendencies. His political sympathies would always lie with republicanism, yet he would often find that his work was supported by royalists and autocrats, in France, Italy and Egypt. So all through his life he would oscillate between the republican and royalist worlds, torn between his love of liberty and his respect for stability, not to mention his ardent admiration for the ancient Egyptian civilization created and maintained by century after century of divine kingship.

A story told about him when he was a little less than 5 years old, in the period following the Terror, and reported by Hartleben, has the ring of truth. He was out walking in the street with his mother when they came across a blind beggar sitting on the threshold of a house, holding out his torn hat to passers-by. Jean-François was in the process of putting a coin in the hat while carefully avoiding the outstretched legs of the old man when a leader of the revolutionary party, puffed up with his own importance, struck the beggar with his walking-stick in order to make him rise and get out of the way. Jean-François, furious at the injustice, tried to grab the stick, crying out: 'Wicked stick, you obey this bad man that you should rather thrash!' 'Citizenness,' said the Jacobin to his mother, apparently amused that she did not know how to react, 'you would do well to trim right away the beak and claws of your fledgling so that others are not obliged to do it.' Champollion recalled the encounter for the rest of his days. When, as an adult, he was attacked by one or other of his numerous adversaries, he liked to remark: 'Fortunately, I was given a beak and claws.'

At around the same age, Jean-François taught himself to read and write – a result of his rather shadowy mother's help, combined with his own fierce love of independence (according, once again, to the family tradition reported by his first biographer). Throughout her life Jeanne-Françoise apparently remained illiterate, despite her husband's profession, but as a pious Catholic she committed to memory long extracts of her missal by hearing them sung and intoned during the Mass. She taught these extracts by ear to her young son, who repeated them uncomplainingly. Soon he took a copy of the prayer book from the stock in his father's bookshop and settled himself alone among piles of old books and prints in a corner of the shop (which was probably often closed in this troubled period) along with paper and pencils. There, by copying out letters and words from the missal – which would also have encouraged his drawing skills – he succeeded, through a process of trial and error, in matching the words of the prayers memorized in his mind with the same words printed on the page, and also grasped the different sounds of the letters in the alphabet ('his first work of decipherment', in Hartleben's phrase). Perhaps he was aided by the missal's illuminated letters, somewhat comparable to the pictures and cartouches of the hieroglyphic script; undoubtedly he would have been helped by the frequency of proper names and religious terms in the text. As a result, he was able to read passages of the book that he had not committed to memory, which came as a great surprise to his parents. One must assume that his father had been too busy, or maybe disinclined, to teach him to read while they spent time together in the bookshop. But his brother Jacques-Joseph, impressed by this literary achievement, began to give the 6-year-old more methodical instruction in the spring of 1797, during his rare moments of leisure.

Once he had cracked the alphabetic code, Jean-François's reading must have developed with exceptional rapidity. By the age of 10, before he left Figeac in 1801, he was said to have been able to recite long passages from Homer and Virgil by heart in the original Greek and Latin. His relations recalled enjoying the family's youngest son act out dramatic scenes from these classics in his own French translation during winter evenings spent around the fireplace at home. Sometimes their friends would slip into the room and gaze with curiosity at the unheard-of spectacle of the boy, seated on a stool next to the hearth (Champollion always relished physical warmth as a child and as an adult) with his eyes sparkling, bringing alive for his family the ancient stories he had learned how to read.

Jean-François's precocity in languages had little to do with any formal schooling. The primary schools in France had closed down during the Revolution. Festivals every ten days – the length of the official 'week' in the new calendar – were the stuff of revolutionary education in the years before Napoleon's *coup d'état* of November 1799. Attendance was poor, and the festivals were a failure. Reading reports of them now, comments Richard Ballard, 'We can feel the yawns two centuries later ... Liberty was celebrated to extinction.'

In 1796 the primary schools began to reopen as restrictions on priests gradually started to ease, though more by default than through any official policy. Jacques-Joseph, who had been teaching his brother for nearly a year and a half, left home in the summer of 1798, after cousins had offered him a job with an export firm in Grenoble. (His father had arranged matters with the relatives at the Beaucaire Fair, with Jacques-Joseph in tow.) Now bereft of his tutor, Jean-François was made to attend school in Figeac in November that year, just before his eighth birthday. He proved to be a bad pupil, unable to stomach the monotony of rote learning and too wilful to accept the discipline of the teachers; mental arithmetic was a particular torture for him. The school was abandoned, and early in the following year, at the insistence of Jacques-Joseph, the boy was instead committed to the personal care of Dom Calmels, Jacques-Joseph's own former teacher. It was Calmels who was responsible for starting Jean-François on Latin and Greek. He also took him for walks in Figeac and its surrounding countryside. The town's historical buildings, including an old chateau and a gateway decorated with numerous grotesques, helped to stimulate the boy's interest in history. But it was nature, not architecture, that really appealed to him. The fields, forests and hillsides opened the boy's eyes to a new world and a more scientific way of thinking. But his questions soon exhausted his teacher's knowledge, as Jean-François delightedly collected insects, plants and stones, to be classified later at home in the Rue de la Boudousquerie, perhaps in the well-lit *soleilho* at the top of the dark house. Here was the beginning of a fascination with the natural world that would suffuse all his research on Egypt, ancient and modern.

In Figeac, Egypt was not on the boy's educational menu. Indeed, there is no record of any interest in that country from Champollion *le jeune* until he moved to Grenoble. This was not the case with his elder brother, however, who had made enquiries about joining the French army's expedition to Egypt during the first half of 1798. 'If I have any regret,' Jacques-Joseph wrote in his unpublished autobiography the following year, 'it is that of not being part of the army of Egypt. I would also say that if I were forced to choose between all the estates, I would probably favour a military career.' Family tradition had it that in September 1799 the Champollion bookshop received from Cairo a copy of the *Courier de l'Égypte*, announcing the discovery and potential significance of the Rosetta Stone, intended for Jacques-Joseph. It is quite plausible that it was sent by Captain André Champollion, Jacques's brother and an army officer, who would have known of his nephew's interest in Egypt. Conceivably, Jacques Champollion showed the copy to his youngest son before forwarding it to Jacques-Joseph in Grenoble, but if he did, it made no impression on the 8-year-old Jean-François.

At any rate, Calmels was an inspired choice of teacher. Nevertheless, despite being fond of his pupil, he was eventually compelled to admit that he could not develop the 'particular genius' of Jean-François in the intellectually unstimulating atmosphere of Figeac, partly for lack of suitable books and qualified teachers. It was clear that the boy's studies were languishing and that he was suffering from a form of depression, not least because of a lack of attention from his parents, as one strongly suspects. At the end of December 1800, the worried tutor wrote to Jacques-Joseph in Grenoble about the situation. After mentioning the boy's considerable progress in Latin, he added more generally: 'He has plenty of taste, plenty of desire to learn but this taste and this desire are swamped by an apathy, a negligence that is difficult to reverse. There are days when he appears to want to learn everything, others when he would do nothing.'

A few days later, in early January 1801, Jean-François himself took up the pen to write to his brother, probably at the dictation of his tutor. Apart from showing great respect for his 'very dear brother', mentioning 'our dear sisters' and making the minimum possible reference to 'Papa' and 'Maman', he asked to be excused for his somewhat 'fickle' mind, which he hoped that 'your lessons will correct'. A sample of his Latin prose, decorated with many flourishes, was attached to the letter.

At the end of February, Jacques-Joseph replied to his brother. By now he had clearly decided to take charge of Jean-François in the long term, including meeting the future cost of his education. But first he gave him a warning:

Since you have confessed to me that your mind is fickle you must try to acquire some perseverance. Never forget that time lost is irreparable, apply yourself well to your studies. Consider that nothing is more shameful for a pupil than laziness and negligence … If you desire to come here with me, it is necessary that you learn something quickly – ignoramuses are good for nothing. If it is your wish that I should obtain permission from our dear father to have you here, from your side you must give him all possible satisfaction.

Note that Jacques-Joseph referred only to their father, as if their mother's opinion about so momentous a decision were irrelevant.

As for Champollion *père*, he seems to have given his permission readily. Solid evidence for his motives is lacking, as usual, but his decision was of a piece with his unexplained lack of involvement with his youngest son's education thus far. (Oddly enough, a similar situation pertained with Thomas Young, an eldest son who was parted from his parents even earlier than Champollion, and who avoided reference to his father or mother as an adult.) From this point on, the father in Figeac and the youngest son in distant Grenoble would have remarkably little to do with each other, until Jean-François was compelled to return to Figeac during his exile from Grenoble in his mid-twenties. One possible explanation for the father's ready agreement might be that he had already started to drink too much.

At the end of March 1801, Jacques's 10-year-old son set out on the first major journey of his life. At Figeac he boarded the *diligence* (public stagecoach) to Lyons, where he changed to a second *diligence* heading for Grenoble. There is no evidence that his father accompanied him, or that his brother or anyone else came to meet him in Lyons. In modern-day terms, this was something like sending an unaccompanied child on a long-distance flight to an unfamiliar city. Evidently, Jean-François, for all his fickleness of mind, possessed an unusual amount of self-confidence. His sisters in Figeac, who had cheerfully indulged the whims of the little tyrant, said of his departure: 'Our house is no longer what it was.' After Jean-François's death decades later his brother, his new guardian in Grenoble, would say memorably: 'I was, by turns, his father, his master and his pupil.'

III

RELUCTANT SCHOOLBOY

*The deputy head fearing a revolt made us say prayers in the
study rooms and go to bed. At half past nine people threw stones
at the dormitory windows after snuffing out the lights:
the panes were smashed. The deputy head came and made
a speech that only served to excite. When he withdrew, people again
broke windows and chamber pots by throwing them
against the casements. The deputy head did not know what to do;
he went to the garrison and had soldiers placed in the dormitory,
with fixed bayonets, to skewer the first person who moved.
People did nothing more but they were baying for blood.
No one had any sleep all night. I don't know to what extremes
they were ready to go; but I did not join in.*

(letter from Jean-François Champollion to his brother
from boarding school in Grenoble, probably summer 1805)

Grenoble, capital of the province of Dauphiné since the 11th century
and headquarters of the post-Revolution *département* of Isère, where
Jean-François arrived at the age of 10, would be almost his sole place
of residence for the next two decades. For all the many tensions in his
relationship with Grenoble, including a period of official exile after the
fall of Napoleon Bonaparte in 1815, the city became his home – far more
than either Figeac, the place of his birth, or Paris, the city that would
make him famous. Writing from the southernmost reaches of Egypt on
New Year's Day 1829 to a close school friend from a Grenoble family,
Augustin Thévenet, Champollion claimed that 'I am always basically a
frenzied *Dauphinois!*' The phrase represented his gleeful acceptance of
the hostile label ('Dauphinois endiablé') attached to him by the royalists
who had earlier exiled him from Grenoble.

Grenoble in the 19th century, where Champollion made his home for two decades from 1801. He always preferred Grenoble to Paris, but his relationship with the city was often tempestuous.

Liberal and republican sentiments were strongly evident in Grenoble's intellectual and cultural life, although it lacked a university until Napoleon began to establish one in 1805, at which the Champollion brothers would be appointed founding professors. But this republicanism had not led to extremism in its politics. Grenoble had managed to avoid the most violent excesses of the French Revolution, including the Terror, because its nobility had been in the vanguard of reform in 1789. In 1815, Grenoble became the first city in France to welcome back Napoleon from his exile on Elba, with the active support of the Champollion brothers.

The city's most famous son in literature, Marie-Henri Beyle – known by his pen name, Stendhal – had a less flattering response to Grenoble than Champollion. Stendhal was born there in 1783 and left his native place for Paris not long before Jean-François's arrival. In his thinly disguised autobiography, *The Life of Henry Brulard* (written 1835–36), he writes: 'All that is base or exhausted in the bourgeois type reminds me of Grenoble, all that reminds me of Grenoble fills me with horror; no, horror is too noble a word – sickness of heart. Grenoble for me is like the memory of dreadful indigestion.' Yet Stendhal protested too much, even by his own standard, for he could not refrain from showing his respect towards the inhabitants of Dauphiné. He admired what he called the 'temperament' of the *Dauphinois* – a 'way of feeling for oneself, quick, stubborn, rational … a tenacity, a depth, a spirit, a subtlety'. These were all qualities that Champollion *le jeune* would in due course display.

Since coming to Grenoble in 1798, elder brother Jacques-Joseph had been lodging in two rooms on the city's Grande Rue, near his place of employment at Champollion, Rif and Cie, a company that exported goods to the French Antilles, probably with the support of two rich *Dauphinois* families. But his mind was now increasingly focused on scholarly research rather than commerce. One of his two rooms he had converted into a library, which he continually added to, often purchasing books at very low prices from those whose estates that had been ruined by the Revolution. Thus the 10-year-old Jean-François found himself sleeping in a cocoon of ancient works written in several Oriental languages, which would soon induce him to start upon his life's research.

Jacques-Joseph had social ambitions too. His decision to change his surname from Champollion to Champollion-Figeac occurred some time after he moved to Grenoble. The longer name served to distinguish him from his Champollion cousins living in the area (and now, of course, from his younger brother); in addition, the adoption of a double-bar-relled name was an accepted mark of someone seeking to move up the social scale. Another step on the ladder was his election in December 1803 to the Society of Arts and Sciences of Grenoble, the successor to the celebrated Académie Delphinale that had been suppressed ten years earlier. Champollion-Figeac quickly became active within the society and through it started to work for the influential Joseph Fourier, the mathematician who had recently taken up his appointment as the prefect of Isère after returning from his labours among the savants in Egypt. Four years later, Champollion-Figeac married into an established, if not notably wealthy, local family of lawyers, the Berriats. However, it would be wrong to give the impression that Jacques-Joseph's worldly networking turned him into a 'pompous, cunning and venal' man, even in middle age, notes Jean Lacouture. 'Nothing of what is known of his relations with the majority of his contemporaries gives credence to such ideas.' He was both a real gentleman and a committed scholar. Nonetheless, Champollion-Figeac would always be a much more conventional person and thinker than Champollion *le jeune*.

As soon as Jean-François arrived, in March 1801, he received private tuition from a primary-school teacher – an arrangement made by his brother and always kept under his direction. In addition, Jacques-Joseph taught the boy himself, as he had started to do back in Figeac. After some months, Jacques-Joseph informed their old teacher Dom Calmels about Jean-François's progress in a letter written in January 1802:

His ordinary work is a translation in the morning, a prose piece in the evening, the rudiments, French grammar; l'Encyclopédie des enfants, and the second book of the Aeneid supply his lessons, to which I add some fables of La Fontaine … I correct his exercises twice a day and as often I ask him to return them and we argue over them word by word … So, Monsieur, these are the means I use to give my brother a little education.

But it was not all bread-and-butter tuition. Six months later, Jacques-Joseph told Calmels: 'I take care to look for moments of relaxation and then, by all possible means, to resuscitate his taste buds. I give him new food with a subject that is spicy and fresh; sometimes I pilot into port an aptitude floating in the immense space of the imagination. My brother works a lot, he achieves a lot and well.'

In November of that year, Jean-François became a day-boy at a school run by the Abbé Dussert, which had a high reputation in Grenoble. Although it was private, it collaborated with the city's public education system by sharing some particularly good teachers. One of these was a botanist, Dominique Villars, who took Jean-François on collecting trips into the mountains surrounding Grenoble and treated him as a favourite pupil. The school clearly suited the boy, who received a very good report from Dussert at the end of the first school year, in 1803. Now he was permitted to begin studying not only Hebrew, but also three other Semitic languages: Arabic, Syriac and Chaldean.

Champollion's first published paper, written in 1804 when he was 13 years old. At top right, writing in 1814, he calls it 'ma première bêtise' ('my first stupidity').

Initially, Jean-François's desire was probably to imitate his beloved elder brother and to help him in his research for the Society of Arts and Sciences, such as the decipherment of Latin inscriptions found on Roman antiquities recovered from the swamps at Bourgoin in Isère, then being drained under the supervision of Fourier. During 1803, however, he launched himself into his own studies, too – his first passion being the origins of mankind and a 'chronology from Adam up to Champollion *le jeune*'. Despite his youth, he was already in touch with leading scholars; the same year the count of Volney sent him his *Simplification des langues orientales*, followed by his *Voyages en Syrie et en Égypte*, and in due course a pressing invitation to visit him in Paris. In 1804, aged 13, Jean-François wrote his first published paper, 'Remarks on the fable of the Giants as taken from Hebrew etymologies', which was delivered two years later to the Society of Arts and Sciences by General de La Salette, since its author was considered too young to speak on his own behalf. Although within a few years Champollion dismissed the paper as foolish, its theme was an intriguing one: the Oriental origins of European fables about giants. In his own precocious words:

It is without doubt rather singular that almost all of the ancient peoples in the world have introduced into their religion giants, always in rebellion against the gods who have much difficulty in reducing them. It would be a very interesting thing to go back to the origin of this fable and find the meaning of these allegorical beings … It may appear strange perhaps that I search in Oriental languages for the etymology of proper names that appear in Greek myths, but one must not forget that it is from the Orient, and from the Egyptians above all, that the Greeks took most of their fables.

From around this time, ancient Egypt began to interest Jean-François more and more – a development that will be discussed in the next chapter, after we have covered his school career.

Dussert's school was expensive – far too expensive for Jacques-Joseph, whose pocket as a commercial assistant was limited, especially given his burgeoning bibliophilia. Early in 1804, therefore, he asked Jean-François to sit the examination for Grenoble's government-run *lycée*; the boy was accepted and given a bursary to cover his boarding fees. Following the summer holidays in 1804, when he returned to Figeac to visit his parents after a gap of more than three years – the last time that Jean-François would see his mother, as it turned out – he reluctantly left his brother's lodgings and became one of 180 boarders at the new school.

The forty-five *lycées* spread throughout France had been established by a Napoleonic law of 1802, but the one set up in Grenoble in the building of a former school did not open its doors to pupils until November 1804. The basic syllabus consisted of Latin and Greek literature, and mathematics, with the additional subjects of natural history, chemistry, technical drawing and geography. History, being controversial, was little studied, and philosophy was altogether absent, in deference to Napoleon's 1802 concordat with the Vatican. Discipline in the school was military: there were uniforms, companies, ranks and drum rolls between events in the timetable, which lasted from reveille at five-thirty in the morning to nine o'clock at night. A draconian prospectus addressed to parents in 1806, apparently intended as reassuring, noted: 'There is, every day, a period of up to ten hours for work; and a surveillance at all hours, at every minute, at night as well as in the daytime, during recreation time as well as during the period set aside for study, covering even the sleep time of the pupils – does not leave them alone for a single instant.' Such strictness may have been imposed in response to the dormitory revolt, described at the head of this chapter, that probably occurred in the summer of 1805; the uproar ended only after the arrival of soldiers from the local garrison, bayonets fixed. Although Jean-François claimed to his brother that he was a spectator, not a participant, this seems unconvincing. While it is unlikely that he was a ringleader, surely the injustice of the school's regime would have induced him, willy-nilly, to show his 'beak and claws' along with his fellow pupils.

No wonder, then, that Jean-François – used to living at home with unfettered freedom and to falling asleep while reading his brother's library books – disliked the *lycée* and rapidly came to see it as a prison. At one desperate point in his two-and-a-half years as a boarder, he even considered quitting and enrolling at the military school in Fontainebleau. Yet, although he was never happy at the school, he in fact worked hard there during term time, not only on the course work, but also on his private studies. By the time he left in 1807 he was considered an excellent pupil, if hardly a model one. The *lycée* may not have encouraged Champollion's particular genius, but it did not try to suppress it.

Indeed, most probably during his first year there, 1804–5, Jean-François played an active role in several school societies concerned with scholarship, very likely with the support of his brother. Signing himself 'president-treasurer, Champollion' of the so-called Academy of Muses, he wrote a flowery appeal (undated in its surviving form) to twenty distinguished *Grenoblois*, inviting them to become corresponding members of the school's nascent academy. Part of the epistle read as follows: 'Being too young to judge your work, it is to you that we have recourse ... Be for us an Apollo: show us the true path that leads to Parnassus.' Many of the recipients were probably already aware of who the signatory was, as a result of his brother's involvement with the Society of Arts and Sciences, and may well have indulged his invitation. Ironically, given this youthful enthusiasm for academic collegiality, Champollion's later dealings as an adult with a leading French scholarly academy in the humanities, the Academy of Inscriptions and Belles-Lettres in Paris, would always be ambivalent and at times bitter.

Notwithstanding some stimulating school activities, Jean-François's health began to suffer, leading him to faint periodically. From this point until his death some thirty years later, he would never be entirely well. The health problems he experienced at the school were partly self-inflicted. Disallowed by the authorities to study privately during the day, he decided to work secretly at night. After lights out in the dormitory, he would lie slightly propped up in bed, with a cotton bonnet on his head, his body angled to the right so as to catch the faint light from an oil-burning streetlamp that fell on his open book; as a result he acquired a slight squint in his left eye as an adult. But presumably most of the deterioration in his health was due to the effects of the school's spartan regime on a sensitive mind. Extracts from his letters to his brother, quoted by his biographer Hermine Hartleben, make for poignant reading. 'Send me a little money, because when they let us out it is a real pleasure to be able to drink a bowl of milk, above all when one is really tired.' Again:

'I feel that I am not well. I do not know what is hurting my chest, I think I may have an abscess ... Besides, the doctor in the infirmary prescribes only herbal tea for coughs to treat all such illnesses, even for toe ache!' And again: 'I have a fever, I can't go on like this. Your obedient brother.'

Some relief came near the end of the first year. The well-known mathematician and physicist Jean-Baptiste Biot – who would later become fascinated by the very same ancient Egyptian astronomical inscription as Champollion – came to hear of Jean-François through his scientific colleague, the prefect Fourier, who was friendly with Champollion-Figeac. Biot met the novice scholar and took pity on his predicament. He asked his friend Antoine Fourcroy, the director-general of public education in Paris, to examine Champollion's case. During Fourcroy's inspection of the Grenoble *lycée* on 1 June 1805, he gave Jean-François a brief examination and then granted him official permission to follow his personal studies during his free hours.

Naturally, this special dispensation irritated some of the school staff, who may have reacted by trying to make the gifted pupil's life difficult. Things came to a head, probably in June 1806, when Jean-François was 15 years old. We have only his side of the event, as described in an anguished letter to his brother. In this he speaks of a friend in the same division at school (unnamed, but known to have been Johannis Wangehis) 'whom I have loved with my heart and whom I will always love. He loves me as much as I love him, he helps me to endure the hurts and harshness that people direct at me.' Now, writes a furious Jean-François, his friend has been deliberately moved to another division by the school authorities. 'They have counselled him not to spend time with me any more because, they say, I am *corrupting* him – as if they could not corrupt him better than me' (the word is underlined in the letter). In Jean-François's view, the real reason for the move was that the director of studies was a 'bigot' and a 'hypocrite' who had taken against him, and who also spoke disobligingly of Jacques-Joseph. Any imputation of adolescent homosexual feeling to Jean-François is probably not justified – not least because there are not the slightest hints of such an inclination in his later life, though plenty of examples of male camaraderie. More likely the 'Wangehis incident' was an early example of Champollion's passionate romanticism, his frequent tact-lessness (especially towards those in authority) and his lifelong talent for creating enduring enemies at the same time as loyal friends.

A more reliable indicator of the school's attitude towards Champollion *le jeune* is that, in August 1806, Champollion was among those chosen to give a speech in front of the prefect, Fourier, when he visited the *lycée* to assess the quality of public education. Although Jean-François tried to wriggle out of the honour by appealing desperately to his brother for help, his public appearance went ahead, and he acquitted himself well. The *Journal administrative de l'Isère* reported on 31 August that 'the young J.-F. Champollion, national pupil' explained part of the Hebrew text of Genesis in the Bible and answered several questions put to him about Oriental languages; 'the prefect, who crowned the winners, displayed great satisfaction'. Shortly afterwards, in his report to the government in Paris, Fourier further noted that Champollion *le jeune* had shown knowledge of beetles, butterflies and minerals, which had been encouraged by his teacher, Villars, who taught him biology at the *lycée* as he had done at Abbé Dussert's school.

Jean-François's own linguistic research work, wholly independent of the school syllabus (which included no Oriental languages), was now taking off in earnest. His correspondence with his brother became a stream of demands for books and scholarly assistance. One letter mentions that he lacks buckles for his trousers, and in the very next sentence requests a Latin work on the grammar of the Ethiopic script, the *Ludolphi ethiopica grammatica*. Another letter asks: 'I beg you to be so kind as to send me the first volume of the *Magasin encyclopédique* or that of the proceedings of the Academy of Inscriptions and Belles-Lettres, because it is not always necessary to read serious things like Condillac'. By the middle of 1806, Champollion-Figeac was no longer able to supply all of the works that his brother needed, and asked advice from a leading Parisian antiquary and naturalist, Aubin-Louis Millin de Grandmaison, the founder of the *Magasin encyclopédique*. Millin advised that Champollion *le jeune* come to study in Paris with Silvestre de Sacy or go to the University of Göttingen, which was then admired for its scholarship in languages.

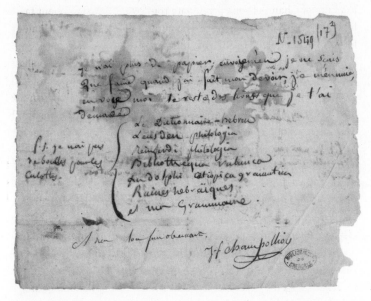

Undated letter from Champollion while at school in Grenoble, requesting from his brother both trouser buckles and scholarly books, including the *Ludolphi ethiopica grammatica* in Latin.

After 1 April 1807, Fourier gave Jean-François official permission to move out of the dormitory and return to his brother's house, so that he might concentrate on his own research while completing only those basic courses required for the *lycée's* leaving examinations. In the last of his school reports – which had varied erratically during his two-and-a-half years, between the top grade, A, and almost the lowest grade – Jean-François received five As and three Es, and was even, astonishingly, awarded a prize in his weakest subject, mathematics: 'what is known as a switchback career!' comments Lacouture. On his very last day at the *lycée*, at the end of August, as the usual patriotic speeches were made and the pupils celebrated the beginning of the holidays, Champollion was so overcome at the thought of putting the gates of the school behind him for ever that he fainted into the arms of his friend Thévenet.

A day or two later, on 1 September 1807, barely out of school uniform and a few months short of his seventeenth birthday, Jean-François read his first paper to Grenoble's Society of Arts and Sciences. Its title was 'Essay on the geographical description of Egypt before the conquest of Cambyses'. Probably Fourier, prompted by the society's joint secretary Champollion-Figeac, had proposed this precocious lecture. Even so, the members of the society greeted the adolescent speaker with warmth and genuine respect. On the spot, they moved to elect him a corresponding member, until one of their number, a Dr Gagnon, mildly protested that 16 was too young an age for election (it is noted in the minutes of the meeting). Some months later, now turned 17, Champollion *le jeune* was formally elected, about four years after his brother. The mayor of Grenoble, Charles Renauldon, uttered some prescient words on the occasion: 'In naming you one of its members, despite your youth, the Society has counted what you have done; she counts still more on what you are able to do. She likes to believe that you will justify her hopes and that if one day your works make you a name, you will remember that you received from her the earliest encouragement.'

IV

EGYPT ENCOUNTERED

I wish to make of this ancient nation a
thorough and continual study. The enthusiasm with which
the description of its vast monuments transports me,
the admiration with which its power and its
knowledge fill me, are sure to increase with the
new ideas that I shall acquire. Of all the peoples whom
I admire the most, I shall confess to you that not one
of them outweighs the Egyptians in my heart!

(letter from Jean-François Champollion to his parents, probably June 1807)

In the summer of 1806, the mayor of Grenoble, Renauldon, overheard his schoolboy son having a serious discussion about botany with his friend Champollion. The mayor asked the 15-year-old Jean-François if he intended to specialize in the natural sciences. 'No, Monsieur,' he replied solemnly. 'I wish to devote my life to knowledge of ancient Egypt.' By the time Champollion left his *lycée* a year or so later, there can be no doubt that he, his brother and his close contemporaries knew that penetrating the mysteries of Egyptian civilization was going to be the dominant passion of his life. What is not so clear, however, is how Champollion first encountered and embraced Egypt, and exactly when this happened, though it must have taken place between his arrival from Figeac in the spring of 1801 and his departure from Grenoble for Paris to study Oriental languages in the autumn of 1807.

If we are to believe the celebrated legend created by his devoted first biographer, Champollion experienced a sort of eureka moment before his twelfth birthday. It occurred 'in the autumn of 1802', according to Hartleben, in the following way. Some time after Joseph Fourier's arrival in Grenoble in April 1802 to take up his new appointment as prefect of

Isère, he was visiting various educational establishments when he met the 11-year-old Jean-François. After a short conversation the scientist–prefect, seeing the boy's zeal for all aspects of the ancient world, issued a thrilling invitation: to come and see his private collection of Egyptian antiquities kept at the prefecture.

Some months went by while the prefect got to grips with the complexities of his new position. Then the appointed hour arrived for the visit of the young admirer. 'But on entering the prefecture, [Champollion] was struck with such fear that the questions of the savant could not draw him out of a respectful silence,' writes Hartleben:

This only made him more attentive in listening to everything that the prefect was saying about Egypt; his excitement increased still further when his host showed him several hieroglyphic inscriptions on stone, as well as some fragments of papyrus, and his joyful admiration at last made him recover his habitual animation.

Fourier immediately explained to him the meaning of the zodiac [in the ancient Egyptian temple of Dendera], undoubtedly in the accepted manner of his time and without suspecting that exactly twenty years later (in September 1822) the 11-year-old boy then standing beside him would provide the definitive solution to this enigma. Struck by the precocity of his small guest, the prefect gave him advance authorization to come to the 'intimate soirées' that he intended to organize, so as to enable physical experiments and the latest discoveries to be studied by a group of handpicked specialists. François left the presence of his noble patron in deep happiness and he maintained many times afterwards that at the time of this first visit to Fourier he had experienced not only an ardent desire to be able to decipher the writing of ancient Egypt one day, but also the conviction that he would attain this goal.

It is an irresistible story of a child prodigy, full of charm and romance, which was touchingly dramatized in Carl Sagan's award-winning 1980s television series *Cosmos*. Since Hartleben's time several other writers on Champollion have been seduced by it, and have respectfully described the Fourier–Champollion encounter: Lesley and Roy Adkins in *The Keys of Egypt*, for example, published in 2000, and even the historians of science Jed Z. Buchwald and Diane Greco Josefowicz, in their academic study

Portrait of Joseph Fourier, prefect of Isère, mathematician, physicist and Egyptologist, who played a key role in the introduction of the young Champollion to ancient Egypt.

The Zodiac of Paris, published in 2010. The latter pair write of Fourier: 'He invited the boy to visit him at the prefecture, where he explained the significance of the Egyptian zodiac to the no doubt awed youngster, which indicates how much the issue was on Fourier's mind for months after his return from Egypt.'

Sadly for lovers of a good story, however, this one as told by Hartleben is almost certainly false, although it probably contains some elements of what really transpired between Champollion and Fourier. The historical evidence is firmly against such a fateful meeting. In the first place, contrary to Hartleben's claim, Champollion never once mentioned a schoolboy epiphany involving Fourier in any of his letters or published writings, and it was never alluded to in the memoirs of his friends and collaborators. Nor was it mentioned by his elder brother Champollion-Figeac, who was close to Fourier for much of his tenure as prefect, and who after the latter's death wrote a book about Fourier, Napoleon and Egypt. Nor did Fourier himself refer to it, though he did later on describe Champollion as 'a fiery colt demanding a triple ration'.

There is also no trace in the historical archives of Isère of such a visit by Champollion around 1802, despite searches made by sceptical biographers such as Lacouture and Faure. The earliest definite reference to a *tête-à-tête* between Fourier and Champollion *le jeune* comes as late as July 1809, in a letter from Jacques-Joseph encouraging his brother to visit the prefect – apparently for the first time, though this is not quite certain from Jacques-Joseph's phrasing (and 1809 seems surprisingly late for their first private meeting). 'There is no reason that this visit should annoy you,' writes Jacques-Joseph to Jean-François. 'M. Fourier is an excellent man, as good as he is kind. He is as Egyptian as you, he likes you because he knows your tastes and your works, and, let this be *entre nous*, he thinks better of you than of many of the members of the [Egyptian] Commission. You will be delighted to make his acquaintance in private.'

Also significant is the fact that Champollion-Figeac probably did not know Fourier as early as 1802, so he could not have had any intermediary role in a meeting between the prefect and his brother at that time. The first correspondence between Champollion-Figeac and Fourier dates from October 1803. Moreover, during most of 1802 Jean-François was actually not studying at school, but receiving tuition in private: he joined Abbé Dussert's institution only in November. So how could Fourier have met the boy on a school visit in mid-1802, as Hartleben claims?

Historical evidence aside, a private meeting between Fourier and an unknown schoolboy in 1802 seems psychologically implausible for a recently appointed prefect with pressing commitments to the running of his department. In addition Fourier, a well-known mathematician and physicist, is known to have taken up his surprising political appointment with great reluctance and purely at Napoleon's insistence; he feared that, residing in far-off Grenoble, he would be totally forgotten in Paris as a scientist. It is doubtful, therefore, that Fourier would have spent time in unnecessary meetings in Grenoble as early as 1802. (Incidentally, there is today a respected scientific institution in Grenoble, the Joseph Fourier University, the nucleus of which was founded by Fourier in 1811.)

More likely than a meeting à deux in 1802, it would seem, is that Champollion may have been a member of a school group from the lycée invited to the prefecture some time in 1804–6 to see the Egyptian antiquities, to whom Fourier offered a guided tour. Still more likely, Jacques-Joseph might have asked Fourier's permission to bring his brother along to one of the soirées held at the prefecture during the same period, where Jean-François would have been able to see the antiquities and perhaps hear about them from Fourier in the attentive presence of his elder brother.

This is a convincing thesis for a number of reasons. From late 1803, Champollion-Figeac, then a newly elected member of the Society of Arts and Sciences, began researching Roman inscriptions at Fourier's request, and the two men formed a working relationship. In June 1804, Champollion-Figeac sent a scholarly communication to the society about the inscriptions on the Rosetta Stone, which demonstrates his own growing interest in Egypt. The following year, with the help of a bibliophile friend, Champollion-Figeac was able to provide Fourier with an invaluable gift: the correspondence of the great mathematician Leonhard Euler, which a grateful Fourier himself presented in a paper read to the society. In 1806, Champollion-Figeac sent a second communication to the society, about the Greek inscriptions in the temple of Dendera, and this was formally addressed to Fourier. Throughout the period from 1804 onwards, Champollion-Figeac, privately helped by his younger brother, also gave Fourier crucial unofficial assistance as he undertook demanding research for his prestigious 'historical preface' to the first volume of the government's Description de l'Égypte. This publication was based on the work of the savants in the Egyptian Commission, including, of course, Fourier himself. Given these various and close connections between Champollion-Figeac and Fourier, what could have been more natural than for Jacques-Joseph to have brought his schoolboy brother to a soirée at the prefecture on an evening when a discussion of Egypt was scheduled?

Thus, rather than having a eureka moment with Fourier, Champollion must have developed his passion for Egypt somewhat more gradually, as a result of exploring the books on Egypt in his brother's library as he helped his research. In all probability this exploration began in 1803–4, at the time when Jean-François started to study Oriental languages and before he became a boarder at the detested *lycée*. One day at home in his brother's lodgings, as reported by Hartleben, he got hold of various books by ancient authorities such as Herodotus, Strabo and Diodorus, and enthusiastically tore out the pages from each one that seemed particularly informative about ancient Egypt. He spread them out in front of him and was about to plunge into a comparison when a cry of astonishment from his elder brother made him jump up. Only then did he realize his offence. But instead of roundly scolding him for the sacrilege, his brother in fact gave him a hug and made him promise to pursue his study of ancient Egypt with all possible assiduousness. Champollion's first ever published paper, the one written in 1804 examining the possible Egyptian roots of ancient Greek myths about giants, may have been an early outcome of his promise.

At this novice stage, Champollion's fascination for ancient Egypt seems to have been broadly focused, covering its art and history, its geography and natural history, its language and literature, and its religion and science. No doubt he was enthused by the early contributions of savants to the *Description de l'Égypte*, as the papers were submitted to Fourier during 1805 and subsequently passed across the desk of his elder brother in the course of his research for Fourier. Thanks to the prefect, Jean-François was able to look at a reproduction of the Rosetta Stone in 1804. The following year, he studied for the first time the faithful and detailed drawings of the current state of the country, including its ancient monuments, in the two entrancing volumes that described Denon's travels in Upper and Lower Egypt. Champollion's breadth of interest in Egypt would remain undimmed until his death, as is evident from the diary of his own Egyptian voyage, which speaks as much of nature and human life beside the Nile as it does of ancient tombs and temples. But within a year or two of his initial flush of excitement, he realized that he would have to focus on the Egyptian language and script if he were to make real progress in understanding the civilization as a whole.

A key moment – which can be dated fairly precisely, to June 1805 – was a meeting Fourier arranged at his house. A guest with Egyptian connections had come from Paris to stay briefly with the prefect; this was Dom Raphaël de Monachis, a senior Greek Catholic priest. Born Rufa'il Zakkur in Egypt, Monachis had lived in Syria, studied in Rome and acted as a cultural adviser to the French expedition in Egypt, where he had become friends with Fourier. In 1803, in gratitude for services rendered, Napoleon had appointed Monachis assistant professor of Arabic at the Special School of Oriental Languages in Paris.

From the professor–priest Jean-François obtained a manual of the Arabic dialect spoken in Egypt and started to learn the language for himself. In conversation with Monachis, he also began to grasp the importance of two other vernacular languages of Egypt, Coptic and Ethiopic, and their scripts. The three scripts – Arabic, Coptic and Ethiopic, belonging to the three most important languages spoken in the Nile Valley – might each be essential in elucidating the language of ancient Egypt, Champollion dimly perceived. Monachis knew enough Coptic to help his young companion get started on its study before he returned to Paris. With the help of published Coptic grammars such as Athanasius Kircher's, the language quickly became one of Champollion's favourites. Later, as a student in Paris, he would become convinced that Coptic should form the basis of his attempt to understand the ancient Egyptian language.

Studying Kircher's writings led him inevitably to the ancient source of Horapollo's *Hieroglyphika*, which Kircher had fancifully interpreted. At this point, Champollion was far from being critically aware of the unreliability of both these authors. Returning again and again to old Horapollo, he wrote a mass of notes on 'the symbolic signs of the Egyptians'. This was perhaps the first of dozens of digressions and blind alleys that he would follow over the next decade and a half of trial-and-error decipherment.

Mainly, however, Champollion concentrated on learning those Oriental languages that might serve to promote his Egyptian studies. During the summer holidays of 1806, for instance, while staying with a cousin, he wrote 'a little treatise on Hebraic numismatics of around 20 pages'. In the same break from school, he practised his translation skills on the biblical book of Exodus, studied the works of Arab geographers and wrote a commentary on the worship of Isis.

In a similar spirit, at the start of 1807 he began to edit a map of Egypt and to compile a 'geographical dictionary of the Orient' with particular reference to the Nile Valley. His general idea was to use the historical sources written in Greek, Latin, Arabic, Coptic, Hebrew and other Oriental languages to try to rediscover original ancient place names. The place names in contemporary use dated back to the Arab conquest of Egypt in the 7th century, and were presumably in many cases phonetic imitations of the names Egyptians used in the Greco-Roman period, which must, in turn, have derived from their ancient Egyptian names. From the midst of this research at the *lycée*, Jean-François wrote to his brother:

Would you have the kindness to ask M. de La Salette for the first volume of the Bibliothèque orientale. *It is a book I wish to read and that one cannot consult too much in order to keep to the right path in this maze of Oriental dynasties, and besides it is only there that one can familiarize oneself with the Oriental names and furnish one's memory with knowledge that is entirely necessary for someone who is destined to make a special study of Orientals.*

It was this research that culminated in the paper he addressed to the Society of Arts and Sciences in September 1807. Entitled 'Essay on the geographical description of Egypt before the conquest of Cambyses', it focused on the country before the Persian invasion in the 6th century BC. The map of Egypt he had created was given to the society.

Since the previous year, following enquires made by Jacques-Joseph to his scholarly contacts, it had been settled that, after leaving school, Jean-François would go on to study Oriental languages in Paris. He would receive financial support from his brother and the active assistance of the prefect Fourier and his connections in the capital. On 17 June 1807, probably at the dictation of Jacques-Joseph, Jean-François wrote formally to his parents asking for their permission – a letter part-quoted at the beginning of this chapter, which spelt out his commitment to the study of Egypt beyond any doubt. But before the letter could reach Figeac, his ailing mother died, on 19 June. Rather than visiting their widowed father in Figeac, the two brothers arranged to meet him at the Beaucaire Fair in July. So far as is known, Jacques Champollion fell in easily with the future plans of his eldest and youngest sons.

In the meantime, on 1 July 1807, Jacques-Joseph, who was now in his late twenties, married Zoé Berriat of Grenoble. At one time he had apparently considered marrying for advantage, but in the event he married chiefly for love, with the encouragement of his young brother. His bride's dowry was a country house at Vif, a beautiful *commune* just south of Grenoble, where she and her husband would now live. Theirs would prove a happy marriage, and for Jean-François something of a blessing in a life that had thus far been signally lacking in parental affection. He and his sister-in-law quickly established a natural, teasing relationship. On the morning of the wedding, she joked that he should consider whitening his brown skin for the ceremony. She also insisted that he change his family nickname from 'Cadet', French for 'youngest', to 'Seghir', an Arabic word of similar meaning. From now on this would be his name within the family.

In mid-September, about two weeks after leaving school and delivering his well-received paper to the Society of Arts and Sciences, Champollion *le jeune* set off for Paris by *diligence*, accompanied by Champollion-Figeac. He was not yet 17 years old and was hardly heard of outside Grenoble. By the time he returned to the city two years later, he would be widely recognized as a prodigy and already entitled to call himself 'Professor'.

V

PARIS AND THE ROSETTA STONE

You think to terrify me with your learned world.
But do you know what it really is, this learned world? The learned
world is like the political world, blindly led by a chief
who may or may not deserve to command, a chief whose every opinion
is believed because it is held by him … until someone else
stronger, more cunning and more skilful comes along to overthrow
the received wisdom, and put another system in its place …
Didn't people believe for a long time the earth was flat? …
The learned world of those days believed that.

(letter from Jean-François Champollion to his brother, September 1808)

The Paris that greeted Champollion and his elder brother in 1807 was far
from the Neoclassical city of grand monuments, spacious boulevards and
elegant bridges over the Seine that we know today. The building of the
Arc de Triomphe, for example, commissioned by Napoleon Bonaparte
in 1806 to celebrate his victory at the battle of Austerlitz, did not start
until 1810 and was not completed until the 1830s. The Egyptian obelisk
in the Place de la Concorde, where Louis XVI had been guillotined in
1793, was erected only in 1836, after Champollion's death (though partly
as a result of his persistent lobbying in Egypt and France, as we shall see).
The boulevards – and the new sewers – that obliterated the medieval city
date from the 1850s and 1860s, during the rule of Napoleon III, which
was also the final period of Champollion-Figeac's long life.

In 1807, by contrast, Paris was an astonishingly squalid, smelly and
disease-ridden place, with little public drainage and many buildings
still awaiting repair after the damage sustained during the Revolution.

Champollion, used to the relative cleanliness, pleasant atmosphere and beautiful surroundings of Grenoble, immediately disliked the capital and would never feel healthy or at ease there. He began to suffer from violent headaches, pains in other parts of his body, breathing difficulties and a chronic cough. 'The air of Paris drains me, I spit like a rabid person and I lose my vigour,' he complained to his brother, who had soon returned to Grenoble. 'This place is horrible, one's feet are always wet. Rivers of mud (without exaggeration) flow down the streets'. He was always very short of money and lacked respectable clothes for paying formal visits on behalf of Jacques-Joseph – a source of perpetual tension with his brother, because Jean-François felt embarrassed by his stocky, ill-dressed appearance. 'Here I look like a sans-culotte' – the famous term meaning 'without knee-britches', used for the extreme republican, working-class foot-soldiers of the Revolution who made a virtue of being able to afford only ordinary trousers – 'but without having either their principles or intentions,' he grimly joked. He was also lonely, without a single family member to offer him support. Although he would soon make many interesting scholarly and social contacts, as well as have an unsatisfactory love affair with a married woman, none of his friendships in Paris was comparable to those in Grenoble or Figeac. Privately he dubbed Paris 'Babel'; as an adult he came to dread living there.

Nonetheless, in this decade of Napoleonic ascendancy Paris offered Champollion unique opportunities as a scholar. Apart from the learned world of linguistic scholarship he had anticipated, the city was unexpectedly full of cultural treasures appropriated by the French from European countries overrun by Napoleon's victorious armies since his Italian campaign of 1796. Denon, as director-general of museums from 1804 – the year that Napoleon declared himself emperor – was deputed to oversee this cultural glorification of Paris. In a few years, the Louvre Museum and the Imperial Library (as the National Library was then known) became akin to 'the caverns of Ali Baba', notes Jean Lacouture. Indeed, the first Egyptian object Champollion saw in Paris was a colossal statue of Isis at the Louvre, discovered on the site of Hadrian's Villa at Tivoli and ceded to the French by the pope in 1797. Even though the statue was from the Greco-Roman period and Romanized in style, it made a big impact on Champollion. As for books and manuscripts, he soon found himself able to study rare Coptic works at the Imperial Library that had been 'borrowed' from the library of the Vatican in Rome. After Napoleon's fall in 1815, much of this loot would be forcibly returned by the victorious Allies. An English antiquary in Italy noted in 1827: 'I think there are few Coptic books in Europe [Champollion] has not examined: a very learned friend of mine told me there is no book in the Vatican in that language, that has not remarks of Champollion in almost every page, which he made when the MSS. were at Paris.'

Throughout his nearly two years in the capital, Champollion drove himself – and was driven by his brother, via long letters from Grenoble – extremely hard. His rather basic lodging (arranged by a somewhat grudging Jacques-Joseph) consisted of a single room in the house of a financially demanding landlady, centrally located in the chic district near the Tuileries Palace. He took his modest meals nearby, in the company of an impecunious husband-and-wife couple from Dauphiné, and had to do a lot of walking to reach the four institutions where he would carry out most of his studies: the College of France, the Special School of Oriental Languages, the Imperial Library and the Egyptian Commission.

An early letter to Jacques-Joseph, dated 27 December 1807, gives an idea of his relentless programme of learning:

On Mondays, at a quarter past eight, I leave for the College of France where I arrive at nine o'clock: you know it is quite far away: it's in the Place Cambrai, near the Pantheon. At nine o'clock, I take the Persian course with Monsieur de Sacy, until ten. As the course in Hebrew, Syriac and Chaldean is scheduled for midday, I go right away to M. Audran, who has suggested that I come to him on Mondays, Wednesdays and Fridays, between ten o'clock and midday. He resides inside the College of France. We pass these two hours in talking Oriental languages, and in translating from Hebrew, Syriac, Chaldean and Arabic. We always devote half an hour to working on his 'Chaldean and Syriac Grammar'. At midday, we go downstairs and he gives his Hebrew course. He calls me the 'class patriarch' because I am the ablest one … After leaving the course, at one o'clock, I cross Paris, and go to the Special School to follow at two o'clock the course of M. Langlès, who takes particular care over me. We talk until evening.

Imperial Library, Paris. The teenage Champollion was permitted to consult rare manuscripts in Oriental languages, including Coptic, as part of his course of studies.

On Tuesdays, I attend the course of M. de Sacy at one o'clock in the Special School. Wednesdays, I go to the College of France at nine o'clock; at ten, I climb up to M. Audran's residence. At midday, I attend his course. At one I go to the Special School (two hours) for the course of M. Langlès; and in the evening at five o'clock I am with Dom Raphaël, who makes us translate the fables of La Fontaine into Arabic.

Thursdays at one o'clock is the course of M. de Sacy. Fridays, I go as on Mondays to the College of France and with Messieurs Audran and de Sacy. On Saturdays, to M. Langlès at two o'clock …

I'm definitely overheated, so I'm going to take several baths that will give me enough strength to continue with my courses.

And this was just Champollion's formal tuition. There was, in addition, his pursuit of Coptic at the Imperial Library and the church of Saint-Roch; his involvement with research for the *Description de l'Égypte* at the Egyptian Commission; his articles for Millin's journal *Magasin encyclopédique*; the researching of Chaldean or Syriac music for General de La Salette in Grenoble; and much running around in pursuit of commissions from his demanding and ambitious scholar brother.

Silvestre de Sacy, Prosper Audran, Louis Langlès, Dom Raphaël de Monachis – these were Champollion's four main teachers in Paris. There was also a fifth teacher, who did not give formal lecture courses but played a crucial role in his training by instructing him in Coptic names and the pronunciation of Coptic letters. When visiting Grenoble, de Monachis had alerted Champollion to the importance of Coptic in studying Egyptian. In Paris, Monachis steered him towards the city's small Egypto-Oriental colony and in particular towards a Coptic priest at the church of Saint-Roch on the Rue Saint-Honoré. The priest, Yuhanna Chiftichi, had accompanied the French army to Egypt and subsequently given occasional assistance to the Egyptian Commission with its *Description de l'Égypte*. Champollion now began to have discussions in Coptic with Chiftichi at the church. Among the manuscripts at the Imperial Library he also discovered a few Coptic grammars by Arabs, which were superior to the grammars written by Europeans such as Kircher; he immediately copied them for his own use. He became fluent in the language. Coptic, he enthused to his brother in 1809, was 'the most perfect and the most rational language known'; for amusement he was now mentally translating everything that happened to him into Coptic. This, he said, was the best way to fix 'pure Egyptian' in his head. Watching his priest friend celebrate Mass, Champollion could listen to the liturgy in Coptic and dream that he might be hearing a sound like that of ancient Egyptian priests conducting their ceremonies. Significantly, after Champollion died in 1832, the catafalque for his funeral was kept at the church of Saint-Roch.

Inevitably, given his past struggles with educational institutions and individual teachers, Champollion's relationships with his Paris teachers ranged from very warm to downright hostile. With Audran, he was such a favourite that the teacher sometimes invited his gifted student to teach Hebrew to the rest of the class, most of whom were clergymen wishing to study the Bible. His relationship with de Monachis was also warm, as is implied by an incident related in a letter to his brother: one day a visitor, Ibn Saoûa, called in to see de Monachis,

Portrait of Silvestre de Sacy, professor at the Special School of Oriental Languages, would-be decipherer of the hieroglyphs and Champollion's most influential teacher.

encountered his companion Champollion and took him for an Arab. 'He began to make his salaam to me, to which I responded as is expected, upon which he proceeded to overwhelm me with never-ending politeness' – until, that is, Dom Raphaël tactfully intervened and put a stop to the unintended comedy.

With Langlès, Champollion was also a favourite to begin with, but after an incident they were at daggers drawn. Langlès was the founder-director in 1795 of the Special School of Oriental Languages, where he taught Persian and specialized in India. In March 1808, without consulting his student, the director put Champollion's name forward to be a French consul in Persia: a potentially dangerous posting for which he was totally untrained, ill suited and, not least, ludicrously young, being a mere 17 years old. When Audran confidentially shared this information with his pupil, Champollion was naturally horrified. Only the high-level political intervention of his mentor Fourier, who was alerted by Champollion-Figeac, scotched the unwelcome appointment. But Langlès took many years to pardon Champollion for his refusal. In addition, he regarded Champollion's attraction towards Egyptian, rather than Persian, as something of a personal betrayal, given his evident gifts as a student of Persian. Champollion, in return, pointedly nicknamed Langlès 'L'Anglais' – an unfriendly reference to the English.

Champollion's relationship with de Sacy – his most influential teacher, because he had a professional interest in the Egyptian scripts – was neither warm nor hostile, though it would swing between these two extremes at other points in Champollion's career, under the impact of both revolutionary scholarship and tumultuous politics. De Sacy was a reserved, even etiolated personality, disinclined to get carried away by enthusiasms – the polar opposite of Champollion. He was also a royalist, without any sympathy for republicanism – again unlike his student. But he was a major scholar and at times an inspiring teacher, able to put himself in the shoes of his students and to some extent turn them into his collaborators through his discussion of difficult texts in Persian and other Oriental languages. However, having failed to make much progress himself with the decipherment of the Egyptian scripts, de Sacy chose to give Champollion little encouragement in this direction as a student. Although there can be no doubt of Champollion's enduring respect for de Sacy's mind, despite their dramatic personal ups and downs, there would always be a mutual wariness in their relationship. Comparing de Sacy with Langlès in a letter to his brother towards the end of his first sojourn in Paris, Champollion wrote: 'As for M. de Sacy, he is different. He is a real savant, and, what is more, modest. But he does not strike up friendships with anyone; I hope through my work to come closer to him.'

One might have expected Champollion to have enjoyed a strong relationship with the Egypt-returned savants of the Egyptian Commission, given Champollion-Figeac's close association with Napoleon's appointee Fourier, who was in the midst of preparing a preface to the *Description de l'Égypte*. But this was not the case. Champollion was on good terms, if not always in agreement, with two young engineers, Édouard Villiers du Terrage and Jean-Baptiste Prosper Jollois, who were charged with writing most of the articles on ancient Egypt. But almost from the outset Edme Jomard, the geographer in overall charge of the *Description*, treated Champollion with coldness, then with sourness, and finally – once Champollion's decipherment had been announced, while the *Description*

Portrait of Edme Jomard, the geographer who travelled in Egypt with Napoleon's army and later edited the *Description de l'Égypte*.

was still in the process of publication – with bitter enmity. Rather than supporting Champollion's system, Jomard would argue for the rival claim of Thomas Young. Of all Champollion's detractors in France, Jomard would be the most persistent and vitriolic.

To some extent, one can sympathize with Jomard. After all, Champollion had not yet worked in Egypt, was egregiously ambitious for a mere student in his Egyptian goals, and was, moreover, only just out of school. 'Jomard considered him a young greenhorn who intended to produce a toponymic study of the Nile Valley without ever having been there, whereas he himself had just written his own geographical commentary for the *Description*,' comment Robert Solé and the Egyptologist Dominique Valbelle in *The Rosetta Stone: The Story of the Decoding of Hieroglyphics*. 'Worse than that: having acquired a solid knowledge of several Oriental languages, Jean-François Champollion could hardly wait to begin deciphering hieroglyphics. Jomard saw himself as the man for that job.'

On the other hand, Jomard was undoubtedly inadequate to the task of decipherment, as is revealed by the feebleness of his future correspondence on the subject with Young. He should have had the humility to accept this and to stick to other aspects of Egypt that he understood better, such as geography. Champollion recognized in 1808–9 that neither Jomard nor anyone else in the Egyptian Commission had sufficient expertise to tackle the Egyptian scripts. He noted that the illustrations of Egyptian geography, architecture, inhabitants and customs in the *Description* were generally fine (they are still appealing two centuries later), and that the engravings made from Egyptian manuscripts were excellent; but he thought that the depictions of the hieroglyphs carved on the monuments were inaccurate and sometimes seriously misleading – indeed, inferior to those in Denon's Egyptian travel books of

1802. After the first volume of the *Description* (dated 1809) appeared in the second half of 1810, Champollion told his brother dismissively: 'I do not have a great respect for [its authors], they may be able to give us some very good drawings, but their commentaries are just pudding water [*eau de boudin*]' – that is to say, fit only to be ditched. With each succeeding volume of the *Description*, Champollion's comments on the hieroglyphic sections would be equally, if not more, scathing. When he at last reached Egypt and checked the inscriptions for himself, his derision for the Egyptian Commission's published drawings was fully validated by the actual monuments.

Word of Champollion's private criticism reached Jomard, which no doubt increased his antagonism. But the young would-be decipherer could not restrain himself. Barbs against his contemporaries and rivals, whether they were French, English or of any other nationality, were integral to Champollion's personality and way of working. Far from being the restrained, mistreated, almost saintly figure portrayed by his first biographer, Hartleben, he was more like a revolutionary agitator emotionally committed to a great intellectual cause. Lacouture, as a well-known journalist and biographer of political figures such as Charles de Gaulle, André Malraux and Gamal Abdel Nasser, gives the true measure of this aspect of Champollion: 'He was a virulent polemicist, at times viperish, an implacable arguer, intolerant, a mixture of a Gascon musketeer, springing like other intrepid swashbucklers from his origin in Figeac, and a strong head from Dauphiné *à la* Stendhal. Very little found favour in his eyes or under his pen; and least of all those who claimed to precede him on the road to the great decipherment.' These characteristics would reveal themselves in Champollion's caustic reaction to those French scholars, such as Alexandre Lenoir, Étienne Quatremère and Jomard, who ventured into the hieroglyphic field in these early years, and to the far more serious challenger Young during the 1820s.

Champollion's polemicism was understood and tolerated by his brother, although he did not approve of it. But even Jacques-Joseph from time to time became exasperated when Jean-François's aspersions on the scholarship of others appeared to cloak a lack of progress in his own work. Why had he allowed himself to be discouraged in his study of a papyrus? Jacques-Joseph upbraided his brother in September 1808. 'You have read a line and a half – you have an alphabet and you rest there. I do not recognize you any more.' Where was his taste for Egypt? 'I have always told you that you lack perseverance in your enterprises. Must I carry out the job? I have associated myself with your work and you abandon me'.

To understand what had happened here, we should recall that in 1804 Champollion-Figeac had submitted a paper to the society in Grenoble on the Greek inscription of the Rosetta Stone. Since 1807, he had been pushing his brother to investigate the Rosetta Stone too. In April 1808, Champollion took his first serious look at the Egyptian scripts on the stone, using a copy borrowed from the Abbé de Tersan, a major collector of antiquities. Since the copy had come directly from the British Museum, it was likely to be accurate. (Champollion probably did not feel in a position to request a copy from the Egyptian Commission, which chose not to publish the Rosetta Stone until as late as 1822.)

By this time, thanks to his elder brother, Champollion had read the unsatisfactory 1802 analyses of the Rosetta inscription by the Swedish diplomat Johann Åkerblad and by de Sacy, which identified some proper names and a few words in the demotic section, and claimed (but did not prove) the existence of an alphabet in the demotic script. Champollion's aim was to see whether or not, using his new knowledge of Coptic, he could translate the Greek sentences on the Rosetta Stone into Coptic equivalents, and then somehow match the Coptic equivalents with the demotic sentences, assuming that the demotic words were spelt alphabetically, as were Coptic words.

However, he warned his brother in June 1808: 'I am afraid that our efforts will be in vain, because our Coptic dictionaries include too few words to hope to produce a complete translation of all the Greek sentences in precisely Egyptian words.' And this was what transpired, as he wrote a few days later: 'The attempt made on the Egyptian text produced no result ... The proper names that I read as Åkerblad did (though differing in our manner of breaking up the simple letters) are not in exact concordance with the Greek text.' That is, the proper names did not occur in the same positions in the demotic text as in the Greek text. So discouraging was this attempt that Champollion did not bother with any analysis of the hieroglyphic text (Åkerblad and de Sacy had made the same decision).

This setback notwithstanding, in August 1808 Champollion boldly tried to apply his own version of Åkerblad's demotic alphabet to a papyrus published by Denon, which he presumed to be written in a cursive form of the same script that appeared on the Rosetta Stone (wrongly, since the hieratic script of this type of papyrus is very different from the demotic of the stone). Again, unsurprisingly, the attempt was a failure. He informed his brother in September:

I have read a line and a half, with an alphabet based on a very well-known monument; I have found clear sense analogous with the context and in an acceptable style. And I cannot advance more than this. I cannot go further, some groups prevent me – I have studied them, pondered for entire days and I have understood nothing. It is true that, without flattering myself, I have gone much further in this matter than all previous antiquaries, since I am able to prove that all the papyri (in cursive script) use the same closely related alphabets, which no one else had suspected until now.

This last claim was hopelessly mistaken. And there was worse to come. The Abbé de Tersan had a large and fascinating collection of Etruscan objects in his private museum. Champollion, baffled by the Rosetta Stone and Denon's papyrus, now lit upon a wild theory, as has quite often happened with scholars attracted by the mystery of the Etruscan language and its script. (Interestingly, an Etruscan 'solution' to the decipherment of Minoan Linear B, Europe's earliest readable writing, would temporarily derail another brilliant decipherer, the schoolboy Michael Ventris, who eventually deciphered Linear B as an archaic form of Greek in 1952.) Perhaps, Champollion hazarded, the Etruscan alphabet of Italy, contemporary in age with the Greek alphabet, was historically linked with the more ancient alphabet of Egypt through the Phoenician alphabet; found around the Mediterranean, including in both Italy and North Africa, Phoenician was older than the Greek alphabet but younger than the Egyptian script. 'The Etruscans occupy me at the moment: the language, medallions, inscribed stones, monuments, sarcophagi, they have all engraved themselves in my head; and why? Because the Etruscans came from Egypt. There's a conclusion that will really irritate all your dusty scholars of Greek and Latin!'

No wonder that Jacques-Joseph was so exasperated with his brother at this time. Not only had Jean-François admitted to being defeated by the Rosetta Stone, he had also embraced an absurd theory worthy of Athanasius Kircher at his most fantastical, and added insult to injury by abusing the community of classical scholars to which Champollion-Figeac very much wished to belong. After an acid exchange of correspondence, in which Champollion *le jeune* gave further vent to his contempt for the learned world, the relationship between the two brothers reached a nadir in late 1808 from which it would not recover until the spring of 1809.

Champollion was forced to abandon his analysis of the Rosetta Stone in 1809, and did not take it up again in earnest until 1814. He made no progress to speak of in deciphering the Egyptian hieroglyphs while in Paris, apart from better appreciating the difficulty of the task he had set himself. But he was far from idle, and in his second year in Paris continued to study ancient Egypt. Not only did he perfect his knowledge of Coptic and complete a Coptic dictionary, he also drafted most of his first book, *L'Égypte sous les Pharaons*, which would be published in part in 1811 and fully in 1814, with a dedication to Louis XVIII.

In July 1809, it was officially announced that Champollion-Figeac had been appointed professor of Greek literature and secretary of the faculty of letters scheduled to open in Grenoble. Champollion *le jeune* was made assistant professor of ancient history in the same faculty. There was also some bad news: the French army was threatening to conscript the 18-year-old Champollion, having tried to do so without success the previous summer. Once again, Fourier came to the rescue, pleading with Napoleon I in the name of the Society of Arts and Sciences in Grenoble, to which Champollion had rendered service as a member. On the third attempt, Fourier's plea seems to have reached the ear of the emperor, and the threat was lifted. In mid-October 1809, Champollion arrived back with pleasure in his favourite city, ready for a new phase of his life in Grenoble, now as both a teacher and a scholar.

VI

TEENAGE PROFESSOR

The natural tendency of the human mind [is] to judge
events according to their results. Too often the writer, having sold
himself to blind fortune, so to speak, lavishes praise on some
reprehensible enterprise that has been crowned with success ...
This way of assessing facts is a natural consequence of cowardly
and criminal complacency born out of forgetting principles,
which finds justice wherever it sees triumph.
This slavishness shows itself in all periods and all places.

(Jean-François Champollion's inaugural lecture as assistant professor
of ancient history in Grenoble, May 1810)

Upon his return to Isère in 1809, by a quirk of fate Champollion found
himself back in his old school, the disliked *lycée* – in body, if not in spirit.
It so happened that the municipal library was located on the *lycée's* first
floor. Here, a room was set aside for the meetings of the Society of Arts
and Sciences, the former Académie Delphinale founded in 1789 and
suppressed in 1793. Champollion-Figeac, besides being joint secretary
of the society, was assistant librarian, and then chief librarian from 1812
onwards, when his brother was officially appointed as assistant librarian.
Between 1809 and 1821, the year he was forced to leave Grenoble, the
municipal library was Champollion's base in the city: 'the cradle of his
thought process', in the phrase of Lacouture.

   This was no ordinary library catering for a provincial city of 20,000
inhabitants. It had come into existence in 1772 to house the 40,000
volumes that had belonged to the late Monsignor de Caulet, bishop
of Grenoble from 1726 to 1771, which the city had bought by public
subscription upon his death. The books were located in rooms that had

belonged to the former college of the Jesuits before it had been turned into a school building. By 1809, the library's inventory had roughly doubled in size. During Champollion-Figeac's reign as librarian, during which he was aided by his fervently bibliophilic brother, the library acquired almost 3,000 further titles, mainly from two collections: a legacy from the Abbé Gattel (of whom more later); and much of the library of the Grande Chartreuse monastery, located in a remote mountain valley north of Grenoble. This foundation had been closed after the Revolution and handed over to the nation, including its more than 300 precious manuscripts and incunabula (books printed before 1500) – an extraordinary and unique resource for Champollion's research.

In the two years that Jean-François had spent in Paris – during which he had quarrelled with his brother about the learned world – Champollion-Figeac had ceased to be a mere assistant in a commercial firm and established himself as a socially prominent, politically liberal citizen of Grenoble. His marriage to Zoé Berriat in 1807 had given him the large family house at Vif and two children: Ali (a name suggested by his 'Arab' brother), born in 1808, and Amélie, born in 1809. It had also made him the brother-in-law of a future mayor of Grenoble, Hugues Berriat. His membership of the Society of Arts and Sciences had brought him into close contact with the prefect of Isère, Fourier, and turned him into the prefect's right-hand man. This had, in turn, led to his official appointments: as assistant librarian; as editor of the government journal *Annales du département de l'Isère*, in 1808; and then as professor of Greek literature at the fledgling university of Grenoble, despite his total lack of formal educational qualifications and his decidedly limited knowledge of ancient Greek – at least as compared with his younger brother. (By imperial decree, both Champollion brothers were awarded the diploma of Doctor of Letters after their university appointments had been announced.) During 1809, Champollion-Figeac conducted a campaign for the post of inspector of education against a rival candidate from the Catholic hierarchy. Although he eventually lost this particular battle, it helped mark him out in Grenoble as a liberal with political ambitions – a reputation that Napoleon Bonaparte himself would recognize and reward during the Hundred Days of his return to power in 1815.

In modern political parlance, writes Lacouture, Champollion-Figeac would be styled not only as a man of the left, but also as an 'intellectuel engagé'.

There was, however, precious little evidence of any willingness to challenge the ruling political or intellectual orthodoxy – Napoleonic or otherwise – in the official speech given at the opening of the university in 1810, which appears to have been written by Champollion-Figeac. It was delivered by the university's seniormost member, the 82-year-old Jean-Gaspard Dubois-Fontanelle, then the chief librarian of the municipal library and the newly appointed professor of history. He told the assembled worthies: 'The double object of education is the formation of men and of citizens. ... Individuals ... must contribute towards the general good, some through their virtues, others through their fortunes, yet others through their knowledge and talents, and everyone through their submission, their zeal and their faithfulness. Thus are enlightened governments seized by public education.' As for the teaching of the controversial subject of history – Champollion's future role at the university – the speech recommended 'a criticism that holds before itself the torch of philosophy: not the philosophy whose name has been prostituted, but the kind and sweet philosophy that teaches men to cherish and love themselves'.

The elderly Dubois-Fontanelle was kind enough to give up half of his professorial salary to the 19-year-old assistant professor Champollion, who had been offered a salary much less than that of the other professors on account of his exceptional youth. However, it is not difficult to imagine Champollion's derision for the sentiments contained in this speech. His own lectures on ancient history, which began in May 1810, caused some sensation in Grenoble. With splendid insolence and considerable courage in the French political circumstances of the age, he lambasted historians for their general slavishness to power, as demonstrated in the comment quoted at the head of this chapter. By way of contrast, he held up the example of the ancient Greek playwrights (perhaps partly to prod the conscience of his brother, the new professor of Greek?). He said:

Sophocles and Euripides, by representing in the theatre the crimes of the House of Atreus, performed a service to the Ancients, by inspiring in the Greek republicans a

hatred of kings and of government by a single person. But before the invention
of tragedy, Greece, like India and Persia, had poets as its first historians ...
They alone were the tutors of nations, they alone wrote about nature and the
power of the gods, and they alone related the history of princes and ruling families.

Not content with this implied criticism of the emperor, in his inaugural lectures Champollion also made it clear that, as a historical source of dates and geography in the ancient world, he would treat the Old Testament – which he of course knew in the Hebrew version – with scepticism. Moreover, he would place the Christian scriptures on the same footing as the writings of other religious traditions, such as Hinduism and Islam. While this comparative stance towards religion was not so controversial during the anti-clerical Napoleonic period, it would become a hot topic after 1815, with the restoration of the king and the ascendancy of the Catholic Church, especially when the age of Egyptian civilization appeared to challenge biblical chronology.

Champollion-Figeac did not approve of such blatant attacks on established authority, but he could not restrain his irrepressible younger brother. 'One can see that our pedagogue, though scarcely launched on his professional life, was already cultivating the art of making himself enemies,' observes a recent Champollion biographer who hails from Grenoble, Alain Faure.

One who was already provoked, if not yet an enemy, was his former teacher in Paris, de Sacy. In March 1810, while Champollion was preparing his lectures on ancient history, de Sacy wrote unexpectedly to Grenoble – not to his former student, but to Champollion's elder brother Champollion-Figeac. De Sacy advised: 'I do not think he [Champollion] ought to attach himself to the decipherment of the inscription from Rosetta. Success in these kinds of researches is more the result of a happy combination of circumstances than of stubborn effort that sometimes leads us to mistake illusions for realities.' If anything, this letter had an effect opposite to that intended by de Sacy. A few weeks later, Champollion told a student friend in Paris, Jean-Antoine Saint-Martin, who had attended de Sacy's course with him in 1807–9 and had enquired about the progress of his obsession with the hieroglyphs, that he hoped to take up the Rosetta Stone again 'with ardour', once his history lectures were done – 'although M. de Sacy has written on this subject to my brother and may hardly encourage me himself …'. He commented: 'All that is very wise; however, *audaces fortuna juvat'* – a Latin tag that translates as 'Fortune favours the bold'.

De Sacy was not misguided in his reasoning; in fact, he turned out to be fairly prescient about the combination of circumstances in 1821–22 that would produce Champollion's breakthrough, as we shall see. Yet his motive for trying to deter Champollion was surely other than the honourable one he implied to Champollion-Figeac: that he did not want Champollion to waste his time and energy on fruitless work. In truth, it looks as if de Sacy did not care to be upstaged by his own student, however brilliant; this much is evident from the professor's open disparagement of Champollion after 1814.

Just a few months later, Champollion proved as good as his promise to Saint-Martin. In August 1810, he delivered a significant lecture before the Society of Arts and Sciences, entitled 'Ancient Scripts of the Egyptians'. Although most of what he proposed was almost pure illusion, just as de Sacy had feared, there was one idea that would prove to be fertile.

The illusion was that he had discovered four types of Egyptian writing. Two of them (now known as demotic and hieratic) were simply alphabetic, he maintained. From these had developed two different types of non-phonetic writing, hieroglyphic and 'symbolic', which used signs to represent ideas, not sounds. In other words, Champollion had reversed the real historical order of development, which is from hieroglyphic and hieratic to demotic. According to him, the reason that the hieroglyphic (and the symbolic) script developed later, and not earlier, than the first two scripts was that it was more refined and expressive than them, having been created in order to suit the more complex requirements of the priestly and ruling elite rather than the simpler needs of merchants and ordinary worshippers. As he confusedly explained:

The result of all that we have said is that there are four scripts of the Egyptians, one of which [demotic] served for common usage and was employed in commerce, the second of which, hierogrammatic [hieratic], served to write the liturgy …

and was understood by the educated class of people, along with the hieroglyphic
script, which was properly speaking a monumental script only. The true priestly
script, which was understood only by the priests, was the symbolic script, the
principles of which they communicated only to initiates and to the highest class of
the State. This was not at all to mislead the people nor to hold them in slavery ...
but rather to hide from them august verities that were outside their grasp.

His good idea was more logical. He simply observed that, if the
hieroglyphic section of the Rosetta Stone was a translation of the Greek
section, then it must represent the Greek proper names present in the
Greek section, such as Ptolemy, Berenice, Arsinoe and Alexander. This
was impossible, he noted, 'if these hieroglyphs did not have the power to
produce sounds'. For the first time in his career, Champollion was pro-
posing a phonetic element in hieroglyphic – but only in the hieroglyphic
spelling of non-Egyptian proper names, not in the rest of the script.

Champollion's suggestion preceded a similar proposal made in
1811 by de Sacy regarding the hieroglyphic cartouches (mentioned in
Chapter 1), yet it postdated a remarkable paper presented to the Society
of Arts and Sciences by the Abbé Gattel. Gattel had argued that European
alphabets probably derived from Egypt, and therefore that Egyptian hieroglyphs must be a mixture of 'abbreviated symbols' representing things
(i.e. pictograms) and other, 'purely arbitrary' signs representing sounds
(i.e. alphabetic letters). Gattel had presented his phonetic theory to the
society in 1801. He was a former teacher of grammar to Champollion
at the *lycée* and was also a *habitué* of educated gatherings in Grenoble,
including the soirées held by the prefect Fourier, where Champollion
himself was something of a star turn in the period after his return
from Paris. It seems highly likely that Gattel and Champollion would
have discussed Gattel's theory in person, and practically certain that
Champollion would have read Gattel's paper by 1810. But Champollion
made no reference to it in his lecture.

Someone else who also failed to make due acknowledgment – this
time to the Champollion brothers – was Fourier himself. His historical
preface to the *Description de l'Égypte* appeared at last in 1810, without the
slightest reference to their help. How much the Champollion brothers

actually contributed will never be clearly known, owing to lack of documentary evidence, but it is plain from Champollion's correspondence with his brother that he had freely shared with Fourier the content of his forthcoming book, *L'Égypte sous les Pharaons*, during 1809. The prefect's lack of acknowledgment was beyond doubt deliberate, especially in the case of Champollion-Figeac, and it led to a cooling of relations on both sides. But the brothers needed Fourier more than Fourier needed them – after all, he had supported their appointments at the new university and had saved Champollion more than once from being conscripted by the army – so they had little choice but to accept his public silence about their help. It did, however, put Champollion in the awkward and unfair position of having to cite Fourier's preface in the work he published in 1811, even though some of the ideas he was citing had originated with him and not with Fourier. Had Champollion, too, kept silent about his sources, he might easily have been accused of plagiarizing Fourier's preface by detractors such as Edme Jomard.

Anxious worries about allegations of plagiarism were at the forefront of Champollion's mind in the second half of 1810, because he had got word that an earlier student of de Sacy, Étienne Quatremère, had nearly completed a book in the very same field of ancient Egyptian geography as that covered in *L'Égypte sous les Pharaons*. Eight years his senior, Quatremère had published a book in 1808 aiming to demonstrate the already familiar suggestion that the Coptic language was identical to the language of the ancient Egyptians. As a curator of manuscripts at the Imperial Library, Quatremère must surely have had personal dealings with Champollion during the latter's student researches into Coptic, but the two of them had not become friendly. Quatremère's new book, Champollion learnt, was to be a fuller study of the same subject, relating the Coptic names of Egyptian towns and villages to their ancient names. Champollion immediately recognized that his as-yet-unpublished *L'Égypte sous les Pharaons* risked being pre-empted by Quatremère's work. Worse still, there was a danger that, when his own study was published, he would be accused of having plagiarized Quatremère's book.

In consultation with his brother, Champollion decided that he should pre-empt Quatremère by publishing as soon as possible.

He would produce his long introduction to *L'Égypte sous les Pharaons* as a self-contained 67-page booklet, which would also include an 'Analytical table of the geography of Egypt under the Pharaohs' discussing the names of 174 towns and villages. (Quatremère would manage 104 names.) Champollion's booklet was printed in Grenoble in October 1810, but its publication was delayed by its distributors and it was not officially released until the beginning of March 1811, two months after his rival's book became available.

To Champollion's chagrin, exactly what he had feared transpired during 1811. De Sacy, who liked Quatremère personally, published a favourable review of Quatremère's book. More woundingly, Champollion's former teacher seems to have persuaded himself that there was some truth in the notion of plagiarism, despite the clear evidence against it and the remonstrations of Champollion's friends in Paris, including an over-zealous Saint-Martin. Yet when a pained Champollion-Figeac raised the allegation directly with de Sacy in a letter, de Sacy denied that he believed Champollion to be guilty of plagiarism. The whole sorry episode – following the recent imbroglio surrounding Fourier's preface – was understandably an upsetting experience for Champollion, which affected his health. Not only did it make him distrust de Sacy, it also hardened his resolve to ensure that in future he would receive the maximum possible public credit for his ideas; this would become only too obvious in his dealings with Thomas Young a decade later, after Champollion's decipherment of the hieroglyphs had been announced. Once bitten, he became determined to use his 'beak and claws'.

Between 1812 and 1814, when the complete *L'Égypte sous les Pharaons* appeared in Paris – a politically turbulent period both in Grenoble and in Paris – Champollion published very little on Egypt. But he continued to research and to speculate on all aspects of the subject, including its ancient writing. In November 1812, he carefully examined some ancient Egyptian objects in the small museum attached to the municipal library. They included two human mummies, one of which had given to the library in 1779 by the French consul-general in Egypt at the request of his doctor cousin, a member of the Académie Delphinale; two other mummies, of ibis; and two alabaster funerary vessels of the type known to antiquaries as canopic jars, whose lids were in the shape of animals, in this case an ape and a jackal. The smaller jar, 30 centimetres (12 inches) tall, was still sealed. Champollion decided to remove the ape-head lid and discovered a dark-coloured, coagulated lump at the bottom of the jar. He then immersed the jar in boiling water for two hours, which melted the embalming fluid and allowed him to extract a cloth-wrapped object. (Today, 'the ape-head lid is slightly blackened where the tar-like contents spilled over during the experiment,' note Lesley and Roy Adkins.)

Champollion's brief 'laboratory' notes, which survive, show that he was excited by his experiment:

In the bain-marie
The straw finely chopped
The object wrapped in a cloth …
The object 4 inches by 2
Very clearly of animal nature
Fibrous tissue
In the lamp: animal odour
Hardening of the animal part
And boiling of the balm, reduction to black carbon
Found at the bottom of the vase
The object impregnated and recovered with a thick layer of balm
Wrapped simply in the cloth
Two small splinters of sea-green
Egyptian porcelain
It is from the liver, the brain or the cerebellum.

M. Bilou, a taxidermist from the Museum of Natural History in Paris who happened to be visiting Grenoble, thought that the embalmed organ could be a liver, a heart or a spleen; Bilou favoured a spleen on the grounds of its volume.

The more important conclusion, however, was one that Champollion shared with Saint-Martin in a letter in early 1813. Classical authors on Egypt had written that the heads that appear on the lids of such jars were images of the god Canopus. In fact, said Champollion, such a god did not exist: the four different kinds of head must represent not the non-existent Canopus, but four different 'geniuses', or aspects of God. (Nevertheless, Egyptologists still use the term 'canopic' for these vessels.) Later in his career, after he had deciphered the inscriptions on canopic jars, Champollion was able to be more specific. Today we know that the ape head is associated with the cardinal direction north and guarded the lungs; the jackal head with the east and the stomach; the human head with the south and the liver; and the falcon head with the west and the intestines.

As for the Egyptian writing system, Champollion's ideas in this period continued to flounder over-confidently in a morass of confusion and error, with occasional glimpses of the truth. Wisely, he published nothing, but we can gain some knowledge of his thinking from his letters to Saint-Martin in 1813–14. 'I am always working on my inscription from Rosetta and the results are not coming as quickly as I would have wanted … I have plenty of ideas but I do not dare to trust them until I have obtained some successes … One cannot guard too much against oneself,' he admitted in May 1814.

To give some examples of how Champollion's thoughts ran at this time, he abandoned the incorrect notion set out in his 1810 lecture that the hieroglyphic script had developed out of the demotic and hieratic scripts (to use current terminology, not Champollion's terminology in 1814). He also gave up the idea of a fourth, 'symbolic' script used only by the priests. But he still clung to the erroneous belief that the demotic script was alphabetic, and that its letters could be substituted with their Coptic equivalents to produce ancient Egyptian words. He also visualized a somewhat larger element of phoneticism in the hieroglyphic script, but came up with far too few phonetic signs: 'In the hieroglyphs, there are two sorts of signs: 1. the six alphabetic signs indicated; 2. a considerable but indeterminate number of imitations of natural objects.' And he began correctly to perceive the complex nature of the hieroglyphic system: 'It is my conviction that a single hieroglyph, that is to say in isolation, has no value, but that they are arranged in groups which I can already distinguish with ease.' But then he went on to contradict himself with an absurd error: 'The system of the hieroglyphs is, like that of the Egyptian language, entirely syllabic'.

In *L'Égypte sous les Pharaons*, Champollion made this astounding claim about his study of the Rosetta Stone:

The first step to be taken, and no doubt the easiest, in this study whose object makes it so important was the reading of the Egyptian text of the Rosetta inscription: I have been fortunate enough to see my efforts crowned by almost complete success; several passages of the Egyptian text are cited in the two volumes I am publishing, while I await the moment when the order of study I have adopted will focus my attention on this precious monument.

He was, however, sensible enough not to publish these passages in 1814 and thereby invite the well-deserved scorn of de Sacy and others. He knew that he was very far indeed from having cracked either the demotic or the hieroglyphic systems. Rather than having achieved a true decipherment of the stone, he had merely made deductions about the meaning of some groups in the Egyptian part of the inscription by comparing them with their Greek equivalent, and by using additional evidence from Coptic manuscripts and the reports of European and Arab travellers, classical authors and the *Description de l'Égypte*.

It may not be much of a stretch to say that the febrile hieroglyphic musings of Champollion in 1812–14 were a reflection of the agitated temper of France in this period. In late 1812, after Napoleon's catastrophic military retreat from Russia, Fourier removed Champollion-Figeac from his position as editor of the *Annales du département de l'Isère* for publishing uncensored 'harmful information'. Although Champollion-Figeac managed to repair his relationship with the prefect to some extent at a personal interview in early August 1813, by the autumn it was clear that Napoleon's throne, and hence Fourier's position, was under threat from a military coalition of Austria, Prussia and other German states, Russia, Spain, Sweden and the United Kingdom now arrayed against France. In October, Allied forces (led by the duke of Wellington) invaded southern France from Spain and, when Napoleon refused to capitulate, the enemy threatened to enter deeper into France. In the spring of 1814, Grenoble was at the mercy of an Austrian army, and the city's inhabitants, including the Champollion brothers, were enlisted for its defence. Only the fall of Paris on 31 March, and the abdication of Napoleon on 6 April, relieved Grenoble of an imminent armed attack, but the city had nonetheless been occupied by the Austrian army by the time of the restoration of Louis XVIII in Paris in early May. In the very period when Champollion was writing his letter to Saint-Martin about hieroglyphs, he was also receiving Austrian army officers at the municipal library in search of interesting reading matter.

Restoration of the Bourbons. Louis XVIII stands outside the Tuileries Palace after his return from his English exile to Paris on 8 July 1815, following the defeat of Napoleon at Waterloo.

The Champollion brothers reacted differently to the fall of Napoleon and the restoration of the Bourbons. Both welcomed the return of peace with relief, and with 'a terrible pleasure', in Jean-François's case. He had never supported autocracy, militarism and empire building, and had openly said so in his lectures at the university in 1810. But whereas Jacques-Joseph headed for Paris as soon as possible to ingratiate himself with the new regime of Louis XVIII, whatever his personal views may have been, Jean-François stayed in Grenoble and regarded the return of royalism and the power of the clergy with the gravest suspicion. He took to composing anonymous satirical songs against the regime, which the *Grenoblois* sang late at night, 'above all in the least well-lit streets of the city, to the great exasperation of the police,' reports Hartleben. As in 1808, the brothers exchanged harsh words about careerism in their letters, without either persuading the other he was right. 'I do not recognize you, you who protest so learnedly against vice, pride and pretentions,' the younger told the elder in June 1814. 'As for me, my fate is clear: like Diogenes, I shall try to buy a barrel.'

In Paris, Champollion-Figeac did well for himself, picking up two honours: a Décoration du Lys from the new government, and a corresponding membership of the Academy of Inscriptions and Belles-Lettres. Yet he also, as ever, did his best to help his brother's Egyptian research. Having found a Paris publisher for *L'Égypte sous les Pharaons*, Jacques-Joseph promptly requested that the book be dedicated to the king, and was able to present Louis XVIII with a luxuriously bound copy at a personal interview on 12 August 1814. Jean-François's letter to him from Grenoble stopping the royal dedication arrived too late. Although Champollion was not to know it, in the 1820s Louis XVIII and his brother Charles X would become key supporters of his Egyptian career.

Two months later, Champollion sent the newly dedicated book to the Royal Society in London, with a request for an accurate copy of the Rosetta Stone inscription held in the British Museum. The request landed on the desk of the society's foreign secretary. By chance, he happened to be the one person in Britain who shared Champollion's urge to decipher the Stone: Dr Thomas Young. The race between Champollion and Young was about to commence.

VII

THE RACE BEGINS

M. Silvestre de Sacy, my former professor, has passed on to
me no information about your paper on the Egyptian part and the
hieroglyphic text of the inscription from Rosetta:
which is as much as to say, Monsieur, that I would eagerly receive
the copy that you have been kind enough to offer me.
I beg you to address it to M. Champollion-Figeac, Rue de Lille, No. 73,
in Paris, who receives my packages and my letters …
I dare to hope that it will permit me to continue a correspondence
in which the entire benefit is certain to be entirely on my side.

(Jean-François Champollion's first letter to Thomas Young,
from Grenoble, May 1815)

Thomas Young's name has already cropped up numerous times in this book. Given the pivotal role he played in the decipherment of ancient Egyptian writing between 1814 and 1819 – which even Champollion, and certainly all but Young's severest detractors, would concede in the following two centuries – it is time to say something more substantial about the background, career and personality of Young. In nearly all significant respects, these differed fundamentally from those of his rival, Champollion.

Partly for this reason, no doubt, and because of their admiration for their subject, and possibly also because of their lack of knowledge of science and English culture, Champollion's biographers have tended to underestimate Young or to misunderstand him (or both). Champollion himself started the trend by referring to Young as simply a medical doctor, which indeed he was, professionally speaking. Champollion's first biographer, the German-speaking Hermine

Hartleben, preferred instead to call Young simply a physicist – which he also was. However, Young was very much more than a doctor and a physicist.

Reading Hartleben's enormous biography, one receives not the faintest hint that Champollion's English rival was one of the great physicists and scientists of his age – a scientist whom Albert Einstein would compare with Isaac Newton for his discovery of the interference of light in 1801, and certainly one of great polymaths of any period. Besides being a doctor attached to a major London hospital and a physicist associated with the Royal Institution, Young was a leading physiologist. He discovered the phenomenon of astigmatism and was the author of the three-colour theory of vision, which explains how the retina responds to light. He was an accomplished classical scholar, whose Greek calligraphy was admired by Edmund Burke and published in a well-known classical teaching text; and he was a friend of the leading British classicist of his day, Richard Porson. He was a highly gifted linguist, who compared the vocabulary and grammar of some 400 languages and in 1813 coined the term 'Indo-European' for the language family that contains Greek, Latin and Sanskrit. And he had expertise, which the British government and other institutions drew upon, in many other areas, such as bridge building, ship construction, the astronomical calculation of longitude for nautical almanacs, the mathematics of life insurance (for which he received a considerable salary from a life insurance company) and the tuning of musical instruments. Had Nobel prizes existed in the 19th century, Young would have received one – and perhaps even two, in physics for his work on the wave theory of light, and in physiology for his studies of the human eye and vision.

Champollion biographers more recent than Hartleben may have a better awareness of Young's range and stature, but they still cannot really figure him out. Each biographer struggles to place Young in a suitable niche or to fit him into a comfortable stereotype.

For instance, the Egyptologist Michel Dewachter makes virtually no reference to Young's polymathy, presumably because Dewachter regards science and polymathy as irrelevant to Egyptian decipherment. The historian Alain Faure, by contrast, emphasizes this aspect: 'In France we hardly know this genius savant … He was an original, very much in the tradition of British savants, capable of galloping upright on two horses or of playing on the bagpipes in his consulting room: Sherlock Holmes is not far away!' Yet in fact Young was often criticized by scientists and mathematicians precisely for relying too much on intuition and neglecting in his published work the kind of logical, step-by-step proofs beloved of a Sherlock Holmes. The political journalist Jean Lacouture writes admiringly that Young 'was to light what Joseph Fourier was to heat' – which is true enough. He emphasizes both Young's science and his polymathy. But then, despite being highly perceptive about Champollion, Lacouture gets carried away with his personal passion for Enlightenment ideals, claiming that Young:

> passed through life on a cloud of light, from success to triumph, seeming to find in each of his discoveries the key to unlock the following one, multifaceted and idolized, magnificent and princely, so accustomed to the top rank that he was indignant that in a domain he had casually skimmed, as in a game, following so many illustrious philologists, he should fail to vanquish straight away, exactly on the mark, and for ever. Nothing destined Young to be the decipherer of the hieroglyphs, except his genius for success. And perhaps also his desire to be at this point a man of light, in all its forms, and of the Enlightenment. Lavish, kind, curious about everything, skilled in dancing, in music, happy in society, he was born for triumphs. How could such a man put up with not being recognized by everyone as the sole conqueror?

Most of this character sketch, however striking, is a far cry from the truth. The real Young, who was no aristocrat, was far indeed from being obviously destined for success and triumph. In this respect he was like Champollion. Born in an obscure village in the county of Somerset in 1773, distant from London, first-class education and social connections, Young was the eldest son of a large and undistinguished family of moderately educated, commercially none-too-successful, generally rigid-minded Quakers. His parents largely abandoned him as a very young child to the care of his grandfather, apparently for lack of income and room in their house.

Although Young had some limited school education and later attended three universities (Edinburgh, Göttingen and Cambridge), he was essentially self-taught, as he often declared, and had no intellectual mentors. His early penchant for polymathy did him no favours in the professional world, and indeed provoked self-doubt and the worry that he would be viewed as a dilettante. In his career as a doctor, Young received little honour and enjoyed a comparatively small practice, largely because he preferred medical research to visiting patients and could not fake the over-confident 'bedside manner' necessary for a successful doctor in this period of yawning medical ignorance. In his career as a scientist he faced both surprising indifference and vitriolic criticism in Britain (although, ironically, he received consistent admiration and honour from scientists in France); in 1804 this criticism became so stinging that it almost persuaded him to give up science. Although he was socially accepted and conservative (with a small 'c'), he was politically uninvolved, not at all lionized for his gifts, and was not awarded the knighthood he plainly deserved. At the Royal Society, where he was foreign secretary for a quarter of a century, he gave not a single speech at a council meeting. Compared with many of his immediate contemporaries, such as the chemist and president of the Royal Society Sir Humphry Davy, Young, far from being egotistical, was a paragon of modesty. He seldom used his own name when he published his writings in Egyptology and many other subjects, preferring anonymity as a scholar; and he showed no envy and very little rancour towards his contemporaries, even towards Champollion at the height of their dispute in 1823. Married but childless, Young spent most of his adult life as quietly and uncontroversially as other gentleman scholars living in the wealthier parts of the metropolis. Although he was comfortable financially, his lifestyle was never excessive: he was careful with money, a teetotaller, and had inexpensive habits apart from bookbuying. His chief pleasure was intellectual: to read, to think, to write and occasionally to experiment, alone in his study.

One might even say, contra Lacouture, that the solitary decipherment of ancient scripts was an activity to which the polymathic Young was predestined – not least because decipherment belongs to both the sciences and the humanities. There is a beguiling story that a friend of Young, a former army doctor and a fellow of the Royal Society, was once out stargazing in London at two o'clock in the morning, armed with a telescope and accompanied by his wife and another couple, when he happened to notice a light in the window of Young's house; clearly Dr Young was burning the midnight oil again. When he rang the door-bell at 48 Welbeck Street, Young appeared personally in his dressing gown, and the little group was invited inside to see a piece of Egyptian papyrus, which Young was in the midst of translating. It appeared, said the polymathic physician, to be a Ptolemaic horoscope.

Thus Young and Champollion, despite their shared fascination, had highly contrasting careers and personalities that would influence their approach to decipherment. Champollion had tunnel vision about Egypt ('fortunately for our subject', writes the Egyptologist John Ray); was prone to fits of euphoria and despair; and would help to lead an uprising against the French king in Grenoble, for which he would be put on trial. Young, besides his polymathy and a total lack of engagement with party politics, was a man who 'could not bear, in the most common conversation, the slightest degree of exaggeration, or even of colouring' (recalls Young's close friend and first biographer, Hudson Gurney).

Consider their respective attitudes to ancient Egypt. Young never went to Egypt, and never wanted to go. He felt no attraction to its ancient customs and religion, which he regarded as foolish supersti-tion. In founding an Egyptian Society in London in 1817, to publish as many ancient inscriptions and manuscripts as possible, so as to aid decipherment, Young would remark to Gurney that funds were needed 'for employing some poor Italian or Maltese to scramble over Egypt in search of more'. Champollion, on the other hand, had dreamt of visiting Egypt and of doing exactly what Young disparaged ever since his teenage years. When he finally got there, he would be able to pass for a native, given his swarthy complexion and his excellent command of Arabic, and in due course would try to improve the harsh lot of Egyptian peasants by giving unwelcome advice to the country's autocratic ruler, Muhammad Ali Pasha. On Egypt, as on most matters, the two scholars were poles apart intellectually, emotionally and politically.

By strange chance, Champollion entered Young's world at the time when the English polymath had chosen to apply himself assiduously to the Rosetta Stone, in late 1814. Champollion's letter from Grenoble formally addressed to the president of the Royal Society, accompanied by his new book on Egypt, was dated 10 November, about six months into Young's Egyptian investigations. Possibly Champollion had confused the Royal Society, a scientific body, with the Society of Antiquaries, because his letter mentioned that he already had access to two different reproductions of the Rosetta Stone: the facsimile made by 'your Society' (that is, the copy made by the Society of Antiquaries in 1802, soon after the Rosetta Stone reached London), and the reproduction intended for future publication in the *Description de l'Égypte* (presumably the French copy made in Cairo in 1800). The two copies were somewhat inconsistent. Champollion noted: 'They present differences, sometimes of little importance, sometimes large enough to leave me in a position of awkward uncertainty.' Would the society be kind enough to check some passages of the inscription transcribed by him from the two copies and attached to his letter? He then confidently (and not too tactfully) continued: 'I am convinced that I would already have settled the reading of the entire inscription if I had had under my eyes a plaster cast made from the original using the simplest process.' In conclusion, he requested the society to create and deposit such a cast in each of the principal libraries of Europe: a gift that would be 'worthy of the zeal and disinterestedness that animates the Royal Society'.

It so happened that at this very time in 1814 Champollion's enemy Edme Jomard went personally to London to make a fresh plaster cast of the Rosetta Stone for the *Description*, with the support of the president of the Royal Society. Whether or not Champollion knew about Jomard's visit when he wrote his letter is unclear. Nor is it clear if he knew about Young's interest in the Rosetta Stone. Champollion-Figeac was well informed via his network in Paris and might have passed both pieces of intelligence to his brother in Grenoble.

Young, on the other hand, was unquestionably aware of Champollion's interest – through Champollion's estranged former teacher de Sacy – though he had seen nothing written by Champollion until he received

L'Égypte sous les Pharaons. Shortly before hearing from Champollion, Young had sent de Sacy his own 'conjectural translation' of the Rosetta Stone, leading to a significant correspondence between Young and de Sacy in 1814–16 that would have importance consequences for Champollion. To understand the state of play in the decipherment at this time, and the way it would later develop, we need to follow the evolution of Young's ideas as reported in his various letters in 1814–15, which were published with his 'conjectural translation' in a Cambridge classical journal, *Museum Criticum*, in 1816.

One might have expected Young to have become involved with the Rosetta Stone earlier, when it first went on display in London, in 1802. However, he was totally occupied with a series of scientific lectures at the Royal Institution, on 'Natural philosophy and the mechanical arts', delivered in 1802–3, and, after the mammoth task of publishing these papers in 1807, he devoted himself mainly to medicine. His active interest in Egypt thus started almost a decade after Champollion's.

What finally triggered it, Young tells us, was a review he wrote in 1813 of a massive work in German on the history of languages, *Mithridates, oder Allgemeine Sprachenkunde*, by Johann Christoph Adelung. This contained a note by the editor 'in which he asserted that the unknown language of the Stone of Rosetta, and of the bandages often found with the mummies, was capable of being analysed into an alphabet consisting of little more than 30 letters'. When an English friend returned from the East shortly afterwards and showed Young some fragments of papyrus he had collected in Egypt, 'my Egyptian researches began'. First he examined the papyri and reported on them to the Society of Antiquaries in May 1814. Then he took a copy of the Rosetta Stone inscription away with him from his home in London to the relative tranquillity of the seaside town of Worthing, where he was known as the resident physician, and spent the summer and autumn of 1814 studying Egyptian when he was not attending to his patients.

Apart from his exceptional scientific mind and his broad knowledge of languages, Young brought to the problem one other extremely valuable and relatively uncommon ability. He had trained himself to sift, compare, contrast, retain and reject large amounts of visual linguistic data in his mind. This ability has been a *sine qua non* for serious decipherers ever since Young and Champollion, as I have described in my two books on decipherment: *Lost Languages: The Enigma of the World's Undeciphered Scripts* and *The Man Who Deciphered Linear B: The Story of Michael Ventris*. (Although outsiders to decipherment often like to imagine that, in today's world, computers could be programmed to accomplish such sifting, in reality the human factor remains all-important – mainly because a human being can spot that two signs that objectively look somewhat different are in fact variants of the same sign. We can all learn, from our knowledge of a language, how to recognize the same phrase written in two very different kinds of handwriting; but this task is extremely difficult for computers.)

In his teens and twenties, Young had been celebrated for his penmanship in classical Greek, leading to the publication of John Hodgkin's *Calligraphia Graeca* in 1794, which contained script examples by Young. From this skill he developed a minutely detailed grasp of Greek letter-forms. In his mid-thirties, he was called upon to restore some Greek and Latin texts written on heavily damaged papyri dug up in Herculaneum, the Roman town smothered along with Pompeii by the eruption of Mount Vesuvius in AD 79. The fused mass of papyri had first to be unrolled without utterly destroying them, and then interpreted by classical scholars capable of guessing the meaning of illegible words and missing fragments. The unrolling required Young's chemical skills (and those of Davy); the interpretation demanded his forensic knowledge of classical languages. In neither activity was Young at all satisfied with his results, but his experience with the Herculaneum papyri made him keenly aware of the relevance of his copying skills to the arcane arts of restoring ancient manuscripts. As he noted in his biography of his classicist friend Porson, 'those who have not been in the habit of correcting mutilated passages of manuscripts, can form no estimate of the immense advantage that is obtained by the complete sifting of every letter which the mind involuntarily performs, while the hand is occupied in tracing it'.

The mass of unpublished Egyptian research manuscripts by Young, now kept at the British Library, bear out this claim. Much of his success in

An Explanation of the Hieroglyphics of the Stone of Rosetta.

ΤΟΝ ΕΜΟΝ ΠΕΠΛΟΝ ΟΝΗΤΟΣ ΑΠΕΚΑΛΥΨΕΝ.

ℓ. 14, 13, 12, 12, 8, 6 . Εὔχαριστος, ⟨ΥΣΥΣ⟩, ΘΡΕΝΛΝΕΣ, or ΣΕΜΛΛΝΕΣ, liberal or munificent, giver of good gifts: ‡ in the singular must be good, the plural is made by the repetition. In ℓ.5 seems to be ἀγαθὰ πάντα [: ‡ occurs in ℓ. 4.4:] again ‡ ἀγαθῇ τύχῃ : must be doer or giver.

ℓ. 14, 13, 13, 12, 12, 8, 6 . Επιφάνης, perhaps ΝΧΕΝΙΨΤ ΦΕΡΣ; illustrious conspicuous, not simply present, as Heyne is disposed to think: this the Egyptian inscription proves by the comparison of its parts, without reference to the Coptic. ΟΟΥ or ΟΠ is a day. ℓ. 1.12,3, perhaps honorary.

ℓ. 14, 13, 12, 12, 8, 6; ℓ.10. Θεὸς, which is rather a hieroglyphic than ΝΟΥΟΥ, like ΝΟΥΤΕ though it is barely possible that it may have been read ΝΟΥΤ, and with the frequent addition, ΝΟΥΤΗ, perhaps of all the gods, or each god; of the gods; probably the great gods crowned with asp-bearing diadems; perhaps derived from this character:, probably a temple. probably sacred or solemn, from the three points following a word always making a plural: and in one or two instances preceding a word, after a preposition. Thus ℓ.5 seems to be of the gods. This preposition seems to be the ⟨⟩, or of the Egyptian inscription. ℓ.14, 12, 7, 6,6,6. surrounding the name of Ptolemy, and sometimes including some of the titles: as an honorary distinction. Thus in the Egyptian the name is generally followed by ΙΣ or Κ, which appears to be borrowed from this character. In ℓ.6 means sacred to, Eg. the character is also found in Egypt.

ℓ. 14, 6 . Probably ἠγαπημένος and the character resembles the in the Egyptian: to or by; it may also imply something sacred, ℓ.4.4: but seems more likely to imply beloved: in ℓ.14,14 again it seems to answer to a termination ar, ℓ.13 private, ℓ.10, must be an article.

ℓ.14, 6 . Αἰωνόβιος, a character pretty obviously borrowed from this: it is true that elsewhere means life; but the other parts of the character do not admit of any such explanation, nor does it agree with any Coptic word. ℓ.10 occurs probably in the same sense as an epithet of Γ, or ΙΣ: ℓ.5, for ever, εἰς τὸν ἅπαντα χρόνον, ℓ.4 113. ℓ.5, probably long life, health, ὑγίειαν: ℓ.5,5. perhaps Apis.

β'. ℓ.14, 12, 6, 6, 6. Ptolemy. The animal seems a lion. The bent staff seems to imply superiority or divinity, being allied to life; and is found in a contrary direction in a priest.

ℓ.14, 7, 6 . Probably young, νέου, the only epithet interposed between king and Ptolemy. (ΣΛΟΥ): in ℓ.10, probably only. ℓ.14, 10, 10, 9, 7, 6, 5, 2. King. 10, probably kingdom: 5, the same.

97

Drawing of the last line of the Rosetta Stone (in hieroglyphic, demotic and Greek), published by Thomas Young in his *Encyclopaedia Britannica* article 'Egypt', 1819.

this field would be due to his indefatigable copying – often exquisitely and occasionally in colour – of hieroglyphic and demotic inscriptions taken from different ancient manuscripts and carved inscriptions, and also from different parts of the same inscription, followed by the word-by-word comparisons that such copying made possible. By placing groups of Egyptian signs adjacent to each other, both on paper and in his memory, Young was in a position to see resemblances and patterns that would have gone unnoticed by other scholars. As his biographer George Peacock wrote, after immersing himself in Young's manuscripts, 'It is impossible to form a just estimate either of the vast extent to which Dr Young had carried his hieroglyphical invest-igations, or of the real progress which he had made in them, without an inspection of these manuscripts.' They also serve as a reminder, if one is still needed, of how unfounded are some modern claims that Young was a dilettante scholar.

It was Young's exacting visual analysis of the hieroglyphic and demotic inscriptions on the Rosetta Stone that gave him an inkling of a crucial discovery, which Champollion would later claim to have made independently of Young. Young noted a 'striking resemblance' (as he told de Sacy), not spotted by any previous scholar, between some demotic signs and what he called 'the corresponding hieroglyphics' – the first intimation that demotic might relate directly to hieroglyphic and not be a completely different script, somewhat as a modern cursive hand-written script partly resembles its printed equivalent. We can see this relationship from the drawing Young published showing the last line of the Rosetta inscription in hieroglyphic (it includes a cartouche), demotic and Greek, reproduced opposite. If one examines the hieroglyphic and the demotic signs, one can see that some signs show a similarity. Equally clear, however, is that other 'corresponding' signs do not.

The clinching evidence confirming this partial resemblance came with the publication of several manuscripts on papyrus in the *Description de l'Égypte*, the most recent volume of which Young was able to borrow in 1815. He later wrote:

I discovered, at length, that several of the manuscripts on papyrus, which had been carefully published in that work, exhibited very frequently the same text in different forms, deviating more or less from the perfect resemblance of the objects intended to be delineated, till they became, in many cases, mere lines and curves, and dashes and flourishes; but still answering, character for character, to the hieroglyphical or hieratic writing of the same chapters, found in other manuscripts, and of which the identity was sufficiently indicated, besides this coincidence, by the similarity of the larger tablets or pictural representations, at the head of each chapter or column, which are almost universally found on manuscripts of a mythological nature.

In other words, Young was able to trace how the recognizably pictographic hieroglyphs, showing human figures, animals, plants and objects of many kinds, had developed into their cursive equivalents in the hieratic and demotic scripts. (Unlike Champollion in 1810, Young never doubted that demotic postdated hieroglyphic.)

But if the hieroglyphic and demotic scripts resembled each other visually in many respects, did this also mean that they operated on the same *linguistic* principles? If so, it posed a major problem, because the hieroglyphic script was generally supposed to be purely conceptual or symbolic (except for the foreign names in the cartouches, as suggested by de Sacy in 1811), whereas the demotic script was assumed (by Åkerblad in 1802) to be purely alphabetical. These two views could not be satisfactorily reconciled if the demotic script were somehow derived from the hieroglyphic script.

So Young took the next logical step and made another important discovery. He told de Sacy in a letter in August 1815: 'I am not surprised that, when you consider the general appearance of the [demotic] inscription, you are inclined to despair of the possibility of discovering an alphabet capable of enabling us to decipher it; and if you wish to know my "secret", it is simply this, that no such alphabet ever existed.' His conclusion was that the demotic script consisted of 'imitations of the hieroglyphics ... mixed with letters of the alphabet'. It was neither a purely conceptual or symbolic script, nor an alphabet, but a mixture of the two. As Young wrote a little later, employing an analogy for the demotic script that perhaps only a polymath such as he could have come up with, 'it seemed natural to suppose, that alphabetical characters might be interspersed with hieroglyphics, in the same way that the astronomers and chemists of modern times have often employed arbitrary marks, as compendious expressions of the objects which were most frequently to be mentioned in their respective sciences'. A modern, non-scientific example of the same idea would be such 'compendious' signs as $, £, %, =, +, which represent concepts non-phonetically and often appear adjacent to alphabetic letters.

Young was correct in these two vital discoveries about the relationship between the hieroglyphic and demotic scripts. But we must also note that the discoveries did not now lead him to make a third discovery. He did not question the almost-sacred notion that the hieroglyphic script was essentially conceptual, without phoneticism or any alphabetic signs, although he admitted to being puzzled as to how such a non-phonetic script might have worked in practice. Bearing in mind the large but nevertheless limited number of pictographic characters in the Chinese script, he told de Sacy:

It is impossible that all the [Egyptian hieroglyphic] characters can be pictures of the things they represent: some, however, of the symbols on the stone of Rosetta have a manifest relation to the objects denoted by them, for instance, a Priest, a Shrine, a Statue, an Asp, a Month, and the Numerals, and a King is denoted by a sort of plant with an insect, which is said to have been a bee; while a much greater number of the characters have no perceptible connection with the ideas attached to them; although it is probable that a resemblance, either real or metaphorical, may have existed or have been imagined when they were first employed: thus a Libation was originally denoted by a hand holding a jar, with two streams of liquid issuing from it, but in this inscription the representation has degenerated into the form of a bird's foot.

Despite his puzzlement, Young continued to adhere to the view that the only phonetic elements in the hieroglyphic script were to be found in the foreign names in the cartouches, as first suggested by de Sacy. The idea that the hieroglyphic script as a whole might be a mixed script like the demotic script, incorporating a hieroglyphic alphabet, was eventually to be the revolutionary breakthrough of Champollion.

In 1815, however, Champollion remained mostly unaware of the new thinking by Young described in this chapter. There was a very brief correspondence between the two of them in the first half of this year. In response to Champollion's letter to the Royal Society of late 1814, Young wrote personally to Champollion offering to send him his 'conjectural translation' of the Rosetta Stone, and Champollion replied from Grenoble in May 1815, asking Young to send it to his brother in Paris. At the same time, probably mistrusting the mail from London in a troubled period – or maybe out of impatience – a curious Champollion requested his brother to ask de Sacy if he could borrow his former professor's copy of the 'conjectural translation'. De Sacy agreed to lend it to Champollion-Figeac (as de Sacy informed Young), who presumably showed it to his brother. But at this point the Champollion–Young correspondence fizzled out, almost before it had got started, for political reasons that will become evident in the next chapter. From mid-1815, until Champollion announced his decipherment more than seven years later, in 1822, there would be no further direct contact between the two rivals.

As far as can be gauged from his surviving letters, Champollion made little or no progress with the Egyptian scripts between 1814 and 1816, the period of Young's correspondence with de Sacy. For instead of studying ancient Egypt, both Champollion and Champollion-Figeac were enthusiastically caught up in a political maelstrom. In early March 1815, the exiled Napoleon Bonaparte returned from Elba and landed on the south-eastern coast of France. The first French city he reached with his followers was Grenoble, which took the plunge and welcomed him. The Hundred Days had begun. Champollion and his brother were to reap the Napoleonic whirlwind with a vengeance.

VIII

NAPOLEON AND CHAMPOLLION

There is no law of succession for the throne of France.
The people alone award the crown; they gave
it in the past to Hugo Capet and now they have taken it
away from his descendants so as to entrust it to
someone more worthy. Their choice confers sole legitimacy.
Napoleon is therefore our legitimate prince.

(Jean-François Champollion's editorial in the *Annales du département
de l'Isère*, 18 June 1815 – the day of the battle of Waterloo)

When Champollion's former professor Silvestre de Sacy first informed
Young about Champollion's research in September 1814, he noted that
in his former pupil's new book, *L'Égypte sous les Pharaons*, Champollion
claimed to be able to read the Egyptian demotic text on the Rosetta
Stone – as did another of his former pupils, Johann Åkerblad. De Sacy
added tartly: 'I certainly have more confidence in the knowledge and
criticism of M. Åkerblad than in those of M. Champollion, but until
such time as they publish some results of their work it is only just to
suspend one's judgement.'

Champollion, too, had been wary of de Sacy since the plagiarism
'incident' of 1811. Now, following the first restoration of the Bourbon
monarchy in May 1814, de Sacy had been created Baron de Sacy by
Louis XVIII (at the same time as Champollion-Figeac received the
Décoration du Lys). He adopted the new baronial title proudly, and
therefore Champollion felt obliged to use it in writing to him. When
his friend Saint-Martin, yet another former pupil of de Sacy, expressed
surprise, Champollion uncomfortably defended his choice: 'That is
how men are; they like to have a rattle and it is necessary to stroke

their weakness. The title of *pupil* that I carry does not exempt me from paying the tribute that a simple commoner owes to a baron, whatever new scheme the baron may be hatching.'

Within a year, de Sacy had firmly made up his mind about Champollion. In mid-July 1815, just weeks after Napoleon had lost the battle of Waterloo and Louis XVIII had been restored to the throne for the second time, de Sacy sat on a committee of the Academy of Inscriptions and Belles-Lettres. It produced a report that rejected the official publication of the manuscripts of Champollion's Coptic dictionary and grammar, a favourite project of his on which he had been labouring gradually since his student days in Paris. Only three or four months earlier in Grenoble, Napoleon Bonaparte had personally promised Champollion that the government would publish his Coptic dictionary. No doubt that was the chief reason why de Sacy and his academic colleagues (including Louis Langlès, another former professor of Champollion who was unfriendly to him) were determined to reject the manuscripts.

Soon after taking this decision, de Sacy volunteered to Young the following acid, and notably indiscreet, observation on Champollion and his *L'Égypte sous les Pharaons*:

If I might venture to advise you, I would suggest you do not communicate too many of your discoveries to M. Champollion. It could happen that he might afterwards lay claim to the priority. He seeks, in many parts of his book, to make it believed that he has discovered many words of the Egyptian inscription from Rosetta. I am afraid this is mere charlatanism; I may add that I have very good reasons for thinking so.

Six months later, in January 1816, de Sacy delivered his *coup de grâce*. 'I do not intend to speak further of M. Champollion,' he informed Young:

His political conduct, during the three-month reign of Ahriman [the equivalent of Satan in Persian mythology, i.e. Napoleon], did him little honour, and without doubt he no longer dares to write to me. He will have seen, besides, from a report that he himself provoked, and for which I was responsible, that I am not a dupe of his charlatanism. I have given him a copy of the report at his request, and he has not yet thanked me for it. He is prone to playing the role of the jay adorned with the feathers of a peacock. This role often ends very badly.

A silence descended between the eminent professor and his reneg-ade, politically disgraced former pupil. But in the long term baron de Sacy would be compelled to speak further of Monsieur Champollion, whether he desired to or not. In 1822, de Sacy would be among the first to acclaim Champollion's decipherment of the Egyptian hieroglyphs; later he would defend Champollion against Young; and when his con-troversial former pupil predeceased him, the 75-year-old de Sacy would rise to his feet at the Academy of Inscriptions and Belles-Lettres to give a flattering eulogy of Champollion as a great French scholar. Was all this an example of intellectual integrity, or of cynical opportunism, from the royalist son of a Jewish notary, who had survived the French Revolution, the Terror, the reign of Napoleon and then the Hundred Days to prosper again under the Bourbon regime? Such were the twists and turns required in both political and scholarly life in France during the early decades of the 19th century – for the Champollion brothers even more than for de Sacy, as we shall now see.

When Napoleon Bonaparte, on horseback and accompanied by a force of soldiers who had deserted to his side, appeared outside Grenoble on the night of 7 March 1815, knocked on the gates with his snuffbox and cried 'Open!', Champollion-Figeac – and probably Champollion too – were among the crowd eager to receive him. Fourier, who had remained prefect under the royalist regime in 1814, was powerless to contain the popular upsurge and escaped through another gate just before Napoleon's triumphal entry. As Bonaparte rode slowly through the streets, his grey riding coat covering his uniform, a magistrate standing beside Champollion-Figeac cried out just as Napoleon came close to them: 'Long live the Emperor, but long live liberty!' 'Yes,' said Napoleon immediately, 'turning his head towards our side,' as Champollion-Figeac recalled. 'Long live liberty!' replied the former emperor.

This vignette is from *Fourier et Napoléon, l'Égypte et les cents-jours*, the memoir Champollion-Figeac wrote about the Hundred Days three decades later, in 1844, which still quivers with the excitement of

Napoleon's three days in Grenoble. For once, the elder brother would behave with the passion and impetuosity of the younger brother. 'In a career conducted with such circumspection, the extravagant enterprise of spring 1815 rings out like a fanfare of youthful spontaneity,' writes Lacouture.

On the morning of 8 March, at his house in Vif, Champollion-Figeac received the call he had been awaiting and hastened back to Grenoble. The moment he arrived at the modest hotel where Napoleon was staying with his generals, he was greeted by his friend Charles Renauldon, the mayor of the city, who informed him that Napoleon needed a personal assistant and secretary. Renauldon had recommended his friend Champoléon (the old spelling of Champollion, often used in Grenoble), and Napoleon, while writing down the address, had apparently remarked: 'It's a good sign; he has half of my name.' Without further delay, the mayor now introduced Champollion-Figeac, whose memoir takes up the story of the first interview with the 'Emperor' (as he chose to call him).

Napoleon was seated on a sofa when Champollion-Figeac entered. His left leg was stretched out on the sofa, his right foot on the floor.

He got up, came towards me, and said, in that vivid voice, penetrating and in places inflected with intonations and a foreign accent … : 'I am very pleased to see you. I am told that you are a person of note in this city, and of moderate principles. These are the men whom I wish to rally round me in the future. It is necessary to explain to the people why I have returned. Without me you will have a republican revolution. The Bourbons do not know France, and I am convinced today that its destiny can be achieved only in the hands of a liberal government.'

Stranger that I was to the rules of palace etiquette, and perhaps a little influenced by the lack of majesty of the place where I was speaking to the Emperor whom I had never seen before, I interrupted his discourse and blurted out these words: 'Under those conditions, Sire, France will be at your feet.' A prolonged 'EH?', issuing from his immediately scowling face, and a displeased mouth that opened only on the right side, warned me that I had transgressed this etiquette; but I did not withdraw, convinced there and then that if I repeated the words, I would have the benefit of being taken for a lout, but not for an insolent person.

During the Hundred Days, Napoleon is known to have tried hard to change his manners, so as to convince both the court and the people that he intended to be a constitutional monarch. Before 1814, he had often shown his courtiers overbearing rudeness; in 1815, they were treated with unaccustomed kindness. In this case the interrupted interview recovered, Napoleon spoke further about his new love of liberty and his lack of desire for revenge, and Champollion-Figeac got the job of secretary. He was also reappointed, with immediate effect, as editor of the *Annales du département de l'Isère* and instructed to use the position to publicize Napoleon's message.

Champollion-Figeac worked with the Emperor at the hotel until Napoleon's departure for Lyons on 9 March. During the course of less than two days, he was able to speak up on behalf of the university; he claims to have dissuaded Napoleon from arresting the fugitive Fourier (for which Fourier was grateful); and he found an occasion to broach the all-important subject of Egypt. 'This word made a visible impression, and animated his conversation.' Champollion-Figeac requested copies of the *Description de l'Égypte* for the municipal library. Then Napoleon spoke of other important scholarly works published in Paris under his aegis, including a Chinese dictionary: 'They had been working on that for a century, I got it out in three years by decree.' The names of many savants were mentioned. 'Happily,' writes Champollion-Figeac, 'I knew my Paris well, and I could respond to his numerous questions.'

As a result, there was an opportunity to introduce Champollion *le jeune*. It was the only meeting between these two great Egyptophiles, who were both, in their exceptionally different ways, devoted to the republic of letters. Napoleon recalled Champollion's name from Fourier's many requests that he be exempted from military conscription. The Emperor inquired about the research that had justified these requests, which gave Champollion the opening he needed. He now spoke enthusiastically of his Coptic dictionary and grammar, and of Egypt in general. Since Napoleon already had an *ideé fixe* that Coptic was the language of ancient Egypt, he listened with great satisfaction. He commanded: 'Bring it all to Paris – we shall have it printed; this will be a great deal easier than the Chinese dictionary.'

In his parting words, Napoleon invited Champollion-Figeac to come and work for him in Paris. Jacques-Joseph took up the offer, set off for Paris as soon as he could, and the die was cast. Judging from his memoir, he was simply overwhelmed by Napoleon's personality. Looking back on the Hundred Days of 1815 from the 1840s, Champollion-Figeac wrote of the 'balance sheet of advantages' that he accrued from his 'curiosity'. In return for his loyalty to Napoleon, he noted wryly, he had been rewarded with:

1. *the decoration of the Legion of Honour, which I wore for all of one or two months –*
2. *the suppression of my position as professor and as head of the faculty of letters at Grenoble –*
3. *my dismissal as librarian of the city of Grenoble –*
4. *exile for 18 months in the south of France.*

In Paris in July 1815, the month after Napoleon's defeat at Waterloo, 'The prevailing atmosphere was ghastly'; so writes the historian Munro Price in *The Perilous Crown: France between Revolutions*. 'The Hundred Days had created something close to a civil war. Everywhere those who had remained true to the Bourbons were turning on those who had rallied to Napoleon.' This explains de Sacy's personal attack on Champollion and his negative report on his Coptic projects. In parts of the south of France, the so-called White Terror held sway, in which arch-royalists, known as Ultras, took murderous reprisals against Bonapartists. The king's brother, the count of Artois, leader of the Ultras, openly supported the terror; the king supported its legal incarnation. By the end of 1815, more than a quarter of public officials – between 50,000 and 80,000 people – had been purged on the grounds of suspected disloyalty. About 5,000 people had been brought before the courts for political crimes, over half of whom were convicted. One of them – Drouet d'Erlon, who was condemned to death *in absentia* for his role as a general under Napoleon at Waterloo – was secretly sheltered by the Champollion family in the winter of 1815–16, before being helped to escape to Munich.

Champollion *le jeune* was obviously a prime target for official attack. Although he had stayed in Grenoble, and had certainly shown less public enthusiasm for Napoleon than his elder brother, he had taken over editorship of the government journal while his brother was in Paris and used it as a mouthpiece for pro-Napoleonic and republican sentiment, even after the battle of Waterloo. Moreover, he had continued to compose anonymous popular satires attacking the royalists that annoyed the police. In early July, he (and his sister-in-law Zoé) had taken part in the defence of Grenoble – which was the last city in France to resist the invading forces – against an attack by combined Austrian and Sardinian troops. When the shelling of the ramparts began, Champollion ran through the bombardment to save the library and its precious manuscripts from fire. The attack, which left about 600 dead and 500 wounded, produced a ceasefire, but very soon the collapse of Napoleon's forces compelled the city to capitulate. Although the worst of the White Terror would not affect Grenoble, there would be severe official repression. Champollion knew that he could expect little mercy from the count of Montlivault and the marquis of Pina – the authoritarian figures who had replaced the ousted prefect, Fourier, and the mayor, Renauldon – not to speak of the new prefect of police and the military commandant.

Champollion immediately lost his professorship at the university and his position at the library, like his brother, which left him without any income. By November he was seriously considering becoming a notary in Grenoble. For his brother he listed five advantages of taking up this respectable occupation:

1. *The certainty of a solid and lucrative state.*
2. *That of finding myself within a short space of time no longer … dependent on my family.*
3. *Of accomplishing a plan of marriage to which I am committed by both heart and honour.*
4. *Of being for a while safe from revolutions.*
5. *Finally it is the only state that … permits me to have commerce with the Muses, without which literary commerce harms financial commerce. I would have the flowers without the thorns.*

Champollion's first declared love, as far back as 1807, had been for a woman six years older than him, Pauline Berriat, who was the sister of his brother's wife, Zoé. But his feelings had not been reciprocated, and she died in 1813. As a student in Paris in 1807–9, he had some kind of affair with a married woman, Louise Deschamp; her husband died, and she remarried in 1811. Pauline Berriat died in 1813. That year, Jean-François began seeing a younger woman, Rosine Blanc, the daughter of a glover from Grenoble. Her father did not favour the match, however, on account of Champollion's financial insecurity. 'M. Blanc has always said that there are only two states in the universe, that of a *Glover* and that of a notary,' Jean-François bluntly told his brother in late 1815. Champollion's new resolve had apparently impressed his prospective father-in-law. For now, though, his plan to marry Rosine had to be put on hold.

In February 1816, the authorities in Paris and Grenoble decided to act against leading dissidents. The prefect of police, the count of Bastard (*sic!*), singled out 'Champoléon', along with two others, as 'dangerous men'. In March, he informed the minister of police in Paris that it was best to act energetically against such men, 'for whom nothing is sacred … For a long time, the brothers Champoléon have been designated by general opinion to be enemies of the government, all the more so since they combine plentiful hypocrisy with plentiful talent, intelligence and knowledge.'

The new prefect of Isère, the count of Montlivault, agreed. Neither of the Champollions would be charged with a crime; instead, they would be exiled from Grenoble. Initially, they were informed that they would be sent to live in an area of France that was firmly monarchist, 'where the name of Bonaparte is one of horror'. But the authorities relented and imposed exile to their native town of Figeac in the *département* of Lot. The brothers were permitted to remain together and to be accompanied by Ali, Jacques-Joseph's 7-year-old son; but his wife, Zoé, and the rest of the surviving children – Jules (born in 1811), Aimé-Louis (born in 1812) and Zoé (born in 1815) – were left behind in Vif. Rosine Blanc, too, remained in Grenoble.

A confidential letter from Montlivault briefed his opposite number in Lot as follows:

Messieurs Champollion are both remarkable for the fervour with which they have embraced the cause of Bonaparte and for the efforts they have made to support it. The elder was the municipal librarian here and head of the faculty of letters. He asked for and obtained from Bonaparte during his passage through this city the editorship of the Journal de l'Isère, *thus he was the first to publish the acts of usurpation. From this, he followed him to Paris and returned from there with the decoration of the Legion of Honour. He is shrewd, witty, well educated, and pleasant to deal with. These qualities are all the more harmful when deliberately misused.*

The second one, as well educated as the first, also a professor in the academy, keeps himself busy with Oriental literature; during the usurpation, he was secretary of the Committee of the Federation; he is perhaps not as pleasant as the other, but has more warmth, which, in a movement, renders him perhaps more dangerous.

The passport issued in Grenoble on 18 March 1816 refers to 'M. Champollion *le jeune* (Jean-François)' and describes him as an 'assistant librarian' who was 1.70 metres high, with black hair, a large forehead, black eyes, a 'flattened' nose, a black beard, a chin 'round and cleft', a 'full and round' face and a 'brown' complexion. It cost two francs.

On 21 March, the two brothers and Ali set off by *diligence*. So that they could travel through the regions least affected by the White Terror against Bonapartists, they were permitted to take longer than usual on their way to their hometown – up to fifteen days. Instead of following a potentially violent route to the south, they at first went northwestwards to Lyons and then travelled south-west through the Massif Central via Aurillac. Within five days of their arrival in Figeac, they were required to present themselves to the prefect of Lot.

Champollion's passport, dated 17 August 1831, issued on the occasion of his last journey, when he returned to Figeac from Paris. It is signed 'J. F. Champollion le jeune'.

IX

EXILE AND REVOLT

Perhaps one day the capture of the citadel of Grenoble by an archaeologist and without any bloodshed will count in my favour in the literary service records of an extraordinary period.

(Jean-François Champollion's reported
comment on the revolt in Grenoble in 1821)

Harsh though their sentence was, the Champollion brothers – as well as two other citizens exiled from Grenoble at this time, a notary and a solicitor – might in retrospect have counted themselves lucky to have left the city when they did. On 4 May 1816, there was an uprising of sorts in the surrounding area, of uncertain political goals, led by a 63-year-old barrister. Jean-Paul Didier, the former director of the law school at Grenoble, was up to his eyes in business debts and ready to do anything that might rescue him from ruin. He recruited four groups of about one hundred men each, consisting of soldiers on half-pay and local peasants in varying states of inebriation, marched them towards Grenoble and attempted to seize the city.

The negligent royalist military commandant was taken by surprise, but even so Didier's small and ill-disciplined rebel force never stood a chance of success. The 'Didier Conspiracy', as it became known, was ruthlessly crushed by the military and the civil administration: eighteen 'conspirators', including a 15-year-old boy, were executed by firing squad on the city's esplanade, and Didier himself, having fled to the neighbouring region of the Savoy, was extradited and guillotined in Grenoble on 10 June. Nothing like this bloodthirsty punishment had been meted out in the city during the Revolution and in the years that followed. In fact, the *Grenoblois* had long prided themselves on the city's lack of violent extremism. The backlash against the official killings took the form of a bitter opposition in Grenoble to the Bourbon regime that would last for many years, with severe consequences for Champollion when he eventually returned to the city a year and a half later.

The authorities took no direct reprisals against the Champollions' circle in Grenoble, since no proof of their participation had been found. Jean-François's old school friend Charles Renauldon, son of the former mayor, was able to prove that he had refused to associate himself with Didier's enterprise and had discouraged his friends from taking part. But there was no lack of sleuthing by the authorities. The prefect, Montlivault, informed the minister of police that the well-known liberal sympathies of the Champollion brothers meant that they could be presumed to have known about the conspiracy in advance. As he admitted, however, 'I have not a single letter, nor a single piece of writing by M. Champollion the elder that might be relevant; one letter written by the younger, in a fairly cryptic style, might give rise to some suspicions but they are too slight and besides as difficult to clarify as they would be simple to deny.' Evidently the police were intercepting the Champollions' letters on a regular basis, as the brothers had already realized. Most probably, like their friend Renauldon, they had known about Didier's plans and wanted no part in them. But if in early May they had been in Grenoble rather than in Figeac, they might conceivably have changed their minds, aided Didier's cause and ended up suffering a fate worse than exile.

The five years between 1816 and 1821, when Champollion finally abandoned Grenoble, were a time of struggle – the most uncertain and onerous period of his life. Exile, a dearth of suitable paid employment, political oppression, tensions with his father in Figeac, separation from his brother in Paris, strains surrounding his marriage, and the sustained opposition of his former professor de Sacy – not to mention the emergence of Young as a serious rival for the prize of hieroglyphic decipherment – adversely affected not only his research, but also his health. And yet Champollion never lost his hieroglyphic obsession in this period, except in his first year or so at Figeac; even in that fallow year he continued to work on the Coptic dictionary and grammar whose publication had been rejected in Paris in 1815, immersing himself more thoroughly in Coptic than perhaps any other contemporary scholar. In a sense, the long struggle in Figeac and Grenoble can be regarded as necessary mental preparation for the sustained burst of achievement in Paris that immediately followed it, leading to Champollion's breakthrough in 1822.

In Figeac, after more than ten years' absence from their native town, Jacques-Joseph and Jean-François were warmly welcomed by their two unmarried sisters, who had always been devoted to their brothers and regarded them now as superior beings. Thérèse, the eldest, had taken over the management of the family's small bookshop; Marie looked after the running of the house in the Rue de la Boudousquerie. Their third sister, Pétronille, had married in 1803 and seems to have played little part in the brothers' stay.

However, there was a cloud hanging over all their lives: their father, Jacques. Widowed in 1807 and now in his early seventies, he had continued to decline under the influence of bad company and alcohol, although he still liked to travel on his annual jaunt to the Beaucaire Fair. Jean-François referred to his father unsympathetically as 'le Patron' ('the Boss') in letters written at this time. As the father's finances deteriorated and threatened even the family property during 1816, relations between 'le Patron' and his two sons would turn extremely sour.

Not surprisingly, the move to the country was more of a wrench for Jacques-Joseph than for his brother. Champollion-Figeac had always enjoyed city sophistication, whether in Grenoble or Paris; and of course he had left behind his wife, Zoé, and his three children. 'One finds [here] scarcely four or five people with whom one can talk good sense,' he wrote in one of many such complaints to Zoé: 'Minutes pass like days, days like months, and months like centuries.' Jean-François felt more at home. True, a week after his arrival he told his school friend Augustin Thévenet, 'I am a *Dauphinois* in my soul. Figeac strikes me as a new country.' But in later letters to another friend he described behaving as a bit of a lad among the local young bachelors, for example singing at night beneath the windows of 'foolishly sleepy' bourgeois, despite the surveillance of the local commissioner of police, and gesticulating in a town square while improvising comic romances set under the window of a forsaken young lady of Figeac. Champollion would remain considerably longer in Figeac than his elder brother, indeed longer than he was compelled to stay by the government. In years to come, he would often do his best to return there. He came to regard the clean air, warm days and nights, and rolling countryside around Figeac – along with its womenfolk – as providing a place for fruitful relaxation from his stressful and unhealthy life in Paris.

Fortunately for the Champollion brothers, the authorities to whom they had been obliged to report themselves on arrival behaved with restraint from the outset. Their fate depended on the prefect of Lot, the count of Lezay-Marnésia, and on the under-prefect of Figeac, the baron of Campagne. Despite some encouragement from the count of Bastard in far-off Grenoble, neither official wanted to make life difficult for the exiles. Apart from confiscating their passports, the under-prefect left the Champollions alone, arguing to the prefect that the brothers presented 'not a single danger' and would spend their time with their families, not consorting with known troublemakers. He added: 'I would avoid employing any means that could wound their self-respect.' As the months went by, relations became decidedly friendly, especially with the diplomatic Champollion-Figeac.

Lezay-Marnésia was passionate about archaeology. He soon persuaded Champollion-Figeac to look for the site of ancient Uxellodunum, the fortress where Julius Caesar finally defeated the Gauls. During the summer of 1816, the two Champollions searched the area on the basis of clues provided by Caesar's *Commentaries on the Gallic War*. Eventually they settled on a dramatic and historic site looking down on the River Lot, Capdenac-le-Haut, about 5 kilometres (3 miles) from Figeac. Champollion-Figeac proceeded to excavate, producing Roman antiquities and discovering a Gallic well (which was finally cleared in 2002). Although subsequent excavations have produced a stronger candidate for Uxellodunum – Puy d'Issolud near Vayrac, further away from Figeac – which was officially recognized by the French Ministry of Culture in 2001, the *Figeacois* continue to advocate Capdenac. At any rate, in 1816 the identification won the Champollions kudos with Lezay-Marnésia and local educated circles.

The other activity that occupied both brothers while they were in exile was the education of local children. They were proponents of 'mutual education' using the principles then being advocated in England by Joseph Lancaster. Essentially, the Lancaster method involved an adult teaching a child who went on to teach another child, and so on. There were examples of this approach in Champollion's own life. One was the request of his Hebrew professor in Paris, Prosper Audran, to teach Hebrew to his fellow students in Paris. Another was Champollion's teaching of his nephews, partly because he liked teaching children and partly out of gratitude to his brother. Among other subjects, he taught Latin to the eldest, Ali, who then instructed Jules, who then taught the 6-year-old Aimé.

In France, interest in the Lancaster method was originally sparked by Edme Jomard, the scientist in charge of the *Description de l'Égypte*, who had seen it in action on his visit to London in 1814. In March 1815, encouraged by Jomard, some enlightened French aristocrats publicly advocated the Lancaster method just before the beginning of the Hundred Days. Despite its royalist provenance, Napoleon's government took up the idea, with the support of Champollion-Figeac (a colleague of Jomard) after his move to Paris. It began to catch on after the second restoration of the king in 1815, notwithstanding opposition from the Ultras and from Catholic priests, supposedly on the grounds of its foreign origin, but really because they wanted to keep the traditional methods of instruction (and indoctrination) under their own control, and also because they disapproved of education for the lower classes on political grounds.

The two Champollions introduced the Lancaster method in Figeac in 1816. In April 1817, the under-prefect at Figeac informed the prefect of Lot that the Lancaster method was being supported by a subscription raised through the zeal of 'several inhabitants', and requested a grant from the ministry in Paris to permit the method to 'surmount small resistances owing to special factors'. The Champollion brothers were not named, but reading between the lines one can assume that they were behind the initiative.

By this time, Champollion-Figeac had in fact departed for Paris. He had been lobbying his friends and contacts in the capital ever since his arrival in Figeac, on behalf of both himself and his brother.

A grateful Fourier and various well-known scientist colleagues, such as Georges Cuvier and even Jomard and Langlès – neither of them friendly to Champollion – made efforts on behalf of the brothers. But de Sacy, the most influential figure of all for Champollion, refused to bend. Jean-François wrote angrily to his brother: 'As for the Rabbi [his name for de Sacy], do not stoop to seeing him ... I do not deny him either his talent or his learning or his superior knowledge. But he has no soul and hence he is no longer a man, he is a walking book.' To add salt to the wound, Champollion's friend Saint-Martin went over to the Ultra persuasion and joined de Sacy's side.

The result of his efforts was that Champollion-Figeac got government permission to leave Figeac in late November 1816, whereas his brother's official period of exile lasted until the following March. In the event, Jacques-Joseph stayed until early April 1817 in order to sort out various domestic matters and to establish a job for himself in Paris. He became the right-hand man of Bon-Joseph Dacier, the 'permanent secretary' of the Academy of Inscriptions and Belles-Lettres. To begin with, he assisted Dacier with his great project, an inventory of French antiquities. Later, he strategically encouraged and directed Dacier's crucial support of Champollion's Egyptian hieroglyphic research under the auspices of the academy. At Champollion-Figeac's suggestion, the title of what has become Champollion's single most famous publication would be the *Lettre à M. Dacier*.

The domestic matters at issue concerned Jacques Champollion, 'le Patron'. Some time in early 1817, it became clear to the Champollion children that certain 'friends' of their father were threatening him with the seizure of the family property – the house, the bookshop and their contents – unless he settled his debts to them immediately. Jacques-Joseph stayed in Figeac as long as he could to deal with his father, but eventually the main burden fell on Jean-François in the months after his brother's departure. It was a horrendous time for him – the worst few days he had ever experienced, he said – despite support from some friends such as Thévenet, who offered loans. In late May, he wrote disgustedly to Jacques-Joseph of their father: 'Provided he eats, he cares about nothing else. This often drives me to fury. I do not know what I may do to him.

Portrait of Bon-Joseph Dacier, permanent secretary of the Academy of Inscriptions and Belles-Lettres in Paris, to whom Champollion addressed his celebrated *Lettre* in 1822.

A man of this calibre is beneath the brute.' Suffice to say that the crisis demanded more than just loans: it became clear that, to preserve the interests of their sisters in the house and bookshop, both brothers would be obliged to abandon all their rights to their inheritance. Even so, 'It will not be enough for them,' Champollion soberly concluded. Jacques Champollion's death, four years later in January 1821, must have come as a profound relief to his sons and daughters.

By now, July 1817, Champollion could easily have left Figeac for Grenoble had he wanted to. In fact, he delayed his departure until October. One reason was that there was a change of prefect in Grenoble in late September: the authoritarian Montlivault was replaced by the more liberal Choppin d'Arnouville. Another was that he had no job in Grenoble to go to. Because of this, he feared the revival of further difficulties in his relationship with Rosine Blanc and her father, since he had made no progress in becoming a notary. But in addition there was a woman, his *maman* ('mummy'), who seems to have held him back in Figeac. In May, he referred to her in a letter to Thévenet: 'The departure of my brother has shaken me deeply; that good and excellent *maman* whom I've sometimes told you about has gone away too to the country. So I am alone.' No one knows who she was. Perhaps she was the same woman as the mysterious 'Madame Adèle' often mentioned in his letters to his brother, to whom he addressed a poem on her twentieth birthday in 1816. Perhaps not. Champollion's biographers Lacouture and Faure speculate that Adèle may have been the wife of the man who became mayor of Figeac in 1817 – a couple who supported him in his battle with his father. His relationship with his *maman* would revive whenever Champollion visited Figeac. Whoever she was, she was probably something of a substitute mother for a man who had never really known a mother of his own.

Until this time Champollion's academic research in Figeac, such as it was, had focused entirely on his Coptic grammar and dictionary. The latter had reached more than 1,000 pages, he informed Thévenet. He was thinking of having it printed in Grenoble in four volumes – de Sacy be damned. His work on the Rosetta Stone and on the Egyptian decipherment had entirely stopped; indeed, all of his Egyptian research papers had remained in Grenoble, stranded in a cabinet in the municipal library that he had locked and left behind in March the previous year. Although Champollion could have sent for these papers earlier, he had not done so because he felt stuck in his Egyptian research, especially in an intellectual backwater like Figeac.

Suddenly, in the mail he received an anonymous review of his 1814 publication *Égypte sous les Pharaons*, probably sent by his brother from Paris. It had been published in London in the *Monthly Review* in April 1816, a year or so earlier, and it was favourable, despite the author's openly expressed anti-French political prejudices. An encouraged Champollion crowed to his brother:

It gives me as much credit as one could wish for. De Sacy is presented as having pushed me forward – me, his pupil, who is bringing him lots of honour. That must have infuriated him. So much the better. The Englishman has only one reproach against me, of having neglected to employ the documentation provided in the Sacred Books, the true source of History, according to him. He adds that my opinion of these books seems to be more the prejudice of an Infidel than the just impartiality of a Philosopher.

Was the anonymous author Thomas Young? Champollion himself does not make this supposition, but at first sight it seems a reasonable one, given Young's strong interest in the subject at this time and the fact that Young had received a copy of the book from Champollion in late 1814. The author is assumed to be Young in an article on the sources of European Egyptology written in 1991 for the bicentenary of Champollion's birth, by the well-known Egyptologist Jean Leclant, permanent secretary of the Academy of Inscriptions and Belles-Lettres. Yet, on the evidence of Young's letters and established writings, he was not much of an admirer of *Égypte sous les Pharaons*. He criticized the book's supposed 'translation' of the Rosetta Stone in a letter to Hudson Gurney in 1814: '[Champollion] certainly has picked out the sense of a few passages in the inscription by means of Åkerblad's investigations – although in four or five Coptic words which he pretends to have found in it, he is wrong in all but one – and that is a very short and a very obvious one'. Young did not even mention Champollion's book in his survey of significant publications on Egypt for the 1819 *Encyclopaedia Britannica*. Nor did the thorough editor of Young's Egyptological papers, John Leitch, attribute the 1816 *Monthly Review* piece to Young. As a final point, one may note that Young was not prone to regard the Bible as 'the true source of History'. On balance, therefore, the review's English author was probably someone other than Young.

At any rate, this unexpected English appreciation triggered Champollion to make a request to Thévenet in mid-July. Would he kindly post to Figeac, as soon as possible, certain papers from 'my ex-cabinet' in the library. Most of these concerned the Rosetta Stone inscriptions, but one was 'a bundle of papers entitled "Egyptian Alphabet"'. The packet arrived in Figeac in early August – at the same time, curiously enough, as Champollion received a visit from a local doctor, named Roulhac, with an interest in etymology, who claimed to offer a key to the decipherment of the hieroglyphs. Although Roulhac's proposal was cranky, it served as a further prod to Champollion that he had rivals in the field, whether genuine or not.

Both events reminded him, too, that he was cut off from contact with Egyptian inscriptions and serious scholars. He toyed with the idea of trying to get to Italy, with the help of a French cardinal known to his brother, in order to study Egyptian manuscripts and obelisks in Rome.

Portrait of Rosine Blanc, Champollion's wife, and their only child, Zoraïde, who was born in 1824. Rosine married Champollion in 1818 in Grenoble, the city of her birth.

But nothing came of this. Then the news arrived in Figeac of the new prefect's appointment in Grenoble. Champollion's decision was quickly made. By the end of October 1817, he was back in Grenoble, where friends such as Thévenet and Renauldon greeted him warmly after his absence of eighteen months.

Without either his former university post or his assistant librarianship to support him, Champollion turned to schoolteaching. With the active support of the prefect, Choppin d'Arnouville, and the equally active opposition of the royalist mayor and the local clergy, he opened a Lancaster-style school in February of the following year; he helped to set up another school to impart education in classical studies; and he even reluctantly accepted a post as professor of history at the Royal College – the renamed *lycée*, his former school. In June 1818, again thanks to the prefect, he got back his job at the library. About six months later, in the cathedral of Grenoble, he at last married Rosine Blanc. Although the couple had eventually overcome the objections of her father, thanks to Champollion's new positions, his brother Jacques-Joseph strongly disapproved and did not return from Paris to attend the wedding, nor were any of the Figeac relatives present. Much more surprising was the absence of almost all of Champollion's friends from Grenoble, except for Jacques-Joseph's brother-in-law Hugues Berriat and one other. It was not an auspicious beginning to what would be a distant partnership, divided by Egypt, as we shall see.

Egyptian research reclaimed Champollion's attention in the spring of 1818, and for the rest of his life it would never let him go. He still lacked a satisfactory reproduction of the Rosetta Stone but was pleased to receive an improved version from Paris in June. He gave a lecture on Egypt to the Académie Delphinale in August. And he began working on what he called, somewhat presumptuously, 'a dictionary of Egyptian hieroglyphs'. But he wisely refused Jacques-Joseph's pleas to publish some of his Egyptian research, and resisted his brother's idea that he move from Grenoble to Paris. 'I would rather be the first in my village than the second in Rome,' he told him. 'You are born for the business, the movement, the manipulation of great things' – whereas his own role in life, he said, was to look beneath the surface of events, an approach reinforced by his interest in Oriental philosophy. No doubt he was also thinking of the fact that his future wife, Rosine, was a woman from Grenoble.

In truth, his research would probably have benefited from a period in Paris at this point. During 1818–20, Champollion seems to have achieved nothing of substance in his study of Egyptian writing. 'During this period of reflection, Champollion considered all sorts of ideas, some of them insightful, others far-fetched, but he was as critical of himself as of others,' is the gentle way that Robert Solé and Dominique Valbelle describe the situation in *The Rosetta Stone*. 'He continued to take an interest in all the Egyptian documents he came across, particularly papyri covered with various kinds of signs.' Living in Paris, however, he would have had access to more of such documents and would have enjoyed interaction with leading minds, notwithstanding de Sacy's persistent opposition to his work.

Champollion would also very likely have encountered Young's most important article on Egypt, entitled simply 'Egypt', completed in 1818 and published as a supplement to the fourth edition of the *Encyclopaedia Britannica* in 1819. In mid-1819 Young despatched it to Jomard, who was in charge of the *Description de l'Égypte*. During the three years since the publication of his 'conjectural translation' of the Rosetta Stone in 1816, Young had made a number of solid contributions to the decipherment of hieroglyphic and demotic, which followed his two insights of 1814–15 into the demotic–hieroglyphic relationship (that demotic was derived from the hieroglyphic and hieratic scripts, and that demotic signs were a mixture of conceptual and alphabetic signs). By way of example, Young identified hieroglyphic plural markers, various numerical notations, and a special sign (a semicircle plus oblique oval) in cartouches to mark feminine names, such as Berenice. But his most important further discovery arose from the idea, developed by the Abbé Barthélemy in the 18th century, that the hieroglyphic cartouches expressed royal or religious names, and from de Sacy's proposal that the foreign names in the cartouches might be spelt phonetically.

There were six cartouches on the Rosetta Stone. According to the Greek translation, these cartouches clearly had to contain the name Ptolemy (Ptolemaios, in Greek). Three of them looked like this:

and the other three like this:

Young postulated that the longer cartouche gave the name of Ptolemy with a title, as suggested by equivalents in the Greek inscription, which read 'Ptolemy, living for ever, beloved of Ptah'.

This enabled Young to match the hieroglyphic signs in the short cartouche with known letters and phonetic values. Here is what he deduced, along with today's accepted phonetic value:

hieroglyph	Young's value	today's value
□	P	P
◠	T	T
⸙	'not essentially necessary'	O
⟐	LO or OLE	L
⸗	MA or simply M	M
⫴	I	I or Y
⎮	OSH or OS	S

And here is Young's reasoning for these values, as stated in the *Encyclopaedia Britannica* (recall that 'enchorial' was Young's name for what we now call demotic):

The square block and the semicircle answer invariably in all the manuscripts to characters resembling the P and T of Åkerblad, which are found at the beginning of the enchorial name [i.e. the assumed name of Ptolemy written in demotic]. The next character, which seems to be a kind of knot, is not essentially necessary, being often omitted in the sacred characters [i.e. hieroglyphic], and always in the enchorial. The lion corresponds to the LO of Åkerblad; a lion being always expressed by a similar character in the manuscripts; an oblique line crossed standing for the body, and an erect line for the tail: this was probably read not LO but OLE; although, in more modern Coptic, OILI is translated as ram; we have also EIUL, a stag; and the figure of the stag becomes, in the running hand [i.e. demotic or hieratic], something

*like this of the lion. The next character is known to have some reference to 'place',
in Coptic MA; and it seems to have been read either MA, or simply M; and this
character is always expressed in the running hand by the M of Åkerblad's alphabet.
The two feathers, whatever their natural meaning may have been, answer to the
three parallel lines of the enchorial text, and they seem in more than one instance
to have been read I or E; the bent line probably signified great, and was read OSH
or OS; for the Coptic SHEI seems to have been nearly equivalent to the Greek sigma.
Putting all these elements together we have precisely PTOLEMAIOS, the Greek name;
or perhaps PTOLEMEOS, as it would more naturally be called in Coptic.*

This passage is worth quoting at length in order to show that Young
was capable of poor reasoning as well as acuity. His analysis of Ptolemy's
cartouche was mostly on target, but he was plainly wrong about the value
of the knot, and also wrong in assuming that some of the phonetic values
might be syllabic rather than alphabetic. He was less successful with the
cartouche of the Ptolemaic queen Berenice, which he guessed to be hers
from a copy of an inscription beside her portrait in the temple complex
of Karnak at Thebes. With the two cartouches taken together, Young was
able to assign six phonetic values correctly and three partly so, while four
were assigned incorrectly: the beginnings of his hieroglyphic 'alphabet'.

In his *Encyclopaedia Britannica* article, Young published a vocabulary
in English offering equivalents for 218 demotic and 200 hieroglyphic
words, including proper names, things and numerals, a portion of
which is shown opposite; his phonetic values for thirteen hieroglyphs,
cautiously headed 'Sounds?'; and a 'Supposed enchorial alphabet' for the
demotic script. 'In all he was able to equate either correctly or nearly
correctly about 80 demotic words with their hieroglyphic equivalents
and, with the help of the Greek words, translate most of them,' notes
the Egyptologist Carol Andrews in *The Rosetta Stone* – an impressive
record, despite a proportion of embarrassing misidentifications and
mistranslations that Champollion and others would later use to ridicule
Young's work. Nothing remotely resembling this article by Young had
been published before on the subject of ancient Egyptian writing. Despite
the fact that his results were 'mixed up with many false conclusions',
noted Francis Llewellyn Griffith, a highly respected Egyptologist working

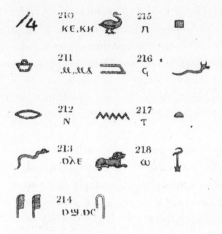

A tentative hieroglyphic 'alphabet' ('Sounds?') and a more definite demotic alphabet ('Supposed Enchorial Alphabet'), published by Thomas Young in his *Encyclopaedia Britannica* article 'Egypt', 1819. Although both contained errors, they stimulated Champollion's thinking.

Part of Thomas Young's hieroglyphic and demotic vocabulary, published in his *Encyclopaedia Britannica* article 'Egypt', 1819. Note the cartouches for Ptolemy and Berenice.

a century or so after Young, 'the method pursued was infallibly leading to definite decipherment'.

Young's article of 1819 for the *Encyclopaedia Britannica* was a landmark. But it was also anonymous: not until 1823 did he publish on Egypt under his own name. Of course, most of those interested in ancient Egyptian inscriptions – including de Sacy, Jomard, the Champollion brothers and a growing number of antiquaries curious and wealthy enough to visit Egypt and collect its antiquities – knew perfectly well who the anonymous author of the article was. Young was by now in constant communication with many of them, in a determined effort to obtain as many copies of new Egyptian inscriptions and manuscripts as he could. One of his contacts was Giovanni Belzoni, the excavator of a great pharaonic tomb at Thebes (mentioned in the Prologue) who, as we know, saluted Young's work in his grand memoir of his Egyptian travels, published in 1820. Belzoni wrote: 'I have the satisfaction of announcing to the reader, that, according to Dr Young's late discovery of a great number of hieroglyphics, he found the names of Nichao and Psammethis his son, inserted in the drawings I have taken of this tomb.' Unfortunately, these two names proved to be among Young's 'false conclusions'.

Portrait of Champollion, aged about 32, holding his hieroglyphic 'alphabet', c. 1823.

above: Portrait of Champollion-Figeac.
below: Portrait of Zoé Berriat, Champollion-Figeac's wife.

Bookcase containing the *Description de l'Égypte*, published in 1809–28 and presented by Louis-Philippe to the upper house of the French parliament in 1836.

The Rosetta Stone in the British Museum, after being cleaned for the bicentenary of its discovery by the French army in 1799. It was first studied by Champollion in 1808.

Reproduction of the Rosetta Stone in the Place des Écritures, Figeac.

opposite: Portrait of Thomas Young, aged about 50, by Sir Thomas Lawrence.
above: Detail from *Study and Genius of the Arts Revealing Ancient Egypt to Greece* by François-Édouard Picot, 1827, in the Louvre Museum.
below: Papyrus Sallier II, 19th dynasty, *c.* 1204 BC, in the British Museum.

Portrait of Champollion in Bedouin dress, probably by G. Angelelli

Naturally, Champollion was far less respectful towards Young than Belzoni was. Champollion first heard of Young's article, possibly in late 1819 but more likely during 1820, from his brother, who sent him some extracts of Young's vocabulary – perhaps obtained from the copy that Young sent to Jomard. Champollion replied from Grenoble with a scoffing disdain: 'The Englishman knows no more Egyptian than he does Malay or Manchu ... The discoveries of Dr Young announced with such pomp are merely ridiculous boasting. The vaunted discovery of the supposed key provokes pity ... I am truly sorry for the unfortunate English travellers in Egypt obliged to translate the inscriptions of Thebes with the master-key of Dr Young in their hands.'

Maybe so – yet Champollion went on to ask his brother to buy Young's article from London and to send it to him as soon as possible. When he finally read the article in full, apparently after he moved to Paris in July 1821, he fundamentally changed his attitude about Young's ideas.

Champollion's own publication record from his final years in Grenoble consisted of a fascicle illustrating 700 hieroglyphic and hieratic signs from various Egyptian monumental and manuscript sources. The most notable of these sources was a collection of papyri that had recently arrived from Egypt at the museum in Lyons, to which Champollion travelled in October 1820. Published in Grenoble in April 1821 under the title *De l'écriture hiératique des anciens Égyptiens*, the fascicle consisted of a mere seven pages of text and seven plates of illustrations. But despite its brevity, it was revealing – if not in quite the way that its author had intended.

The brief fascicle announced three significant conclusions, based on Champollion's comparison of hieroglyphic and hieratic (the cursive script from which demotic derives). The first was that hieratic 'is no more than a simple modification of the hieroglyphic system, and differs from it only in the form of its signs'. In other words, hieroglyphic was the origin of hieratic (and hence of demotic). The second was that hieratic 'is not in any way alphabetical'. The third was that hieratic characters 'are signs of things and not sounds'.

Champollion's first conclusion was correct, and had already been published by Young in 1816 and repeated in the *Encyclopaedia Britannica* article in 1819. In his 1815 letter to de Sacy, as mentioned earlier, Young had noted a 'striking resemblance', not spotted by any previous scholar, between some hieratic and demotic signs and what he called 'the corresponding hieroglyphics' – not only in the Rosetta Stone, but also in some papyrus manuscripts published in the *Description de l'Égypte*. Apparently, Champollion had now made the same deduction working on his own.

His second conclusion contradicted the published work of de Sacy, Åkerblad and Young, and was almost certainly incorrect, since they had shown that demotic (derived from hieratic) almost certainly contained alphabetic elements. In his 1815 letter to de Sacy, Young had written that the demotic script consisted of 'imitations of the hieroglyphics … mixed with letters of the alphabet'. It was neither a purely conceptual or symbolic script, nor an alphabet, but a mixture of the two.

His third conclusion, which implied that hieroglyphic, as well as hieratic, represented 'things not sounds' (since the later script was derived from hieroglyphic), was bound to be incorrect, since his second conclusion (about there being no alphabeticism in hieratic) was almost certainly incorrect. Presumably, Champollion still had faith in the hoary classical notion that all the Egyptian scripts were conceptual rather than phonetic.

Champollion's published denial of phoneticism in any of the Egyptian scripts was a blunder. His biographer Hartleben, with unusual frankness given her loyalty to Champollion, even calls his error 'disastrous'. Just as important, his fascicle was also an admission of how late in his research (1820–21) compared to Young (1815) he had discovered the derivation of hieratic from hieroglyphic.

For whatever reasons, Champollion soon regretted his 1821 publication. In Paris he was alleged to have made strenuous efforts to withdraw all copies, in order that he might suppress the text and redistribute only the plates. The accusation was probably true, given the subsequent rarity of the publication; the fact that Champollion presented only the plates to Young, who would remain unaware of the text until much later; and, most telling of all, that Champollion chose to make no reference of any kind to this embarrassing 1821 publication in his *Lettre à M. Dacier* of 1822. Such a suppression would make sense, because in the year or

Portrait of the baron of Haussez, prefect of Isère, who attempted to put Champollion on trial in Grenoble for high treason, and obstructed his career during the 1820s.

two that elapsed between his 1821 publication and his breakthrough in understanding the hieroglyphic system in 1822–23 he decided that there was, after all, a phonetic component in the Egyptian scripts; and also because Champollion's priority dispute with Young became intense during this period.

The meagreness of Champollion's published output in Grenoble between 1818 and 1821 was at least partly due to the deteriorating political atmosphere, his stressful existence and his poor state of health.

The liberal prefect was at loggerheads with the royalist mayor and military commandant. In 1819, Ultra activity meant that law-abiding citizens could not walk at night in the city without arms. In February 1820, the assassination at the Paris Opera of the duke of Berry, the second son of the leader of the Ultras, the count of Artois, led to a general tendency towards conservatism in the government, which enacted laws to detain suspects for up to three months on suspicion and introduced the pre-publication censorship of periodicals. A hardline Ultra prefect, the baron of Haussez, was sent to Grenoble in February to replace Choppin d'Arnouville. Around this time Champollion, who had been suffering from insomnia, stomach pains and a recurrence of his schoolboy fainting fits, wrote in despair to his brother: 'I would like to give myself up to the sweetness of doing nothing and thinking nothing.' His correspondence was full of critical references to 'les éteignoirs'. The word means 'candle-snuffer', but in Champollion's parlance (used also by Stendhal and others) it referred to any kind of arch-conservative obscurantism, whether priestly or party political. One cannot help wondering whether the policemen now once more intercepting Champollion's mail understood this literary metaphor.

As in 1815, after the fall of Napoleon, Champollion was soon in the prefect's sights. At a stormy personal interview with Haussez in mid-1820 to discuss Champollion's second dismissal from his library post (restored to him in 1818), the infuriated prefect foolishly pulled open a drawer to show a box of what he said were inflammatory letters and writings by the brothers. Champollion, equally infuriated, demanded to know by what right the prefect was reading his private correspondence. From now on, Haussez would show no mercy in his pursuit of Champollion, even making his life difficult a decade later, after Champollion had become a national figure, when Haussez was a minister in the government in Paris.

Matters came to a head in March and April 1821, just as Champollion's brief Egyptian publication was appearing from the press. A revolt by the inhabitants of Grenoble on 20 March saw the white flag of the Bourbons replaced by the Revolutionary tricolour – even on the citadel, Fort Rabot, which had been left almost undefended when the garrison was marched out to control the town. Champollion, it is said, led the party of men that planted the offending flag, though there is some dispute about exactly where he managed to plant it. Later, the prefect Haussez claimed he had seen Champollion shouting seditious slogans in the crowd that confronted him and his armed force, but there were no other witnesses, and Champollion disingenuously claimed he was not involved in the insurrection but otherwise engaged on 20 March. Having suspended him from his post at the Royal College, Haussez attempted to put Champollion on trial for high treason at a court martial. But the government in Paris intervened, and Champollion was tried instead in a civil court and acquitted of all charges against him in early July 1821. He had, however, lost all his positions and income in Grenoble. The prefect got his way in the end by making life impossible for his enemy in his favourite city.

There was no alternative now but for Champollion to move to Paris and stay with his brother. A few days after the trial was over, suffering in both mind and health, Champollion boarded a *diligence* with his nephew Ali, leaving his wife, Rosine, to follow later. His loyal friend Thévenet came to see him off. 'Pitiless fate has arrested me – if at all I survive,' groaned Jean-François at the moment of departure. 'Courage,' replied his old school friend, 'your genius will end by conquering fate.'

X

BREAKTHROUGH

Hieroglyphic writing is a complex system,
a script all at once figurative, symbolic, and phonetic,
in one and the same text, in one and the same
sentence, and, I might even venture, in one and the same word.

(Jean-François Champollion, *Précis du système*
hiéroglyphique des anciens Égyptiens, 1824)

Upon arrival in Paris on 20 July 1821, an exhausted Champollion settled down with his brother and family in their rented house at 28 Rue Mazarine, a central address in easy walking distance of Champollion-Figeac's office at the Academy of Inscriptions and Belles-Lettres, within the French Institute. The situation of the 30-year-old Champollion after leaving Grenoble for Paris is reminiscent of that of the 10-year-old boy after he left Figeac and arrived at his brother's apartment in Grenoble. In both instances, he was dependent on his brother for money and for the necessities of life. But, whereas in 1801 his elder brother had also been his teacher, now the relationship was reversed: Jean-François had become the teacher, Jacques-Joseph the pupil.

Over the next two years, in the house on the Rue Mazarine, without the distractions of university and school teaching, librarianship and the political instability of the previous decade, Champollion was able to devote his every waking minute – and probably his dreams as well – to ancient Egypt. Here, surrounded by his brother's library and immersed in new sources of Egyptian writing on monuments and papyri that reached him from private and public collections in Europe and from travellers in Egypt, he would finally crack the code of the hieroglyphs. His results would be announced, hot off the press, so to speak, in lectures during

1821–23 – most famously on 27 September 1822 – delivered to the Academy of Inscriptions, thanks to his brother's intimate connection with the academy's long-serving secretary, Bon-Joseph Dacier; and in two crucial illustrated texts published in 1822 and 1824.

Unfortunately, the steps that led to his decipherment are hard to discern. The difficulty arises partly from a dearth of correspondence by Champollion in this period, during which he no longer had any need to write revealing letters about ancient Egypt to his brother or to fellow scholars, most of whom were now readily at hand in Paris. But it comes also from the fact that he left important aspects of his thinking in the dark, reporting chiefly his established conclusions in his lectures and publications. This obscurity in itself is not too surprising. Exceptionally creative minds such as Champollion's generally work alone and in private: even the individual is often unaware of his or her own thought processes. Sometimes, however, Champollion's silence about the source of his insights appears to have been polemical subterfuge, intended to diminish the importance of the work of his English rival, Young.

To give a step-by-step account of Champollion's decipherment in 1821–24 is therefore impossible. It is possible, though, to identify three general phases; then, looking more closely at the order in which he tackled the problem, one can use informed speculation to fill in missing sections of his own account. By bearing these phases in mind, we can avoid the confusion present in many published accounts of the decipherment, which rely on an incorrect date stated by Champollion's first biographer, Hartleben.

In the first phase, lasting from April 1821 to September 1822, Champollion was convinced that all of the Egyptian scripts – hiero-glyphic, hieratic and demotic – represented things or ideas, not sounds. This was the belief he stated in his Grenoble publication of April 1821, as mentioned earlier. He repeated it categorically a year and a half later on the first page of his *Lettre à M. Dacier*, which was based on his lecture at the Academy of Inscriptions on 27 September 1822: 'I hope it is not too rash for me to say that I have succeeded in demonstrating that these two forms of writing [hieratic and demotic] are neither of them alphabetic, as has been so generally thought, but *ideographic*, like the hieroglyphs themselves, that is to say, depicting the *ideas* and not the *sounds* of the language.' Although this statement seems to exclude even the slightest phonetic element from the Egyptian scripts, Champollion clearly did not intend such a total exclusion, because he made one vital exception: hieroglyphs *could* represent sounds, not ideas, when used phonetically to write foreign proper names in cartouches, such as Ptolemy and Berenice. The latter deduction provided the *raison d'être* of his *Lettre à M. Dacier*, which proposed phonetic transliterations for the cartouches of many Greek and Roman rulers of Egypt, and a hieroglyphic and demotic 'alphabet' supposedly used only for writing foreign names.

During the second phase of decipherment, from September 1822 to April 1823, Champollion radically changed his mind. Having thought to apply his hieroglyphic alphabet first to the signs in native Egyptian cartouches, and then to other native Egyptian words, he was surprised and thrilled to find that the alphabet produced credible transliterations of historically known pharaohs such as Ramesses and Thothmes, and of ordinary Egyptian words recognizable from Coptic vocabularies. In April 1823, he announced to the Academy of Inscriptions that there was, after all, a major phonetic component in the hieroglyphic script, which had existed not only in the Greco-Roman period, but also throughout Egyptian history, and which had been used not merely in the writing of foreign proper names, but also throughout the script.

During the third phase, from April 1823 to early 1824, Champollion intensively worked out the hieroglyphic writing system, which consisted of a basic alphabet of some twenty phonetic values (the majority of them represented by several equivalent signs), some other, partially phonetic signs, plus many hundreds of non-phonetic figurative and symbolic signs. He showed how these phonetic, figurative and symbolic signs were combined to represent words by applying the system to numerous inscriptions, with consistent results. This analysis was published in his revolutionary *Précis du système hiéroglyphique des anciens Égyptiens* in April 1824, and in a revised second edition in 1828. The revised edition incorporated the text of his *Lettre à M. Dacier* (as its second chapter) but with a crucial emendation. Revealing his change of mind about phoneticism in 1822–23, Champollion silently, without so much as a footnote, altered the statement he made in September 1822 into a fundamentally different assertion that corresponded with his third phase of understanding: 'I hope it is not too rash for me to say that I have succeeded in demonstrating that these two forms of writing [hieratic and demotic] are neither of them <u>entirely</u> alphabetic, as has been so generally thought, but <u>often also</u> *ideographic*, like the hieroglyphs themselves, that is to say, <u>sometimes</u> depicting the *ideas* and <u>sometimes</u> the *sounds* of the language.' (His 1828 alterations are underlined.)

The credit for the second and third phases of the decipherment belonged, without question, to Champollion – a view not disputed by Young, who in fact never wholly accepted the phonetic component in the hieroglyphic script proposed by Champollion, other than in the spelling of foreign proper names. The dispute that arose between them concerned only the first phase, for which Young claimed far more credit than Champollion was willing to give him. Since the first phase laid the foundation for the subsequent decipherment, its authorship was bound to be controversial.

What influence did Young's work of 1814–19 have on Champollion's first phase? There can be no definitive answer. Indeed, the issue has been debated from 1823 until the present day; opinions of Young's importance to Champollion's decipherment cover the gamut from *sine qua non* to none.

French writers have almost universally subscribed to the view that Champollion was intellectually independent of Young – at least those who wrote after the decipherment became generally accepted in the mid-19th century. They have taken their cue from the patriotic tone of Aimé Champollion-Figeac's *Les Deux Champollion*, published in 1887, with its remark that: 'Today Champollion *le jeune* has entered posterity, the petty jealousies have fallen silent, Europe is unanimous in recognizing that his immortal discovery belongs to him in its entirety *and not only to him*, but ultimately to France, which does not hesitate to count him among the innovative geniuses whose glory has made them fellow citizens of all peoples.' Outside France, however, opinion has always been strongly divided. It is worth citing the opinions of three Egyptological experts to provide a flavour of the debate.

The Irishman Edward Hincks was a contemporary of Champollion and an early Egyptologist who later became a highly respected pioneer of the decipherment of Mesopotamian cuneiform. In 1846, Hincks wrote:

Had [Champollion] been candid enough to admit that he was indebted to Dr Young for the commencement of his discovery, and only to claim the merit of extending and improving [Young's] alphabet, he would probably have had his claims to [his] subsequent discoveries, which were certainly his own, more readily admitted by Englishmen than they have been. In 1819 Dr Young had published his article 'Egypt' in the Supplement to the Encyclopaedia Britannica; and it cannot be doubted that the analysis of the names 'Ptolemaeus' and 'Berenice', which it contained, reached Champollion in the interval between his publications in 1821 and 1822, and led him to alter his views.

Half a century later, Egyptology had become an established academic discipline, with Champollion viewed as its 'founding father'. Sir Peter le Page Renouf, a British Egyptologist (though partly of French ancestry) enraged by the continuing allegations that Champollion plagiarized Young, championed him with fierce conviction in 1896:

No one could learn anything from [Young's] famous Essay [of 1819], for even the true things contained in it are logically undistinguishable [sic] from the false. Young was in the habit of calling Champollion's discoveries an extension of his own. But the difference was not one of quantity but of quality. A man who sometimes hits upon the right answer to an arithmetical problem is not on the same level as one who knows the rule for working all such problems … Two undeniable facts remain after all that has been written: Champollion learnt nothing whatever from Young, nor did anyone else. It is only through Champollion and the method he employed that Egyptology has grown into the position which it now occupies.

At the beginning of the 21st century, a third Egyptologist, Richard Parkinson – the curator in charge of the Rosetta Stone at the British Museum – fell somewhere between the extremes of Hincks and Renouf. In 2005, he wrote: 'Even if one allows that Champollion was more familiar with Young's initial work than he subsequently claimed, he is the sole decipherer of the hieroglyphic script: any decipherment stands or falls as a whole, and while Young discovered parts of an alphabet – a key – Champollion unlocked an entire written language.'

Champollion himself was coy about when he first came to know of Young's published contributions, and vague about what exactly he learnt from them.

In the *Lettre à M. Dacier* of 1822, he signally neglected Young, consigning him to one fairly long but uninformative footnote. Here, after accepting the correctness of a few of the signs in Young's alphabetical reading of the Ptolemy and Berenice cartouches but criticizing other sign readings, Champollion grudgingly admitted:

M. le docteur Young has done in England, on the inscribed monuments of ancient Egypt, work analogous to that which has occupied me for so many years; and his researches on the intermediate text [i.e. demotic] and the hieroglyphic text of the inscription of Rosetta, as on the manuscripts that I have made known as 'hieratic', present a series of very important results. See the Supplement to the Encyclopaedia Britannica, *vol. IV, pt. I, Edinburgh, December 1819.*

But in the *Précis du système hiéroglyphique des anciens Égyptiens* of 1824, published after his dispute with Young came into the open, Champollion tellingly devoted virtually the entire first chapter of the book to an attempted refutation of Young's claims. After listing six conclusions about Egyptian writing reached by Young from the beginning of his research until he published his article of 1819, Champollion baldly claimed, without specifying any dates: 'I must say that in the same period, and without having any knowledge of the opinions of M. *le docteur* Young, I managed to arrive, by a fairly certain method, at more or less similar results.' A few pages later, he noted that he had read Young's *Encyclopaedia Britannica* article 'in 1821'; in later life he stated that he read it 'a little after my arrival in Paris, in September 1821'.

These claims, although defensible, are surely economical with the truth. As we know, it is certain that Champollion was aware of Young's work in 1815, because the two of them corresponded after Champollion had written to the Royal Society in 1814. He almost certainly read Young's 'conjectural translation' of the Rosetta Stone, in the copy lent by de Sacy to his brother at Champollion's request in mid-1815. During late 1819 or 1820 (the date is uncertain), Champollion was informed of Young's article in the *Encyclopaedia Britannica* by his brother and scoffed at some of its results. It is likely that he did not read the full article until after he reached Paris in the summer of 1821, because it was hard to obtain, even in England, according to independent witnesses. Notwithstanding, Young is known to have sent personal copies of the article to several scholars in 1819, including Edme Jomard and Alexander von Humboldt in Paris, so Champollion could have received a summary from his brother well before he arrived in Paris in July 1821. It strains credulity to suppose that the well-connected, highly determined Champollion-Figeac, private secretary to the permanent secretary of the Academy of Ancient Inscriptions, could not have procured a copy of Young's article in Paris in 1819–20.

Whatever the true extent of Champollion's knowledge of Young's work in 1815–21, in the introduction to his *Précis* he felt obliged to concede the following achievements to Young:

I ... recognize that he was the first to publish some correct ideas about the ancient writings of Egypt; that he also was the first to establish some correct distinctions concerning the general nature of these writings, by determining, through a substantial comparison of texts, the value of several groups of characters. I even recognize that he published before me his ideas on the possibility of the existence of several sound-signs, which would have been used to write foreign proper names in Egypt in hieroglyphs; finally that M. Young was also the first to try, but without complete success, to give a phonetic value to the hieroglyphs making up the two names Ptolemy and Berenice.

In my view, unprovable as it may be, this statement was a tacit admission that it was Young's 1819 article that compelled Champollion to embrace the existence of a phonetic component in the Egyptian scripts. Since 1810, Champollion had oscillated in his view of hieroglyphic, hieratic and demotic phoneticism; now Young's analysis and results were too decisive to ignore. Phoneticism had to be present in the signs within the cartouches that spelt foreign proper names, at the very least. The plate section of Young's article saliently published what he called 'something like a hieroglyphic alphabet' in the form of a list of fourteen hieroglyphs labelled 'Sounds?', along with a second, longer list of demotic signs labelled 'Supposed enchorial alphabet', modified from those suggested by Åkerblad. As he explained in his accompanying text, Young had derived this rudimentary hieroglyphic alphabet from the cartouches of Ptolemy and Berenice, by attempting to match each hieroglyphic sign in a cartouche with its apparently equivalent alphabetic letter in the names' Greek spelling. Although some of the phonetic values he assigned were incorrect, the 'matching' principle was convincing. Surely, having critically digested Young's articles and accepted both this principle and some of Young's results, however reluctantly, Champollion was now primed to take his own first correct, original step.

The moment came in January 1822, when Champollion saw a copy of an obelisk inscription sent to the French Institute by an English traveller and collector, William Bankes, who was a friend of Young. Bankes had had the obelisk removed from the island of Philae (near Aswan) by Belzoni in 1818 for transportation to London, where it finally arrived by ship in September 1821, though without its base block, which had been accidentally stranded in a cataract of the Nile. Its inscriptions (including those on the base block) were copied in London and published in November 1821 by Bankes, who sent the published drawings to interested individuals and institutions. The object itself – the first ancient Egyptian obelisk to reach Britain – was eventually erected at Bankes's country house at Kingston Lacy in Dorset, where it still stands.

The Bankes obelisk is important to the story of decipherment because it bore two languages. The inscription on the base block was in Greek, while that on the column was in hieroglyphic script. This, however, did not make it a true bilingual inscription, a second Rosetta Stone, because the two inscriptions did not match. Notwithstanding, in 1818 Bankes realized that in the Greek letters the names of Ptolemy and Cleopatra, Ptolemaic queen, were mentioned, while in the hieroglyphs two (and only two) cartouches occurred – presumably representing the same two names that were written in Greek on the base. One of these cartouches was almost the same as a long cartouche on the Rosetta Stone identified by Young as representing Ptolemy plus a title:

Rosetta Stone

Philae obelisk

– so the second cartouche on the obelisk was likely to read 'Cleopatra'. In sending the drawing of the Philae inscription to Young and other scholars – including Denon, who presented his copy to the French Institute – Bankes pencilled his proposed identification of Cleopatra in the margin of the copy.

Unfortunately for Young, the copy contained a significant error. The copyist had expressed the first letter of Cleopatra's name using the sign for t (◁) instead of k (◁). Later, Young noted that 'as I had not leisure at the time to enter into a very minute comparison of the name with other authorities, I suffered myself to be discouraged with respect to the application of my alphabet to its analysis'. In other words, Young was unlucky here; but he was also undermined by his lifelong polymathic tendency to spread himself too thinly. Not long before this, he had been appointed as the superintendent of the Board of Longitude's *Nautical Almanac*, a demanding position that reduced his Egyptian studies.

Champollion, after a decade and a half of effort and frustration, was not about to be diverted from his study of Egypt by other interests and duties, or by a copyist's error. During 1821, he had ascertained the *demotic* spelling of Cleopatra from a bilingual Greek–demotic papyrus recently collected in Egypt by an Italian, Casati, as noted in his *Lettre à M. Dacier*. According to Hartleben, this demotic spelling allowed Champollion to construct a hypothetical hieroglyphic spelling of the queen's name from his knowledge of demotic–hieroglyphic sign equivalences. But this claim has seemed implausible to modern Egyptologists (Henri Sottas, for

Drawing of the Bankes obelisk from Philae, made in 1821 in preparation for its publication. The obelisk stands in Kingston Lacy, Dorset, in the grounds of the former house of William Bankes.

'Cleopatra', a research note in Champollion's manuscripts on the vital cartouche from the obelisk that Bankes acquired from Philae.

example, in his detailed analysis of the *Lettre*), nor was the claim actually maintained by Champollion himself. More likely is that he identified four similar-looking cartouches published in the *Description de l'Égypte* between 1809 and 1817, each containing the feminine termination and the signs from 'Cleopatra' if the name was indeed spelt phonetically – in particular the signs standing for *l*, *o* and *p*, which were known from the cartouche for Ptolemy (as shown by Young). However, Champollion did not claim that this was his method, either. Most likely is that he simply took the pencilled clue offered by Bankes and hazarded some guesses about the phonetic values of Bankes's cartouche. But if this really was what he did, he did not confess it and made no acknowledgment. (An offended Bankes thereafter refused to give Champollion any help, despite his requests.)

Whatever route Champollion may have followed to identify the cartouche, Cleopatra's name proved to be his key to the phonetic system. Just as Young had done, Champollion decided that the shorter of the two versions of the Ptolemy cartouche on the Rosetta Stone spelt only Ptolemy's name, while a second, longer cartouche must have involved some royal title tacked onto Ptolemy's name. Again like Young, Champollion assumed that Ptolemy was spelt alphabetically, and thus, following Bankes's identification, that the same principle must apply in the spelling of Cleopatra on the obelisk from Philae. He proceeded to guess the phonetic values of the hieroglyphs in both cartouches:

c	△	p	▢
l	𓃭	t	◠
e	◊	o	𓃀
o	𓃀	l	𓃭
p	▢	m	⊏
a	𓅄	e	𓏭
t	◠	s	⌐
r	◠		
a	𓅄		

There were four signs in common – those with the phonetic values *l*, *e*, *o* and *p* – but the phonetic value *t* was represented differently in the two names. Champollion deduced correctly that the two signs for *t* were what are known as 'homophones', that is, different signs with the same sound (compare, in English, **J**ill and **G**ill, **C**atherine and **K**atherine) – a concept of which Young was also aware. The real test of the decipherment, however, was whether these new phonetic values, when applied to the cartouches in other inscriptions, would produce sensible names. Champollion tried them in the following cartouche:

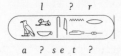

	l		?		r	
a		?		s	e	t	?

Substitution produced *Al?se?tr?*. Champollion guessed the name *Alksentrs*, equating to the Greek *Alexandros* (Alexander): the two signs for *k/c* (⌓ and △) are almost homophonous, as are the two different signs for *s* (—∞— and |). Using his growing alphabet, Champollion went on to identify the cartouches of other rulers of non-Egyptian origin, such as Berenice (already tackled by Young, though with mistakes) and Roman emperors such as Trajan, including their titles of Caesar and Autocrator (which Young had mistakenly identified as Arsinoe).

Drawing of the Dendera Zodiac and its surrounding hieroglyphs, published in the *Description de l'Égypte*. The cartouche immediately to the left of the feet of the full-length figure, which apparently reads 'Autocrator', turned out to be a copyist's error (see page 216).

The last identification, Autocrator, would attract unexpected attention during 1822. The cartouche in question came from a drawing in the *Description de l'Égypte* of an important temple at Dendera, not far north of Thebes. The temple's ceiling was carved with a controversial inscription, the Dendera Zodiac, which had been discovered and drawn by Napoleon's savants. Two decades later, in 1821, an enterprising if unscrupulous French engineer had partially sawn the zodiac off the temple ceiling and shipped it to Paris, where it went on public display. In 1822, the Dendera Zodiac was more celebrated in the French capital than the Rosetta Stone. There was even a vaudeville theatre production, *Le Zodiaque de Paris*, with actors playing each sign of the zodiac and a chorus of wailing mummies, which satirized the popular, official and scholarly reactions to the exotic antique, despite heavy government censorship.

The reason for the furore was that the zodiac had come to stand for a clash between science and religion. Almost from the moment of its discovery in Egypt in the late 1790s, the zodiac's date of origin had been hotly contested. According to some astronomical analysis of the historical star positions supposedly depicted in the zodiac, the object, and therefore Egyptian civilization, seemed to be older than permitted by the biblical account of the creation of man – as much as 15,000 years older than Christ, according to an initial estimate by Fourier in 1802. But according to other astronomical analysis, such as that by the physicist Jean-Baptiste Biot, the zodiac dated from much later: the positions of its stars represented the state of the heavens in about 747 BC. This was the view supported by the Catholic Church, needless to say. For more than two decades, the Dendera Zodiac was a *cause célèbre* for left-wing atheists and the right-wing devout.

In the end, the Gordian knot was cut not by the quarrelling scientists and priests, but by Champollion. From his study of ancient Egyptian religion, Champollion

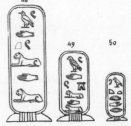

Three variant hieroglyphic cartouches of the title Autocrator, drawn by Champollion and published in the *Lettre à M. Dacier*.

grasped that the Dendera Zodiac was of astrological, not astronomical, significance. Its age, therefore, could not be calculated from its star positions; rather, it could be dated from its hieroglyphic inscriptions. When he read the cartouche from the Dendera temple as a Roman title, Autocrator, a late date for the zodiac seemed assured. (The date given by modern scholars is the 1st century BC, the time of Cleopatra, who is depicted in the temple.) Champollion, despite his belief in the great antiquity of Egyptian civilization and his dislike of the conservative *éteignoirs*, now found himself promoted by the Catholic Church as a saviour of the true Christian faith, whether he liked it or not.

Champollion reached his conclusion about this cartouche in the summer of 1822. By now, it was clear to him that the hieroglyphic code was beginning to break. The decipherment of one cartouche had led to the decipherment of another, and another, and yet another. From many such Greco-Roman proper names and titles written in hieroglyphs, Champollion worked out a table of phonetic signs, in the manner of Young's 'hieroglyphic alphabet', but much fuller than his rival's and more accurate (though still with plenty of errors). He would soon publish his findings in the *Lettre à M. Dacier*.

However, at this juncture – the first phase of the decipherment – Champollion did not expect his phonetic values to apply to the names of native Egyptian rulers, which he persisted in thinking would be spelt non-phonetically. Even less did he expect that his values would apply to the entire Egyptian writing system.

It was a hieroglyphic inscription he received on the morning of 14 September 1822 that launched the second phase of his decipherment. Drawn by a French architect, Jean-Nicolas Huyot, who had recently travelled in Egypt with Bankes, the inscription came from the great temple of Abu Simbel in Nubia and contained intriguing cartouches. They appeared to write the same name in a variety of ways, the simplest being:

The last two signs were familiar to Champollion as having the phonetic value *s*. Using his knowledge of Coptic, he guessed that the first sign had the value *re*, which was the Coptic word for 'sun' – the object that the sign apparently symbolized. (Or perhaps he simply followed Young, who had made the connection clear in his 1819 article.) Did an ancient Egyptian pharaoh with a name that resembled *R(e)?ss* exist? Champollion, steeped in his knowledge of ancient Egypt, thought of Ramesses, a king of the 19th dynasty mentioned in a well-known Greek history of Egypt written in the 3rd century BC by a Ptolemaic historian, Manetho. (Even current Egyptologists use Manetho's text as the basic framework of ancient Egyptian history.) If this speculation was correct, then the sign 𝖒 must have the phonetic value *m*. (Champollion believed that the hieroglyphic script did not represent vowels, except in the case of foreign proper names such as Cleopatra.)

Encouragement came from a second hieroglyphic inscription:

Two of these signs were 'known'; the first, an ibis, was a symbol of the god Thoth (the inventor of writing). The name, then, had to be

Thothmes/Thuthmosis, a pharaoh of the 18th dynasty also mentioned by Manetho. (Young had already identified this cartouche as belonging to Thuthmosis, but he had not attempted to read the signs phonetically.) The Rosetta Stone appeared to confirm the value of 𝖒. The sign occurred there, again with ▯, as part of a group of hieroglyphs with the Greek translation '*genethlia*', meaning 'birthday'. Champollion was at once reminded of the Coptic for 'give birth', '*mise*'. (He was only half right about the spelling of Ramesses: 𝖒 does

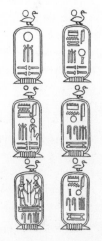

Six variant hieroglyphic cartouches of the name Ramesses II, drawn by Champollion and published in the *Précis du système hiéroglyphique des anciens Égyptiens*.

157

not have the phonetic value *m*, as he thought, but rather the *biconsonantal* value *ms*, as implied by the Coptic '*mise*'. Champollion was as yet unaware of this complexity.)

Once he had accepted that the hieroglyphs were a mixture of phonetic signs and signs standing for whole words, Champollion could decipher the second half of the long cartouche belonging to Ptolemy – i.e. the king's title – on the Rosetta Stone. That is:

According to the Greek inscription, the entire cartouche meant 'Ptolemy living for ever, beloved of Ptah'. Ptah was the creator god of the city of Memphis. In Coptic, the word for 'life' or 'living' was 'onkh'; this was thought to be derived from the ancient Egyptian word 'ankh', represented by the sign ♀ (a whole-word sign). Presumably the next signs ⌓ meant 'ever' and contained a *t* sound, given that the sign ⌓ was now known to have the phonetic value *t*. With help from Greek and Coptic, the ⌐ could be assigned the phonetic value *dj*, giving a rough ancient Egyptian pronunciation *djet*, meaning 'for ever'. (The other sign ═ was silent, a kind of classificatory word sign now known as a determinative; it symbolized 'flat land'.)

Of the remaining signs, ⌓ ⌐ ⌐, the first was now known to stand for *p* and the second for *t* – the first two sounds of Ptah; and so the third sign could be given the approximate phonetic value *h*. The fourth sign – another whole-word sign – was therefore assumed to mean 'beloved'. Coptic once more came in useful in assigning a pronunciation: the Coptic word for 'love' was known to be 'mere', and so the pronunciation of the fourth sign was thought to be *mer*. In sum, Champollion arrived at the following rough approximation of the famous Rosetta Stone cartouche (guessing at the unwritten vowels): *Ptolmes ankh djet Ptah mer* – 'Ptolemy living for ever, beloved of Ptah'.

The events that followed these few hours of logic, intuition and luck are truly worthy of the Romantic movement, the age of Byron and Goethe. It was said in the Champollion family – as Aimé

Champollion-Figeac recorded long after the death of his uncle – that towards noon on 14 September 1822 Jean-François rushed from his house in the Rue Mazarine to the nearby Academy of Inscriptions and Belles-Lettres, flung a bundle of drawings of Egyptian inscriptions onto a desk in Jacques-Joseph's office, and cried: 'Je tiens mon affaire!' ('I've done it!') – his own version of Archimedes's cry 'Eureka!'. But before he could explain what he had done, he collapsed on the floor in a dead faint. For an instant, his brother feared that he was dead. Taken home to rest, Champollion apparently did not revive until eveningtime five days later, when he immediately plunged into work again. On 27 September, he gave his celebrated lecture at the Academy of Inscriptions and Belles-Lettres announcing his breakthrough, which was published in October as the *Lettre à M. Dacier, relative à l'alphabet des hiéroglyphes phonétiques*. The surviving manuscript shows that the letter was originally to have been addressed to de Sacy; this name has been crossed out by Champollion-Figeac and replaced with the name of the faithful Dacier.

By an extraordinary fluke of history, Young happened to be in Paris in late September 1822, accompanying his wife on a foreign visit, and he was present at Champollion's lecture on 27 September. In fact, he was invited to sit next to his rival while Champollion read out his paper. It was the first personal encounter between the two decipherers, who were formally introduced after the meeting by a mutual friend, the physicist François Arago. Although there is no direct report of their conversation, it appears to have been amicable, judging from their significant correspondence during the next three or four months, in which Champollion sent Young details of some of his latest results.

Nonetheless, during the Paris lecture Young could hardly have avoided noticing Champollion's lack of open acknowledgment of his own work. He wrote to his friend Hudson Gurney from Paris:

Fresnel, a young mathematician of the Civil Engineers, has really been doing some good things in the extension and application of my theory of light, and Champollion … has been working still harder upon the Egyptian characters. He devotes his whole time to the pursuit and he has been wonderfully successful

LETTRE

A M. DACIER,

SECRÉTAIRE PERPÉTUEL DE L'ACADÉMIE ROYALE
DES INSCRIPTIONS ET BELLES-LETTRES,

RELATIVE A L'ALPHABET

DES HIÉROGLYPHES PHONÉTIQUES

EMPLOYÉS PAR LES ÉGYPTIENS POUR INSCRIRE SUR LEURS MONUMENTS
LES TITRES, LES NOMS ET LES SURNOMS DES SOUVERAINS GRECS ET
ROMAINS;

PAR M. CHAMPOLLION LE JEUNE.

A PARIS,

CHEZ FIRMIN DIDOT PÈRE ET FILS,

LIBRAIRES, RUE JACOB, N° 24.

M. DCCC. XXII.

Title page of the *Lettre à M. Dacier*, published by Champollion in 1822.

in some of the documents that he has obtained – but he appears to me to go too fast – and he makes up his mind in many cases where I should think it safer to doubt. But it is better to do too much than to do nothing at all, and others may separate the wheat from the chaff when his harvest is complete. How far he will acknowledge everything which he has either borrowed or might have borrowed from me I am not quite confident, but the world will be sure to remark que c'est le premier pas qui coûte ['it's the first step that costs'] though the proverb is less true in this case than in most, for here every step is laborious. I have many things I should like to show Champollion in England, but I fear his means of locomotion are extremely limited, and I have no chance of being able to augment them.

Young's work was conspicuously downplayed in the *Lettre à M. Dacier* – so patently, in fact, that anyone knowledgeable about the recent history of the Rosetta Stone could not fail to conclude that Champollion had done so deliberately. As Young would remark publicly in 1823, with notable understatement: 'I did certainly expect to find the chronology of my own researches a little more distinctly stated.' Champollion's first publication of the decipherment in October 1822 shows that from the very beginning he was set on keeping all the glory for himself, since he could have had no other motive to downplay Young's role at this time, before Young had made a single public criticism of him or his work.

Champollion's attitude to Young is most evident if we consider Champollion's description of how he identified Cleopatra's cartouche and used it, with Ptolemy's cartouche, to construct an alphabet. The following account is Young's own translation from Champollion's *Lettre* (the emphases are also Young's):

The hieroglyphical text of the inscription of Rosetta exhibited, on account of its fractures, only the name of Ptolemy. The obelisk found in the Isle of Philae, and lately removed to London, contains also the hieroglyphical name of one of the Ptolemies, expressed by the same characters that occur in the inscription of Rosetta, surrounded by a ring or border [i.e. a cartouche], and it is followed by a second border, which must necessarily contain the proper name of a woman, and of a queen of the family of the Lagidae, since this group was terminated by the hieroglyphics expressive of the feminine gender; characters which are found at the end of the names of all the Egyptian goddesses without exception. The obelisk was fixed, it is said, to a basis bearing a Greek inscription, which is a petition of the priests of Isis at Philae, addressed to King Ptolemy, to Cleopatra his sister, and to Cleopatra his wife. Now, if this obelisk, and the hieroglyphical inscription engraved on it, were the result of this petition, which in fact adverts to the consecration of a monument of the kind, the border, with the feminine proper name, can only be that of one of the Cleopatras. This name, and that of Ptolemy, which in the Greek have several letters in common, were capable of being employed for a comparison of the hieroglyphical characters composing them; and if the similar characters in these names expressed in both the same sounds, it followed that their nature must be entirely phonetic.

There was not even a nod to Young (or Bankes). The omission stung him, and, with the encouragement of his friend Gurney, spurred him into publishing a book in April 1823 for a general readership, this time under his own name, entitled *An Account of Some Recent Discoveries in Hieroglyphical Literature and Egyptian Antiquities*. Here Young commented on the previous passage by Champollion as follows:

This course of investigation appears, indeed, to be so simple and so natural, that the reader must naturally be inclined to forget that any preliminary steps were required: and to take it for granted, either that it had long been known and admitted, that the rings on the pillar of Rosetta contained the name of Ptolemy, and that the semicircle and the oval constituted the female termination, or that Mr Champollion himself had been the author of these discoveries.

It had, however, been one of the greatest difficulties attending the translation of the hieroglyphics of Rosetta, to explain how the groups within the rings, which varied considerably in different parts of the pillar, and which occurred in several places where there was no corresponding name in the Greek, while they were not to be found in others where they ought to have appeared, could possibly represent the name of Ptolemy; and it was not without considerable labour that I had been able to overcome this difficulty. The interpretation of the female termination had never, I believe, been suspected by any but myself: nor had the name of a single god or goddess, out of more than 500 that I have collected, been clearly pointed out by any person.

'Table des Signes Phonétiques' from Champollion's *Lettre à M. Dacier*. This table of demotic and hieroglyphic signs with their Greek equivalents was drawn up in October 1822. His own name appears in demotic script at the bottom, enclosed in a cartouche.

But, however Mr Champollion may have arrived at his conclusions, I admit them, with the greatest pleasure and gratitude, not by any means as superseding my system, but as fully confirming and extending it.

Indeed, Young added a provocative subtitle to his book: *Including the Author's Original Alphabet, As Extended by Mr Champollion.*

Champollion was duly provoked. On 23 March 1823, having seen only an advertisement for Young's new book, he wrote angrily to him: 'I shall never consent to recognize any other original alphabet than my own, where it is a matter of the hieroglyphic alphabet properly called; and the unanimous opinion of scholars on this point will be more and more confirmed by the public examination of any other claim.' Scholarly war had been declared.

Young's supporters felt that he had taken the vital first steps that had enabled Champollion to advance, and that Champollion had either ignored them or claimed that he had come to the same conclusions independently. 'Nothing can exceed the effrontery of Champollion in thus complaining to Dr Young, the author of the discoveries ... as if he himself were the person aggrieved,' wrote John Leitch, the editor of Young's Egyptological works. Champollion's supporters argued, by and large, that while Young had taken some first steps, not all of them were correct, as witness his misreading of some of the signs in the cartouches of Ptolemy and Berenice. Champollion, they said, had established a *system* that worked easily when applied to new cartouches, as opposed to Young's more ad hoc methods, which in some cases required ingenious manipulation to produce phonetic values. And inevitably they pointed to Champollion's truly revolutionary progress from 1823 onwards, which Young himself generally admired.

At the end of the chapter in his book named 'Mr Champollion', Young summarized his basic wish about his French rival:

[that] the further he advances by the exertion of his own talents and ingenuity, the more easily he will be able to admit, without any exorbitant sacrifice of his fame, the claim that I have advanced to a priority with respect to the first elements of all his researches; and I cannot help thinking that he will ultimately feel it most for his own substantial honour and reputation, to be more anxious to admit the just claims of others than they be to advance them.

This was a reasonable, temperate suggestion, given the pioneering role Young had played in 1814–19, but it fell on stony ground. Champollion's rejection of it was virtually inevitable. For him to have agreed to Young's request would have made a mockery of his long years of obsession with ancient Egypt, beginning with his time as an impecunious student in Paris in 1807, for which he had truly suffered – unlike the comfortably-off Young. Or perhaps Champollion had convinced himself that he had genuinely taken the inaugural steps in the first phase of the decipherment, whether independently of Young or by correcting him. In all probability both thoughts coexisted in his mind. There was, in addition, the fact that his rival was an Englishman – Champollion's least-favoured nationality – and thus a representative of the nation that had taken the Rosetta Stone from its French discoverers. To cap it all, Champollion was always a man attracted to extremes, unlike the moderate Young. In his by no means entirely convincing proof in the *Précis* of Young's lack of system, Champollion dramatically concluded that Young's system applied 'to *nothing*', whereas his own system applied 'to *all*' (the italics are Champollion's). But of course this all-or-nothing distinction, even supposing it were true of Champollion's system (which it was not, as of 1824), implied nothing definite about its *origins*, despite Champollion's indignant insistence to the contrary.

Nevertheless, by sticking intransigently to his claim of sole authorship, Champollion would achieve his ambition and come to enjoy wide acceptance in his lifetime as *the* decipherer of the Egyptian hieroglyphs. But in so doing he would lose his good name, rather like Isaac Newton in physics, who denied any credit to other scientists such as Robert Hooke. Young was right in his moderate warning: Champollion's personal reputation would forever be tainted by his hubris towards Young. An English friend and admirer of both men, the antiquarian Sir William Gell, who had studied their work in detail as it developed, commented aptly of Champollion to Young in 1828: 'I wish he would have the decency to write you a letter in print and confess your originality and his own embryo ideas emanating from your discoveries, without which his real merits seem to me always in a cloud.'

By the time Young's book appeared in April 1823, Champollion was already far ahead of him. He was about to embark on the third phase of the decipherment as explained above, which would lead to the publication of his magnificent *Précis du système hiéroglyphique des anciens*

Égyptiens in 1824. Even in the closing pages of the *Lettre à M. Dacier*, he had hinted at the existence of a single, universally valid hieroglyphic system, by hazarding that 'the phonetic writing existed in Egypt in the far distant past', long before the arrival of the Greeks. Young, in his book, was cautiously sceptical of this claim, even where it concerned the names of the ancient pharaohs, let alone the rest of the hieroglyphs.

What exactly happened to reorient Champollion's mind in the six months or so between the *Lettre* of September 1822 and his next key announcement to the Academy of Inscriptions in April 1823? He gave no direct explanation in his *Précis*. Hartleben maintained that the idea of the hieroglyphic system as a mixture of phonetic, figurative and symbolic signs came to Champollion in December 1821 – on his birthday, 23 December, according to an established 'tradition' mentioned by Hartleben in a footnote to her original German biography (which is omitted from the French translation). But this date, 23 December 1821, is unquestionably wrong – too early – because we know that Champollion firmly dismissed phoneticism in the hieroglyphs (except for the cartouches) as late as the *Lettre à M. Dacier* in September 1822. A far more likely date, if we choose to stick with the birthday story, would be a year later: 23 December 1822. By then, an excited Champollion had transliterated the cartouches of some thirty more pharaohs (as he would inform Young in early January 1823) and was surely having serious doubts about whether his theory of 'things not sounds' was valid for the rest of the hieroglyphs. In other words, by December 1822 the evidence against his theory had reached a 'critical mass' in Champollion's mind, leading to an efflorescence of insights.

Probably a combination of several factors was in play. For one thing, at this time Champollion learnt with surprise from a newly published French grammar of Chinese that there were phonetic elements not only in foreign proper names written in Chinese characters, but also in native Chinese words. If so in Chinese, why not also in Egyptian? For another, he tried counting the characters on the Rosetta Stone, as Hartleben mentions. This is how Champollion explained his analysis in the *Précis*:

The 14 partially damaged [hieroglyphic] lines of which it is composed correspond
more or less to 18 complete lines in the Greek text, which, at 27 words per line
[the average number over 10 lines] would form 486 words; and the ideas expressed
in these 486 Greek words are expressed, in the hieroglyphic text, by 1,419 signs;
and among this great number of signs, there are only 166 signs of different form ...
This calculation therefore establishes that the number of hieroglyphic signs is not
nearly as extensive as is generally supposed; and it seems to prove above all ... that
each hieroglyph does not express on its own an idea, since 1,419 hieroglyphic signs
are needed to represent only 486 Greek words, or alternatively 486 Greek words
are enough to express the ideas noted by 1,419 hieroglyphic signs.

So 1,419 hieroglyphs corresponded to 486 Greek words; and among these 1,419 hieroglyphs there were only 166 individual signs. If each hieroglyph truly represented an idea or word, then one would have expected similar numbers of hieroglyphs and Greek words, and a larger set of separate signs, each one representing a different idea or word. All of a sudden, it must have struck Champollion that the hieroglyphs on the Rosetta Stone could be explained not by a purely 'ideographic' system, but by a small set of frequently employed phonetic hieroglyphs – an alphabet like the one he had published in 1822 – mixed with many more non-phonetic hieroglyphs that stood only for ideas or words.

A few weeks after this revelation, Champollion had a second life-changing experience of a completely different kind. 'The publication of his letter to Dacier had brought him not the least advantage,' noted Hartleben: 'pointless admiration on the one side, jealousy and scepticism on the other.' Champollion needed practical help with his research. In January 1823, he visited a saleroom in Paris in order to copy a text from an Egyptian collection that had come up for auction. He began quickly and surely to sketch the Egyptian inscriptions in his notebook. An older man, watching him at work, engaged him in conversation. Soon, Champollion found himself discussing without reserve the importance of a recent Egyptian collection sold by the French consul-general in Egypt, Bernardino Drovetti, to the king of Sardinia for display in his royal museum in Turin. What a scandal, said Champollion, that these treasures had not been acquired by the French government!

The stranger was none other than the duke of Blacas d'Aulps, one of the most influential and loyal courtiers of the king of France, who had spent many years as French ambassador in Naples and later in Rome, where he built up an art collection that would eventually became part of today's British Museum. Despite their exceptionally different backgrounds and political views, Blacas was drawn to Champollion by a shared passion for ancient Egypt. Perhaps, too, as the first provincial noble to obtain high office in Louis XVIII's court, Blacas felt sympathy for a fellow man from the provinces with high ambitions of a different kind. Both Champollion and Blacas were somewhat arrogant, and outsiders to the Establishment, with numerous detractors. Theirs seems an unlikely partnership, but it would certainly work to the advantage of both Champollion and the French government during the 1820s.

Blacas became Champollion's second mentor after Champollion-Figeac, generously supporting his research and protecting him from enemies. In February 1823, he presented his protégé with a gold box from the king, inscribed as follows: 'King Louis XVIII to M. Champollion le Jeune on the occasion of his discovery of the alphabet of the hieroglyphs'. In early 1824, Blacas arranged for Champollion's forthcoming *Précis* to be dedicated to the king and organized a personal meeting between the decipherer and the monarch. Thanks to Blacas, Champollion would receive the financial help he needed to take him on the next step of his voyage towards Egypt: a study tour of the ancient Egyptian treasures gathered in Italy since the days of ancient Rome.

Portrait of the duke of Blacas d'Aulps, friend of Louis XVIII and Charles X, and mentor and benefactor of Champollion.

XI

AN EGYPTIAN RENAISSANCE

On entering this room in the museum, I was seized
with a mortal chill at the sight of a table 10 feet in length,
covered from end to end with a layer of papyrus debris,
to a depth of at least half a foot ... How to shield oneself from
emotion when stirring this ancient dust of centuries?
I philosophized extravagantly – no chapter of Aristotle or Plato
was as eloquent as these scraps of papyrus. My table spoke
even more than the tablet of Cebes, Socrates' disciple: I have seen
roll through my hand the names of ages whose history is
totally beyond recall, the names of gods who have lacked altars
for fifteen centuries, and I have picked up, hardly daring to
breathe, fearing to reduce it to powder, one little scrap of papyrus –
the last, unique memorial of a king who in his lifetime
perhaps found himself cramped in the immense
Palace of Karnak!

(letter from Jean-François Champollion to his brother describing
the Egyptian Museum in Turin, November 1824)

Developments in Champollion's career had scarcely ever been free from opposition. His visit to Italy in 1824 would prove to be no exception. Without the persistence and resources of the duke of Blacas, it would have stood no chance at all of success. Hartleben recounts how, as he anxiously awaited a decision, Champollion controlled his fever of impatience to apply his decipherment to new Egyptian monuments and papyri by repeatedly telling himself: 'For me, the road to Memphis and to Thebes passes via Turin.'

Near the end of March, Blacas's introduction to Louis XVIII at last materialized. The king graciously received from Champollion the first copy of the *Précis du système hiéroglyphique des anciens Égyptiens*, with its personal dedication; soon after the royal audience, copies of the book were sent to interested scholars and went on sale to the Paris public. But although the king engaged its author in a long conversation, he did not bring up the subject of Champollion's Italian visit. The rumour mill in Paris had raised objections to the official funding of such a notorious republican from provincial Grenoble, and the king had ordered an enquiry into Champollion's suitability. Louis XVIII rapidly took advice from the former prefect of Isère, the count of Montlivault, and from the baron of Haussez, who was still in post as prefect at Grenoble and was of course Champollion's implacable enemy. We may easily imagine what these two gentlemen told the king. Nevertheless, the influential Blacas prevailed over Louis, as he so often had in the past. He advised Champollion-Figeac and Champollion how to write a letter giving details of the proposed Italian research, which was formally submitted to the king on 5 April. In the event, part of the funding came from the civil list and the rest from the pocket of Blacas himself, acting in the interest of the burgeoning science of Egyptology. He agreed that Champollion would depart Paris in mid-May for Isère, then go to Turin to examine its recently acquired Egyptian collection, and after that visit Egyptian collections in other Italian cities such as Naples, where Blacas expected to welcome him in his capacity as French ambassador.

Before Champollion left Paris, it is said (by Hartleben) that he and Champollion-Figeac undertook a lightning visit to London – Champollion's sole journey to England. Their purpose was to see the British Museum's Egyptian collection, which of course included the Rosetta Stone.

A personal sighting of this long-pursued quarry would undoubtedly have been an emotionally stirring occasion for Champollion. Yet he did not once refer in his correspondence to having seen the Rosetta Stone, nor did his brother in his many writings; and there is no record of a visit to England by Champollion in the correspondence or memoirs of his contemporaries, such as Young, Sir William Gell and some known English admirers of Champollion. The sole evidence that such a visit may have occurred is a letter written two years later by the Chevalier

San Quintino, director of the Egyptian Museum in Turin, to Young. San Quintino referred to 'M. Champollion, who, in speaking to me one day of his journey to England, and the British Museum, told me that the English are barbarians'. Since San Quintino had by this time (1826) fallen out badly with Champollion, as we shall see, and wished to cultivate his English correspondent Young by stirring up trouble for the French scholar, his comment must be regarded with caution. Most likely, Champollion never in fact went to England or set eyes on the Rosetta Stone he had for so long laboured to decipher. By April 1824, its inscriptions were no longer of importance to the progress of his work; indeed, he would never bother to publish a translation of the stone, unlike Young.

Champollion travelled to Italy via Grenoble, where he had not been for nearly three years. Here he spent eight days in the idyllic park-like sur-roundings of his brother's family house at Vif, where his wife, Rosine, had preceded him. Their only child, Zoraïde, had been born in Vif on 1 March, while Champollion had been awaiting the royal signal back in Paris. Now he had a chance to hold the baby in his arms and was happy to find that she responded to her name. (A local Catholic priest, possibly less happy than her father at the Oriental name, baptized the child 'Zéroïde'.) The three-month-old already promised to be 'the daughter of her father', Champollion claimed, because she shared his dusky complexion and the same particular cast of eyebrows.

In early June, word reached Champollion that the pass of Mont-Cenis through the Alps – a route to Italy constructed in the time of Napoleon – had become free enough of snow to negotiate in a *diligence*. On the morning of 4 June, Jean-François said goodbye to his wife – who had no idea when she and the baby would see him again – climbed aboard a *diligence* and headed for Chambéry. Two days later, as the sun rose, the most dangerous part of the journey began. Although the route was magnificent, it was 'marked out on the hillsides above terri-fying precipices and there was never enough daylight to guide a large *diligence*,' as Champollion wrote soon after. But he arrived in one piece at Turin, on 7 June.

This was Champollion's first visit to the capital of Piedmont-Sardinia, but it was not his first connection with the city. In 1818, the liberal prefect of Isère, Choppin d'Arnouville, had asked for Champollion's help in sorting out some documents relating to the territories ceded by France to Piedmont-Sardinia at the Congress of Vienna in 1815. As a result, Champollion had become friendly with Count Costa, the secretary of state of the Sardinian kingdom, who had then offered him the post of professor of history and ancient languages at the University of Turin. Notwithstanding the salary – which Champollion very much needed in 1818 – and the prestige of an institution founded in the 15th century, he had turned down the count's offer, since he did not want to desert Grenoble. Now, in June 1824, he was welcomed to Turin by Costa, in whose residence he stayed.

The notably reactionary royal family of Sardinia had little to do with the French visitor, despite his enjoying the official support of Louis XVIII. Yet Champollion proved to be a hit with the nobility of Turin – in stark contrast to his clashes with the royalist authorities in Grenoble. His letters to his brother in Paris are dotted with the names of aristocratic contacts: Count Apremont, the Count and Countess Sclopis and the Count Vidua, who had travelled in Egypt, as well as the duke of Clermont-Tonnerre, the marquis of Cavour and the inspired poet Countess Diodata of Saluzzo (the 'Sappho of Piedmont', then one of the most admired celebrities in Italy). Champollion's aristocratic conquests would be repeated elsewhere in Italy, among kings, queens, dukes, cardinals, and even the pope in Rome. Like Wolfgang Amadeus Mozart in imperial Austria four decades earlier, Champollion was fêted by Italian high society, despite his liberal political views, and he came to regard Italy, especially Florence, as his second home. His unique personality and undoubted charm, not to speak of his hauteur, must have played their part in this warm aristocratic reception. In addition, some of the lustre of the Egyptian pharaohs had rubbed off on ancient Egypt's decipherer. Like many a committed egalitarian, in practice Champollion often got on rather well with the social elite.

But it was the scholars, not the nobility, who naturally interested him the most. Intellectually, Champollion was fortunate in Turin and made a number of lasting friendships. The two most important were with the Abbé Amadeo Peyron, a Hellenist and professor of the faculty of letters

The Egyptian Museum, Turin, showing the Drovetti collection on display.
Champollion studied here for many months during the period 1824–25,
proving the truth of his decipherment.

at the university, and the Abbé Constanzo Gazzera, an Orientalist and
the university's librarian, who had been in touch with Champollion in
Paris during the period of his breakthrough. Other scholars included
another Hellenist, a Latinist, the director of the astronomical observat-
ory, and a mathematician. Champollion would have their support when
the director of the Egyptian Museum, San Quintino, began to intrigue
against him in what Peyron would describe as 'the struggle of a Pygmy
against a giant'.

Today, the Egyptian Museum in Turin is the second most significant
collection of ancient Egyptian antiquities in the world after the national
museum in Cairo, and the only national museum outside of Egypt devoted
solely to Egyptian art and culture. The first Egyptian object to reach Turin

173

Seated statue of
Ramesses II in the
Egytian Museum,
Turin. Discovered
by Bernardino Drovetti
at Thebes, it is
probably the finest
existing portrait of
the pharaoh.

arrived in the late 1620s; it was a puzzling altar table probably created in ancient Rome for the temple of Isis. Housed in the University of Turin, it became the nucleus of a small collection of Egyptian objects during the 18th century. But not until 1824, after the king of Piedmont-Sardinia, Carlo Felice, purchased the Egyptian collection of the French consul-general Drovetti (who was of Piedmontese origin), did the Egyptian Museum acquire its own building: a 17th-century palace built as a Jesuit school that had later passed to the Academy of Sciences. Drovetti's superb trove – which was still being unpacked when Champollion arrived, and even when he left nine months later – consisted of 5,268 objects: 100 statues, 170 papyri, stelae, sarcophagi, mummies, bronzes, amulets and items from daily life. Perhaps its single most famous piece is a granite statue of Ramesses II, excavated by Drovetti at Thebes.

Champollion's first letter to his brother after entering the museum on 9 June showed his growing feeling of astonishment and reverence for Egyptian art:

You are, without doubt, very impatient to get my news. I shall give it to you in a phrase of this country: Questo e cosa stupenda *[sic] [This is a marvellous thing]. I did not anticipate such riches; I find the courtyard filled with colossi in pink granite and in green basalt. One 8-foot group, representing a seated Amon-Ra with King Horus, son of Amenophis II of the 18th dynasty, at his side, is an admirable piece of work; I have yet to see anything of such beauty. Inside are still more colossi: a superb giant statue of Misphra-Thuthmosis, preserved as if it had just emerged from the sculptor's workshop; a monolith 6 feet in height, representing Ramesses the Great seated on a throne, between Amon-Ra and Neith, an exquisite piece. A colossus of Moeris, in green basalt, of astonishing execution; a standing statue of Amenophis II; a statue of Ptah from the time of the same prince. A group in sandstone, King Amenophis and his wife, Queen Atari; a statue of Ramesses the Great, larger than life size, worked like a cameo, in magnificent green basalt. On the uprights of his throne are sculpted, in full relief, his son and his wife. A crowd of funerary statues in basalt, red sandstone, white sandstone, white limestone, grey granite, among which is a squatting man, bearing on his tunic four lines of demotic characters. In the middle of all this, more than 100 stelae of 4, 5 and 6 feet in height, an altar loaded with inscriptions and a mass of other objects.*

Satirical scene from a Book of the Dead, 19th–20th dynasties, *c.* 1295–1069 BC. A cat and a hyena herd ducks and goats; and a lion and a gazelle play a board game known as *senet*.

Not all of these identifications were correct. Nonetheless, Champollion was the first person since the late Roman Empire to have a realistic hope of accurately identifying the Turin statues from their inscriptions. He set to work deciphering frenziedly in this virgin field, describing his discoveries in two lengthy letters to his patron, the duke of Blacas. The first letter was dated July and the second December 1824; both were published as a book in Paris in 1825, with additional material by Champollion-Figeac. But it was a further encounter at the museum later in 1824 that would make the single strongest impression on both him and the nascent discipline of Egyptology. Rather than monuments, this amazing discovery involved manuscripts.

After completing the task of unrolling various historical papyri, in November Champollion heard mention of a room in the attic of the museum containing papyrus debris. He was told that the material was not worth visiting, but he insisted. When he entered the attic, the sight of the debris was chilling, as he described in the extract at the beginning of this chapter. The Drovetti collection's gruelling journey from Thebes by boat and ship, and the cold and damp of northern Italy – where the objects had waited for a long time in the port of Livorno until their demanding owner had agreed a purchase price – as compared to the dry conditions in the necropolis of Thebes where the papyri had originally been stored, had wreaked havoc on the manuscripts. A dismayed Champollion nonetheless began to piece together what he could, as he explained to his brother:

In these remains, so fragile and mutilated, of a world that is no more, I have noticed that like today there is only a small step from the sublime to the ridiculous

– that time reduces to the same level and sweeps up without distinction the great and the small, the serious and the frivolous, the sad and the cheerful: next to some fragment of a regnal act of Ramesses the Great, or a ritual consisting of praises to Ramesses-Meïamun or to some other great Shepherd of his people, I have found a bit of an Egyptian cartoon, showing a cat guarding ducks with a shepherd's crook in its paw, or a cynocephalus playing a double flute; – next to the name and forename of the bellicose Moeris, there is a rat armed for battle letting fly arrows against a ferocious combatant, or perhaps a cat mounted on a war chariot. – Here lies a scrap of funerary ritual on the back of which some interested party has written a contract of sale, and there lie the remains of paintings of a monstrous obscenity that give me a singular idea of the Egyptians' gravity and wisdom.

Champollion had been looking at pieces of what became known later in the century as the 'Book of the Dead' – which he was the first modern scholar to begin reading – and at what is now known as the 'Turin Erotic Papyrus' (first published in the 1970s). But the papyrus that concerned him most, on account of its terrible state, was the one now known as the 'Turin King List' or the 'Turin Royal Canon' – a vitally important manuscript from the period of Ramesses II. In Champollion's own words, once more:

The most important papyrus, the one whose complete mutilation I shall always regret, and which is a real historical treasure, is a chronological table, a true Royal Canon in hieratic script, containing more than four times the number of dynasties as are shown in the Table of Abydos, in its unmutilated form. I have gathered from the dust about twenty fragments of this precious manuscript, but these scraps an inch or two in length at the most still contain the forenames, more or less damaged, of seventy-seven pharaohs. What is even more remarkable about all this is that not one of these seventy-seven forenames resembles any of those in the Table of Abydos, and I am convinced that they all belong to earlier dynasties. It seems to me equally certain that this historical canon dates from the same period as all the manuscripts from which I have gathered debris, that is to say from no later than the 19th dynasty … I confess that the greatest disappointment of my literary life is to have discovered this manuscript in such a desperate condition. I shall never get over it – it is a wound that will bleed for a long time.

Such early dates for Egyptian civilization, however provisional, were a potential challenge to the biblical story of the Creation – perhaps more so in France than in Italy at this time, given the accession to the French throne of the reactionary count of Artois – the leader of the Ultras – as Charles X after the death his elder brother Louis XVIII in September 1824. Charles X introduced notorious legislation against sacrilege in 1825, which encouraged an atmosphere of Catholic intolerance that would directly affect Champollion's work on Egyptian chronology. In Champollion's second letter to Blacas, following the discovery of the Turin Royal Canon, he and his brother (who supplied the letter's appendix on 'Chronology') were careful to make no reference to any potentially embarrassing pre-biblical dates.

Following Champollion's discovery, the Egyptologist Gustavus Seyffarth managed to piece together the Turin Royal Canon in the correct order, though many gaps remained. Modern scholarship has shown that the canon must originally have included about three hundred rulers, all of them named and with the precise duration of their reigns given. Moreover, the canon makes an attempt to go back before the time of known pharaohs to the reigns of unnamed spirits and gods. It must have been a document such as this that provided the ancient Greek historian Manetho with his sequence of thirty dynasties, which proved so valuable to both Young and Champollion.

Champollion, seldom tactful, made known his displeasure at the poor state of conservation of these papyri. He also publicly ridiculed, under the cloak of anonymity, the museum's careless display of its giant statue of Ramesses II (called Ozymandias by Greek travellers), by distributing a delightful but recklessly insolent pamphlet on the streets of Turin under the title 'Petition of Pharaoh Ozymandias to His Majesty the King of Sardinia'. In the pamphlet, Ozymandias complains to King Carlo Felice that he has been relegated not so much to a courtyard as to a farmyard, where he is covered in pieces of straw rather than being allowed to enjoy the 'beautiful yellow costume bordered in green' granted to some other works of art. This was a sly dig at museum director San Quintino's penchant for dressing up certain statues, including even those of cats and other animals, to the unintended merriment of the

Turinese. An outraged Ozymandias cries out across three millennia to his fellow monarch:

What! The Pharaoh who conquered Bactria at the head of seven hundred thousand men, who erected the most marvellous building in Thebes, shall from now on be known only as a Straw King, or, to be blunt, a Stuffed King? No, Sire, Your Majesty cannot stand for this. You now know the long line of my tribulations; I appeal to your fairness – It is as a King that I should be treated.

That word spells out all that I expect. I demand also, as an essential reparation, that the inventor of the ridiculous straw garb with which I am got up should himself be stuffed, for immediate despatch to the Museum of Natural History. This would be justice.

There were frequent spats between Champollion and San Quintino during 1824. Although friction was inevitable, given their respective positions – Champollion as the celebrity outsider, San Quintino as the ignorant insider – not all of it redounded to the credit of Champollion, who might have chosen to be less provocative in trying to bring order to the Drovetti collection. However, San Quintino's bad faith cannot be doubted. In February 1825, at a meeting of the Academy of Turin where the recently elected Champollion was absent, San Quintino put forward as his own research all that he (and others) had heard from Champollion in the preceding few months about the numerical system of the ancient Egyptians. Only energetic protestations against this blatant plagiarism from Peyron and Gazzera, Champollion's colleagues at the university, prevented the communication from being printed under San Quintino's name. For some time afterwards, the embarrassed museum director avoided attending sessions of the academy.

Since January, Champollion had been preparing to leave Turin and continue his odyssey in search of ancient Egyptian objects. Suddenly, at the end of February, he received an unexpected offer to become the consul of Sardinia in Egypt, a result of his longstanding friendship with the secretary of state, Count Costa. The proposal had tremendous immediate appeal, but on the other hand the position would require him to abandon his Italian tour, to change his French citizenship and to dwell far from his brother in Paris. Champollion-Figeac advised firmly against acceptance. To begin with, he wrote by return, 'It is better to be the first among one's own people than among others.' Second, a foreign posting would gratify Champollion's enemies in Paris, such as Jomard: 'Let us guard against satisfying them,' he wrote. Champollion declined the job.

Although his health was poor after his relentless research in Turin, in early March 1825 Champollion set off for Rome. He journeyed via Milan and Bologna, where he conducted brief examinations of Egyptian collections, all the while suffering from endless hours of jolting travel in pouring rain and sleepless nights in uncomfortable inns, which aggravated the gout in his feet and hands that would trouble him for the rest of his life. Having left Bologna on 7 March, he arrived in Rome five days later at six o'clock in the morning without once lying in a bed.

The sight of the Flaminian obelisk at the northern gate of eternal city revived Champollion's enthusiasm. Without even resting at his hotel, he spent the entire day guiding himself on swollen feet around the churches and ancient monuments of Rome, and meeting influential people. His first stop was St Peter's, which provoked the following comment to his brother: 'We are wretches, in France: our monuments are pitiable beside this Roman magnificence.' After St Peter's, he raced to the Piazza Navona, where he saluted the Pamphilian obelisk. At the museum on the Capitoline Hill, he was thrilled to see two Egyptian colossi representing Ptolemy Philadelphus and his wife Arsinoe, and two magnificent Egyptian lions at the base of the staircase leading down from the hill. At seven o'clock that evening he called on the French ambassador, the duke of Laval, whom he had known at Turin; he received a warm welcome, and an invitation to dinner the following night with a party of his fellow countrymen. Returning to his hotel at last, he found a note from the duke of Noailles, who had just arrived from Naples. They passed the evening together at the duke's hotel. 'He gave me news of M. de Blacas, who has requested me to make haste for Naples as soon as possible, given that he must come to Rome for Holy Week; it is likely that I shall depart to join him in five or six days at the latest. So that was my first day in Rome, which I shall never forget,' Champollion told his brother, adding: 'My tender affections to M. Dacier'.

Naples, for Champollion, was 'the first lively city that I have encountered since the Alps'. Blacas introduced him to the king and queen of Naples, who were interested in Egypt. The king asked for a report on some Egyptian vases in the palace, and the queen requested Champollion to give her a private tutorial in the basic principles of the hieroglyphic system. Although Mount Vesuvius was quiet – to Champollion's disappointment – he was excited by the ruins of Pompeii (rediscovered only in the mid-18th century) and even more excited by the Greco-Roman city of Paestum, down the coast from Naples, which he visited alone and on foot, despite the area's reputation for brigands. The perfectly preserved temples, located on a desolate plain, had a profound effect on him: 'From a certain distance, and above all because of the way they stand out golden yellow against the beautiful azure of the sky and the sea, I felt I was looking at *Egyptian temples*: most of all with the temple of Neptune, the grandest of them all, in which the Egyptian origin of the Greek architecture penetrates every part of the building.' Here was a theme – the neglected ancient Egyptian influence on Greek civilization – that would become more and more prominent in Champollion's writing, and that remains controversial to this day.

Back in Rome towards the end of April 1825 and staying with Blacas – his initial host in the capital – Champollion immediately set to work recording the city's many obelisk inscriptions. Conditions were difficult: hot sun, abrupt showers of rain, and dangerous ruins surrounding the ancient monoliths, from which emanated foul smells. But Champollion, ever ardent for Egyptian knowledge, was indefatigable. The more he carefully noted down the hieroglyphs, the more he discovered the inaccuracy of existing copies, especially those made by the fancy-prone Jesuit priest Athanasius Kircher. (This issue would become a great theme of Champollion's expedition to Egypt, especially in regard to the inaccuracy of the *Description de l'Égypte*.) He even suggested the design of a modern obelisk, complete with inscriptions, for the French ambassador's party in Rome to celebrate the coronation of Charles X; the obelisk was made and much admired, but persistent rain unfortunately ruined the grand party.

Champollion also worked in the Vatican on its collection of Egyptian papyri and reacquainted himself with Coptic and other manuscripts that he had studied (and annotated) as a student in Paris nearly two decades earlier. (The Vatican published a catalogue of these papyri the same year.) Moreover, Champollion was presented to Pope Leo XII at a long private audience in June. Aware of Champollion's dating of the Dendera Zodiac to the Roman period (but of course unaware of the dates contained in the Turin Royal Canon), the pope told him three times, in excellent French, that he had rendered 'a beautiful, great and good service to the Church'. He then offered to make him a cardinal. A surprised Champollion sidestepped the unwelcome and impossible proposal with a deft pirouette, by saying that 'two ladies would not agree'. Later, at the suggestion of Leo XII to the French government, Champollion was created a knight of the Legion of Honour.

Although he and his hieroglyphic decipherment were now the toast of the diplomatic community in Rome, Champollion wanted to escape, so as to continue his Egyptian studies. Two days after his papal audience, he reached Florence, where he stayed for only about two weeks. Nonetheless, he was invited by the Grand Duke Leopold II to catalogue his Egyptian collection, initiating a relationship that would soon prove vital for Champollion's future Egyptian expedition. In a letter to his brother, he called Florence 'the only city in Italy where one may enjoy a true and just liberty; it is really the only land here that has a government, and that is certainly something.' Soon after, he went back to Turin and worked with the Drovetti collection at the Egyptian Museum for a further long period. Then, in early November 1825, just before the Mont-Cenis route through the Alps became impassable, he returned to his family in Grenoble.

Before that, however, an important development occurred that would lead to the next major stage in Champollion's career. He received word that a large and probably excellent new Egyptian collection had arrived in Livorno. It had been put together by Drovetti's competitor, the English consul in Egypt, Henry Salt. Sensing a great opportunity, Champollion had called in at Livorno in July 1825 on his way from Florence to Turin. After inspecting the objects, he was determined

Portrait of Henry Salt, Egyptologist and English consul in Egypt, whose collection was purchased for the Louvre Museum. It was painted c. 1815 by John James Halls.

that, having failed to buy Drovetti's magnificent collection, the French government – rather than the British Museum – must buy the Salt collection and make it the foundation of a new Egyptian gallery at the Louvre Museum. He and his brother hoped that he would be appointed the first curator of such a collection.

Inevitably, the two Champollions, supported by Blacas, had a battle royal on their hands. A rival Egyptian collection, belonging to the Italian excavator Giuseppe Passalacqua, had arrived in Paris around the same time and was up for sale. Jomard was determined that the French government should buy Passalacqua's collection and appoint *him* as the new curator of Egyptian antiquities at the Louvre, given his long affiliation with Egypt going back to Napoleon's expedition. Champollion's enemies lined up in support of Jomard. But eventually, in late February 1826, as a result of Blacas's recommendation, Champollion received a royal grant to return to Livorno, study the Salt collection and estimate its value to the government. He departed from Grenoble as soon as he could on his second visit to Italy.

While he was in Livorno, Champollion met two very different people who would influence the rest of his life. Ippolito Rosellini was a 25-year-old professor of Oriental languages at Pisa who had been sent by Grand Duke Leopold II to meet Champollion. Rosellini had been studying the hieroglyphs for a year and now asked if Champollion would accept him as a pupil. Their lessons began there and then, and the two scholars immediately became collaborators and friends. 'I was no sooner taken into his friendship and generously informed about his secrets and discoveries', Rosellini later recalled of this seminal first meeting, 'than I felt a love for Egypt grow more sharply and deeply in my heart; and I immediately determined to follow him wherever he should go.' Champollion, for his part, enthused to his brother about the young Italian professor's 'excellent heart and well-furnished head'.

Bust of Ippolito Rosellini, Egyptologist, student of Champollion and joint leader of the Franco-Tuscan expedition to Egypt.

Portrait of
Angelica Palli,
the poet from
Livorno for
whom Cham-
pollion felt an
unrequited love.

Soon the two of them were travelling together in Italy – to Florence, Rome and Naples – and conceived the idea of a joint French–Italian expedition to Egypt, which they hoped would be supported by Leopold II and the French king. Leopold was interested, and at the end of 1826 Rosellini would join Champollion in Paris for further discussions.

The second important figure was a poet, Angelica Palli, the daughter of a local businessman. Champollion fell in love with her after hearing her improvise a poem in his honour at a meeting of the Academy of Livorno. Although his love was unrequited and the two of them in fact met only a few times during mid-1826, he opened his heart to her in thirty letters written in 1826–29, even after she had ceased to respond. (They were published in 1978 as *Lettres à Zelmire*.) Her replies, such as they were, have not been preserved, so it is difficult to form a clear impression of the relationship, except to say that it had little to do with his passion for Egypt. Champollion's biographers have been divided about Palli: some, including Hartleben, have seen her as talented and sincere in her professed admiration for Champollion; others, including Lacouture, have viewed her as the type of calculating schemer familiar from Italian comic opera. In the end, Palli is probably significant in Champollion's story less for herself than for what his letters to her reveal of his unsatisfying marriage to Rosine Blanc.

Champollion's recommendations regarding the Salt collection, supported by Blacas, carried the day in Paris, against the bitter public opposition of Jomard. In April 1826, the king approved purchase of the collection, and in May Champollion received word from his brother that their wish had been granted: Champollion was to be appointed as the first curator of Egyptian antiquities at the Louvre. He was nevertheless obliged to remain in Italy until mid-October to supervise the despatch of the Salt collection from Livorno to Le Havre, which gave him a chance to visit Venice for the first time. But, by the very end of October, he, his wife and their young daughter, Zoraïde, were on their way from Grenoble to Paris. Champollion had been absent from the centre of French power and influence for two-and-a-half years.

XII

CURATOR AT THE LOUVRE

*Collections of Egyptian monuments … are generally formed with
the sole aim of clarifying the history of art – the techniques
of sculpture and of painting from different periods and diverse
national traditions … But the important and numerous
collections of Egyptian monuments with which royal munificence
has recently endowed the museum of Charles X, must, as
it were, serve as a source and as evidence for the entire history
of the Egyptian nation, and so need to be coordinated on a different plan;
it is necessary, indeed essential, to consider both the subject matter
and the particular purpose of each monument, and that rigorous knowledge
of one or the other of these things should determine the position and
rank that the monument ought to occupy. In short, it is necessary to display
the monuments in a manner that presents as completely as possible
the sequence of gods, and of Egyptian rulers, from the primitive period
up to the Romans, and to label objects in a systematic order that relates
to the public and private life of the ancient Egyptians.*

(Jean-François Champollion's 'Descriptive Notice' setting out his intentions
for displaying the Egyptian collection at the Louvre Museum, 1826–27)

Controversy swirled around Champollion whenever he was in Paris. Part of the reason was his 'all or nothing' personality, which typically inspired loyalty or enmity, seldom tepidity – as witness the unwavering support he received from the duke of Blacas and from Dacier, the permanent secretary of the Academy of Inscriptions and Belles-Lettres, as opposed to the long-standing hostility of baron de Sacy and Jomard, editor of the *Description de l'Égypte*. Even the moderate Young, a man who made very few enemies over his lifetime, was to some extent provoked by his French counterpart's temperamental behaviour.

There was also the unavoidable fact that whatever Champollion did trailed his republican political past in Grenoble, with its whiff of Jacobin sulphur, and his elder brother's obvious support for Napoleon Bonaparte during the Hundred Days in 1815. Some of the French nobility and their supporters certainly overlooked his political reputation, but the majority, such as the baron of Haussez, most likely distrusted Champollion on principle. Indeed, according to Hartleben, when Champollion was due to be appointed at the Louvre in 1826, not just the royal court but half of the capital were apparently under the impression that he had been one of the diehard leaders of the Terror in 1793. To scotch this fantastic rumour, Champollion-Figeac procured his brother's birth certificate, dated 23 December 1790, which the minister in charge of the appointment personally showed to the king.

Yet another reason was Champollion's choice of subject: ancient Egypt. Ancient Egyptian chronology potentially challenged the religious orthodoxy that had become government policy under Charles X – despite the pope's blessing of Champollion's work in 1825. It undoubtedly challenged the prevailing classical and art historical orthodoxy, given Egypt's pre-classical antiquity and the respect in which it was held by classical authorities such as Herodotus and Pliny. Champollion himself believed that ancient Egypt was the source of much that was revered in the civilization of ancient Greece, and that Egyptian art and architecture were in some ways superior to those of the Greeks.

Such revolutionary opinions were bound to displease many Hellenists and Latinists; all of the followers of Johann Winckelmann, the German archaeologist and art historian who had popularized the Neoclassical movement in Europe in the second half of the 18th century; the curator of Greek and Roman antiquities at the Louvre, the count of Clarac; and the director of the Louvre, the count of Forbin, who presided over this great collection of classical and Neoclassical art, for whom Egyptian art was a decided interloper. Even the Egypt-minded Dominique Vivant Denon, Forbin's predecessor as director of French museums until 1816, had doubts. In his fine book recounting his Egyptian travels during Napoleon's expedition, he described the temple of Karnak at Thebes in the following terms:

It is the pomp, then, of the Egyptians that we behold at Karnak, where are piled not only quarries but mountains, fashioned with massive proportions, and where the execution is feeble in the outline and rude in the masonry; barbarous reliefs, and hieroglyphs without taste and without colouring, in a state only of coarse sculpture. There is nothing of the sublime, either in the dimensions or the executions of the work, except in the obelisks, and some facings of the outward doors, which are of a chastity truly admirable.

What is more, Champollion was in a position to provide textual evidence to support his unorthodox views because he could read the hieroglyphs, unlike virtually every other scholar. His response to Egyptian art was therefore not merely an aesthetic one, like Denon's and that of the classical specialists, but also a historical one, based on his rapidly growing knowledge of the individual pharaonic rulers whose works he had identified at Turin. Such a preoccupation with the chronological development of Egyptian art sounds normal to the ears of the modern museum-goer, but in 1826 it was decidedly novel. For those scholars who disliked Champollion and his views, one possible response was simply to deny the truth of his decipherment. This was what several of his philological opponents, notably Julius Klaproth and Gustavus Seyffarth, chose to do, both in the 1820s and in the years after Champollion's death. Another response was to reject his candidacy for the Academy of Inscriptions. Amazingly, Champollion, for all his Europe-wide celebrity, would not be elected to his native academy until 1830, after being turned down in 1827 and 1829.

His early letters from Paris to his friends in Italy, whence he had recently returned, provide a vivid picture of his embattled state as he tried to impose his vision of an Egyptian gallery on the authorities in charge of the Louvre, while dreaming of his embryonic expedition to Egypt. In mid-November 1826, Champollion wrote to Rosellini in Pisa:

In spite of Paris and her pomp and ceremony, I have returned to the past and the present brings me no benefit. Imagine a man who loves peace and quiet yet finds himself all of a sudden thrown by duty into the bowels of machination and intrigue directed against himself and his studies. My life has become a fight.

I am forced to extract everything I need, none of those who are supposed to assist me is willing to do it. My arrival at the Museum has disturbed the whole place, and all my colleagues are conspiring against me, because instead of treating my position as a sinecure, I busy myself with my department, which inevitably makes it appear that they are doing nothing with theirs. This is the nub of the matter. It requires a battle to get hold of a nail. Fortunately the minister is on my side, but I regret having constantly to involve him and weary him with all these political manoeuvres. How I long to be camped on the deserted plain of Thebes! Only there will it be possible for me to find at the same time both pleasure and rest. Come quick, we shall talk in Tuscan, and that at least will be a relief from the muddy bowels of this moral and physical Babylon.

A few days later, he continued in the same vein while writing to the Abbé Gazzera in Turin:

I have a magnificent ground-floor room for my large pieces, and four rooms on the first floor of the [Louvre] Palace. So I shall soon be in the midst of painters, architects and masons, and that will not be without difficulties if things move ahead. You rightly suspect that I have encountered hostility from certain people [i.e. Forbin, Clarac and others] who allow themselves not to approve the decisions in my favour of the duke of Doudeauville [the king's minister] and the viscount of La Rochefoucauld [the king's aide-de-camp, and Doudeauville's son], people who raise, and will continue to raise, a thousand little obstacles to what I require, whatever that might be. I fight each day to the best of my ability, but my side has won only because our excellent duke of Blacas is in Paris and has taken in hand the direction of the business ... May the Great Amun-Ra preserve him for us!

Anyone who has tried to start something original within an established institution will recognize something of Champollion's situation and conflicts at the Louvre. His compensation for all the office politics was, of course, that he was surrounded by a feast of unique and wonderful objects, entrusted to his personal care as curator. The Salt collection consisted of nearly 5,000 pieces: large sculptures; a huge stone sarcophagus; bronze, gold and porcelain objects; paintings; and excellent papyri. Further acquisitions arrived in 1827: a colossus from Rome ('the brother of your Stuffed King', Champollion remarked to Gazzera); some magnificent ancient gold jewellery presented to Charles X by the pasha of Egypt; exquisite enamels; and a gold seal of one of the Cleopatras.

The most important of all these new acquisitions was a second collection put together by the French consul Drovetti. It had been offered to the king of Sardinia-Piedmont, but against the advice of his ministers he had declined to purchase it for the Egyptian Museum in Turin, so the French government had stepped in. Champollion enthused about this bonanza to Gazzera, somewhat tactlessly:

It includes Egyptian jewels of an unbelievable magnificence, necklaces, rings, bracelets, earrings made of gold and enriched with enamel. These are no doubt the cast-offs of a Pharaoh, and the majority of the objects carry royal legends: for example a cup in solid gold, decorated with a bas-relief showing fishes playing in the midst of lotus blossoms, is offered to King Moeris by the 'Royal Secretary in charge of tin, silver and gold' ...

One can hardly wait for the return of the king [Charles X] to deliver these rare objects into my hands. Moreover, this collection contains statues, 50 Egyptian or Greek manuscripts, 500 scarabs, vases, 80 stelae, etc etc. We are finishing up as finer and richer than your collection, which could have been the Premier one and did not wish it.

(Champollion's reading of these hieroglyphs was almost, but not quite, correct. Today's reading would be 'Royal Secretary in charge of lapis lazuli, silver and gold'. Starting from the left, signs 1 and 2 – the sedge plant and the scribal palette – mean 'Royal Secretary'; signs 3 to 7 – concluding with the leg – mean 'lapis lazuli'; signs 8 to 10 – including three dots and a collar – mean 'silver'; signs 11 and 12 – another three dots and another collar – mean 'gold'. The order of the five signs for 'lapis lazuli' is unusual, and must have been adopted for calligraphic reasons, which may help to explain Champollion's failure to recognize the word.)

To understand what Champollion was up against as Egyptian curator, we need to know a little about his chief opponent, the count of Forbin, director of the Louvre. A now-forgotten painter, he was nonetheless a figure of considerable note in the Paris of his day. Born in 1779, and thus only a decade older than Champollion, Forbin hailed from an aristocratic family who had suffered during the Terror; his father had been guillotined in Lyons in 1793. Forbin trained as an artist in Paris, in the studio of the history painter Jacques-Louis David, who championed the Neoclassical style. Then he married an heiress, moved to Rome, turned himself into an accomplished dilettante, and was appointed the chamberlain of the sister of Napoleon Bonaparte, Princess Pauline Borghese, whose lover he also became. Later, he served with distinction in Napoleon's armies in Portugal and Austria, but left the army and retired to Italy in 1809, where he took up history painting, wrote a novel and played no part in the final years of Napoleon's empire. Returning to Paris after the restoration, Forbin was appointed director of museums by Louis XVIII, at a time when Napoleon's loot had to be returned to Italy and other countries. In 1817, Forbin led an expedition of French artists, on board the frigate *Cléopâtra*, to purchase Greek and Roman works of art from the Levant. The expedition eventually reached Cairo in 1818, where Forbin concluded his journey, without going south to Thebes. Not much was acquired from this trip, but in 1820 he enjoyed a coup in purchasing for the Louvre the recently discovered *Venus de Milo*. He also persuaded Louis XVIII to buy David's *Intervention of the Sabine Women* and *Leonidas at Thermopylae*, and Théodore Géricault's controversial *The Raft of the Medusa*.

A clash of taste between Forbin and Champollion was inevitable. Champollion wanted to show 'Egyptian antiquities in Egyptian rooms'. Forbin, unmoved by ancient Egyptian art, wanted a décor of Neoclassical paintings inspired by Greece, Rome and the Bible throughout the museum, as of course did Clarac. Forbin acquiesced in Champollion's demand for a draughtsman assistant, his friend Jean-Joseph Dubois, who had illustrated a book of Egyptian divinities, the *Panthéon égyptien*, for Champollion in 1823–25. But the director got his way with the main décor of the Egyptian rooms.

At least Forbin chose subjects connected with Egypt for the ceilings, which were painted by contemporary French history painters inspired by David's art. For example, Abel de Pujol's *L'Égypte sauvée par Joseph* ('Egypt Saved by Joseph') shows a biblical scene with the addition of a Ptolemaic temple from Philae for décor. Adrien Guignet's *Joseph expliquant les rêves de Pharaon* ('Joseph Interpreting the Dreams of Pharaoh') also takes its cue from the Bible, this time borrowing the papyrus-shaped columns of the hypostyle hall at Karnak. François-Edouard Picot's *L'Étude et le Génie des arts dévoilant l'antique Égypte à la Grèce* ('Study and Genius of the Arts Revealing Ancient Egypt to Greece') is an allegorical tableau. This ludicrous painting depicts Greece as a kind of superwoman, wrapped in a red toga, standing on a cloud and accompanied by angels, while cherubim whisk away a white sheet from bare-bosomed, dusky Egypt, who is seated on a throne flanked by lions and Egyptian paraphernalia. The top of a pyramid and an obelisk – but no sphinx – can be glimpsed floating in the distance. So much for the genuine revelation of Egypt launched by the Greek section of the Rosetta Stone. Champollion's opinion of this particular *avant*-Hollywood travesty of his vision of Egypt and Greece is not recorded, but he was naturally opposed to Forbin's general décor. 'Contrary to all the received wisdom, Champollion vehemently accused Joseph' – Jacob's son in the Bible, appointed vizier of Egypt by Pharaoh – 'of having reduced Egypt to poverty with his usurious speculations,' wrote Hartleben.

For all his professional frustrations and his continuing health problems – made worse by the climate of 'Babylon', which had sickened him even as a teenaged student in Paris – Champollion worked extremely hard on the new gallery. He was keenly aware that France's Egyptian collection was now the finest in the world outside Egypt, and began to refer in correspondence to 'my' pieces and 'my' museum. He also knew from his discussions with the minister Doudeauville that he could expect to receive no royal support for his and Rosellini's proposed Egyptian expedition until the new Egyptian gallery was finished. Its planned formal opening on 4 November 1827 was delayed by the late completion of Ingres's famous painting *Apothéose d'Homère* ('The Apotheosis of Homer') and of Forbin's various commissions for the Egyptian rooms. The opening finally took place on 15 December, in the presence of Charles X, scarcely more than a year after Champollion had begun work; and it brought its Egyptian curator the official kudos for which he and his brother had hoped. The compromises he had been obliged to make with French artistic convention and royalist officialdom were tolerable, Champollion accepted, for the sake of the new knowledge he would gain in Egypt.

He was consoled, too, by a happier home life during this period – perhaps the happiest he would ever experience. The Champollion brothers had now moved from 28 Rue Mazarine to number 19 in the same street, where they lived with their two families as a 'colonie Grenobloise'. Although Jacques-Joseph would never approve of Jean-François's marriage to Rosine, his wife, Zoé, now formed a close relationship with her sister-in-law. They were 'like true sisters', according to Hartleben, and the children of the two families got on well. Jacques-Joseph's children regarded their little cousin Zoraïde 'as a beautiful gift', who behaved with a spontaneity and independence that provoked endless astonishment. At the same time, their affectionate uncle enjoyed entertaining his nephews and nieces with stories, amusing drawings and riddles.

Moreover, Champollion's relationship with his student Rosellini was going from strength to strength. The young professor had arrived from Florence in December 1826 and stayed in Paris for about a year, taking advantage of the golden opportunity provided by the work on the gallery to shadow his teacher. In October, Rosellini married Zénobie Cherubini, the daughter of the composer Luigi Cherubini, who had been born in Florence but worked most of his life in Paris. Champollion was one of the witnesses to the marriage. In the following year, the composer's son Salvador would join the Champollion–Rosellini expedition to Egypt.

There was even an opportunity to repair his ruptured relationship with his erstwhile rival Young. The English polymath had abandoned work on the hieroglyphs in 1823 after observing Champollion's spectacular progress, but had recently taken up the demotic script, partly as a result of receiving a letter in Latin written in May 1827 by Champollion's friend Peyron from Turin. Peyron told Young:

You write that from time to time you will publish new material that will increase our knowledge of Egyptian matters. I am very glad to hear this and I urge you to keep your word. For, as Champollion will witness, and other friends to whom I have mentioned your name, I have always felt, and so do many others, that you are a man of rare and superhuman genius with a quick and penetrating vision, and you have the power to surpass not only myself but all the philologists of Europe, so that there is universal regret that your versatility is so widely engaged in the sciences – medicine, astronomy, analysis, etc. etc. that you are unable to press on with your discoveries and bring them to that pitch of perfection that we have the right to expect from a man of your conspicuous talents; for you are constantly being drawn from one science to another, you have to turn your attention from mathematics to Greek philosophy and from that to medicine, etc. The result is that there are some mistakes in your books that you yourself might well have corrected.

From this time until his death two years later, Young worked assiduously at his *Rudiments of an Egyptian Dictionary in the Ancient Enchorial Character; Containing All the Words of Which the Sense Has Been Ascertained*. And it is pleasant to record that Champollion assisted him. In the summer of 1828, Young visited Paris to accept his recent signal honour of being elected as one of the eight foreign associates of the French Institute's Academy of Sciences. From there he wrote to his friend Gurney that Champollion 'has shown me far more attention than I ever showed or could show, to any living being: he devoted *seven* whole hours at once to looking over with me his papers and the magnificent collection which is committed to his care ... he is to let me have the use ... of all his collections and his notes relating to the enchorial character that I may make what use I please of them.' To the scientist François Arago, the friend who first introduced him to Champollion in 1822, Young wrote of Champollion's 'kindness and liberality', and added: 'I have obtained in this manner a most extensive collection of enchorial documents, many of which are accompanied by Mr Champollion's own interpretations of particular passages, which amply demonstrate how unjustly he has been supposed to have neglected this department of the great field.'

We can only guess at Champollion's motives: no doubt they included some new respect for Young as a foreign associate of the French Institute, but more important must have been Champollion's pride in his invulnerable achievement and in his curatorship. In addition, it would surely be reasonable to assume some feeling of guilt at his unacknowledged debt to Young. Be that as it may, Young was careful to acknowledge Champollion's help in generous terms when he produced his enchorial/demotic dictionary. Although the difficulties of deciphering demotic remained formidable – many manuscripts contain passages that are puzzling even today – Young could justifiably claim that '30 years ago, not a single article of the list [i.e. the words in the dictionary] existed even in the imagination of the wildest enthusiast: and that within these ten years, a single date only was tolerably ascertained, out of about 50 which are here interpreted, and in many instances ascertained with astronomical precision.' The modern Egyptologist John Ray sums up: 'Young was the first person since the end of the Roman Empire to be able to read a demotic text, and, in spite of a proportion of incorrect guesses, he surely deserves to be known as the decipherer of demotic. It is no disservice to Champollion to allow him this distinction.'

Champollion's generosity with his time was noteworthy for another reason. On 26 April 1828, Charles X had finally given him the go-ahead for his Egypt expedition. When Young came to see him and his collection at the Louvre, in late June, Champollion was in the thick of preparing to depart for the Mediterranean coast. On 10 July, he wrote hurriedly to his old school friend Thévenet, now a shopkeeper in Grenoble, asking to meet him en route in Lyons. 'I am leaving on a voyage that is so chancy I am thirsty to embrace those who are dear to me, and you may imagine how happy I would be to see you, before throwing myself into the midst of the tanned faces who await me on the shores of Africa.' Less than a week later, Champollion and Cherubini would leave Paris for what Champollion anticipated would be the greatest adventure of his life.

XIII

TO EGYPT, AT LAST

*The dog in Egypt lives in a state of complete liberty, and in going to
the obelisks we were accompanied by the barking of
a crowd of these animals, which occupied the summits of the dunes one
by one as they pursued us at quite a distance with husky, muffled
cries. These dogs, though of varying sizes, are of one and the same species;
they strongly resemble the jackal, except for their coats, which
are yellow-red. I am no longer astonished that in the hieroglyphic
inscriptions it should be so difficult to distinguish the dog from the jackal:
their defining characteristics are identical. The hieroglyphic
dog differs only in having a tail raised like a trumpet. This trait is taken
from nature; all dogs in Egypt carry their tails curled up like this:*

(Jean-François Champollion's Egyptian journal,
Alexandria, August 1828)

The idea of a joint Franco-Tuscan expedition to Egypt led by Champollion
and Rosellini had been in the air since the two scholars had visited
Florence in mid-1826, when Champollion had seductively written Grand
Duke Leopold II's name as a hieroglyphic cartouche in the grand-ducal
art gallery, along with an accompanying description: 'Most Gracious
Sovereign'. The two had then travelled to Naples and outlined the same
idea to the duke of Blacas, for him to raise with King Charles X. But
even if Leopold II of Tuscany was willing to support the expedition from
the outset, the French government had required more persuasion. Joint
initiatives – with shared responsibilities and shared prestige – were not

Charles X's normal style. The king had been finally won over in the spring of 1828 by a combination of influential courtiers and politicians: Blacas, Rochefoucauld, Doudeauville and the king's new prime minister, the viscount of Martignac, who favoured closer political ties between Paris and Florence – not to mention the appealing possibility of sharing the expedition's total cost, 90,000 francs, with the Tuscans.

In their official proposals, written in mid-1827, Champollion and Rosellini argued that the prevailing level of understanding of Egyptian art – its architecture, sculpture and painting – was essentially inadequate, indeed false. The great French expedition of 1798–1801 and subsequent *Description de l'Égypte* (still not quite completed in 1827) had laid the groundwork for a more informed understanding. Now was the time to go deeper into the subject, the two proposals argued – just as Champollion himself was already arguing on behalf of the displays and captions in the new Egyptian gallery at the Louvre – with the benefit of 'the new knowledge acquired from the writings of ancient Egypt' as a result of the decipherment, which would guide an expedition of savants and artists consisting of 'a small number of well-prepared persons'.

Another point in the expedition's favour was the rapid destruction of ancient Egyptian monuments that had begun soon after the turn of the century. These had survived for more than two millennia remarkably well until the time of Napoleon's expedition, but were now suffering through a combination of disuse (apart from those temples converted into Christian churches), geographical isolation and lack of interest from the surrounding population – except, that is, for local treasure hunters looking mainly for gold and jewels in the tombs and pyramids. Neither the Arabs who ruled Egypt from 642, nor the Ottoman Turks who took over from the Arabs in 1517, regarded ancient Egypt and its remains, including of course the hieroglyphs, as part of their cultural heritage. But in the quarter century that followed the French withdrawal from Egypt in 1801, there had been a highly destructive mixture of pillaging for antiquities (such as the Dendera Zodiac, the Philae obelisk and the sarcophagus of Seti) by European excavators (notably Belzoni, Bankes, Drovetti and Salt) and the demolition of monuments for fertilizer, lime and building stone by the regime of Muhammad Ali Pasha, in his drive to modernize Egypt. In his later years, the pasha even encouraged French engineers to dismantle the Pyramids at Giza to obtain stone for dams across the River Nile. 'Between 1810 and 1828 thirteen entire temples were lost and countless objects were removed from their contexts,' notes Patricia Usick in her biography of Bankes, *Adventures in Egypt and Nubia*. Unless Champollion's expedition were to set off quickly, he would almost certainly find that many of the finest Egyptian monuments and works of art had vanished from their original locations.

In the end, it was agreed between the French and Tuscan rulers that Champollion would have responsibility for the general direction of the joint expedition; Rosellini would be the second-in-command, with responsibility for all the details of its execution; and Charles Lenormant would be its inspector general, representing Rochefoucauld and the French government. The two commissions consisted of seven persons each. On the French side: Champollion and Lenormant; an architect called Antoine Bibent (whom Champollion had met in Naples); three painters named Alexandre Duchesne, Pierrre-François Lehoux and Édouard Bertin; and Nestor L'Hôte, a young customs officer with a passion for Egyptology, who would prove to be a good artist. On the Italian side: Rosellini; his architect uncle Gaetano Rosellini; his artist brother-in-law, Cherubini (who regarded himself as a Frenchman); a painter, Giuseppe Angelelli; a well-known naturalist from Florence, Giuseppe Raddi, and his assistant, Gaetano Galastri; and a medical doctor from Siena, Alessandro Ricci, who had travelled in Egypt with Bankes and had become Henry Salt's physician. After saving the life of the Egyptian pasha's son, Ricci had become the son's personal physician, received a large gift and retired to Italy, where he set up an antiquities museum and sold portfolios of his Egyptian drawings and journals that Champollion had much admired on his visit to Florence in 1825. To Champollion's disappointment, he was unable to include his friend from his days at Turin's Egyptian Museum, the Abbé Gazzera.

Everything now depended on the permission of the Egyptian authorities – which in practice meant Muhammad Ali, who had been the effective ruler of Egypt since 1805 (even if he was nominally the viceroy of the Ottoman sultan), closely advised by the French consul-general in

Bernardino Drovetti, the French consul in Egypt, with members of his expedition to Upper Egypt in 1817–18. Drovetti both assisted and hindered Champollion.

Egypt, who in 1828 was still Drovetti. While the pasha was motivated by politics, with a decided tilt towards France, and was indifferent to Egyptology, Drovetti's motives were more inscrutable – at times almost indecipherable. Drovetti would give some aid to Champollion in Egypt, but would also create many difficulties for him.

Four years earlier, before Champollion left Paris for Italy in 1824, Drovetti had encouraged him through one of their mutual contacts to come to Egypt on a study tour, for which he promised all necessary help. At this time, an official invitation from Muhammad Ali did not appear necessary, because Drovetti was confident that such a leading French scholar as Champollion would be welcomed by the Francophile pasha. But when Drovetti turned up in Paris in mid-1827, at the time of the installation of his second collection at the Louvre, the consul-general was no longer so full of encouragement.

The obvious reason was the deteriorating political relationship between Egypt and France, which reached a nadir in October 1827 after the battle of Navarino. There, as part of the Greek struggle for independence from the Ottoman Empire, a combined French, British and Russian fleet had wreaked havoc on the fleets of Ottoman Turkey and Egypt. French visitors to Egypt, however apolitical, were now unlikely to be welcome, although the pasha had guaranteed the protection of French residents in the period following the battle.

Less obviously, Drovetti now had the excavation of Egyptian antiquities largely to himself, because of the withdrawal of his long-time rival, the British consul Salt, who died in October 1827. The appearance of Champollion on the Egyptian scene, far from having the potential benefit of winning advantage with the pasha over the British, would in fact tend to interfere with the French consul's trade in Egyptian antiquities. Although Drovetti never openly admitted his commercial motive, it was plain from his actions. For, despite his claims to the contrary, he did not inform Muhammad Ali about the planned Franco-Tuscan expedition in order to obtain the pasha's permission; instead he sent two letters to Champollion and Rosellini warning them not to come to Egypt in 1828.

Drovetti's letter to Champollion, written from Egypt on 3 May 1828, advised him to delay his expedition for political reasons:

There reigns in Egypt, as in all of the other parts of the Ottoman Empire, a spirit of animosity against Europeans, which, in certain cases, could produce ferment and seditious unrest against the personal security of those domiciled there or who find themselves travelling there. If the situation depended only on the will of Muhammad Ali to put a stop to the effects of this discontent, it would not be difficult to obtain what you have given me the responsibility of requesting, but he himself is a target of this animosity because of his European principles and sympathies, and he does not dare to give the guarantees that I have requested on behalf of you and your travelling companions.

This letter reached Paris after Champollion had left the capital, heading for Lyons and thence to his expedition vessel waiting in the harbour at Toulon. Champollion-Figeac opened it and immediately smelt a rat: some kind of intrigue by Drovetti, or perhaps Drovetti acting in league with his very close friend Jomard. Champollion-Figeac knew that cancellation of the expedition would devastate his brother. So it appears that the canny Jacques-Joseph sat on Drovetti's disturbing missive for a few days and did not forward it to Jean-François at Toulon until 28 July. The government in Paris did not act until 1 August, when the appropriate minister sent a message to the naval station in Toulon by the new system of telegraphic communication, asking the admiral urgently to inform the prefect in Toulon to detain the expedition. But the telegram arrived too late: around midday on 31 July, the wind was favourable and the commander of Champollion's corvette raised anchor and set sail towards the east. Champollion eventually heard about the letter from Drovetti in person, when he reached Alexandria. Had he known about it before leaving Paris, he wrote to his brother from Egypt in late August, he would not have set out: 'It is the hand of Amun that diverted it.' At this stage Champollion knew nothing of the hand of Champollion-Figeac.

Fortune favoured Champollion in a second way, too, during the week before his departure. Nearing Toulon, he made a detour to Aix-en-Provence to see some hieratic papyri belonging to François Sallier, a local revenue official, former mayor of Aix and a friend of the count of Forbin. On the second day, Sallier showed Champollion some rolls that struck him as being of the greatest importance. Two of them contained what he thought were 'types of odes or litanies' in praise of a certain pharaoh, as he told his brother. Another roll, whose first pages were missing, consisted of 'eulogies and exploits of Ramesses-Sesostris in a biblical style, that is to say, in the form of an ode in which the gods and king converse'. There was no time to study the manuscripts in depth, so Champollion requested Sallier not to show them to anyone else until he returned from Egypt – a request that Sallier apparently granted. (After Sallier's death in 1831, the papyri were eventually sold to the British Museum and catalogued as 'Sallier II'; a note on one sheet of the 'odes and litanies' states that it was 'stuck onto fourteen squared sheets by Champollion at M. Sallier's in the month of February 1830'.)

To Champollion, the importance of the 'eulogies and exploits' lay in their refining of his decipherment and the historical information they imparted. He obtained from them the names of some fifteen conquered nations, including the Ionians, Lycians, Ethiopians and Arabs, and information about the chiefs who had been taken hostage, as well as the payments required from those nations. This enabled him to identify a pair of hieratic signs used to specify the names of foreign countries and individuals given in a foreign language. 'I have carefully noted down all the names of the conquered peoples which, being perfectly readable and in hieratic script, will help me to recognize those same names in hieroglyphic on the monuments of Thebes, and to restore them, if they are partly worn away,' he told his brother in mid-1828, giving us an inkling of his formidable preparation for the expedition and of the comparative working methods he would adopt in Egypt.

For today's Egyptologists, too, Papyrus Sallier II is of great importance – but for literary rather than historical reasons. According to Richard Parkinson in his anthology of ancient Egyptian poetry, 'The rediscovery of ancient Egyptian literature can be dated precisely to the 22 July 1828' – the day that Champollion came across the 'odes and litanies'. In actuality, Champollion had discovered a copy of 'The Teaching of King Amenemhat', a text composed around 1900 BC and probably copied in Memphis in 1204 BC, during the 19th dynasty. It was written by a treasury scribe called Inena in 'Year 1, month 1 of winter, day 20', under Seti II. Amenemhat was the founder of the 12th dynasty, who ruled c. 1938–1908 BC, but he cannot have been the author of the poem, since the king speaks to his son and heir in a dream from the grave, telling him of an attempted palace assassination (apparently his own) and giving him advice on how to rule. Champollion, writes Parkinson, 'did not recognize its literary character, since at that time preclassical literature – with the exception of the Bible – was little regarded'.

The expedition's voyage eastwards along the Mediterranean went smoothly, although the corvette was prevented from landing at Agrigento, where the group wanted to visit the site of the ancient Greek city of Akragas, by Sicilian officials who had heard rumours of plague in France. Champollion's first sighting of Africa was through a telescope. He was able to pick out Berber shepherds, their tents and flocks in the hills and valleys of Cyrenaica (eastern Libya). On the afternoon of 18 August he spotted Pompey's Pillar and the harbour at Alexandria through the telescope. The corvette's commander fired a cannon shot, which beckoned from the harbour an Arab captain, who piloted the vessel past French and English ships charged with blockading the harbour and moored her among European vessels, not far from some Egyptian and Turkish ships still undergoing repair after the battle of Navarino almost a year earlier. The cosmopolitan mingling of ships of all nations, friends and enemies, struck Champollion as a very strange spectacle, characteristic of the period. Then the secretary of the French consulate came on board, welcomed him in the name of Drovetti, and a meeting was arranged with the French consul for that very evening. The Tuscan consul, Carlo Rosetti, also sent a message via his Turkish janissary (a type of retainer), Moustapha.

The corvette's commander wished to meet Drovetti, too, so together with Champollion and Rosellini the three men set off in the commander's rowing boat, weaving their way through the crowded harbour for a good half-hour until they reached the customs house. Champollion's description of their first steps onto Egyptian soil, written for his brother, is vibrant with life and humour:

Preceded by two janissaries from the consulates of France and Tuscany, who, with their white turbans, their flowing red robes and their silver-knobbed canes, recall the ancient doryphores [spear-carriers] of the kings of Persia, we took a few steps towards the gate of the city. But scarcely had we cleared the customs house than a crowd of young boys, clothed in rags and leading rather pretty donkeys, surrounded us with much shouting, and forced us to accept their modest palfreys, which had saddles that looked clean enough and were braided in all colours. Thus we were now in a cavalcade, led by the two janissaries who had also grabbed themselves a donkey each, and made our first entrance into the ancient residence of the Ptolemies. It is fair to say that the donkeys of Egypt, which are the hackney carriages of Alexandria and Cairo, merit all the praise given them by travellers, and that it is difficult to find a mount with a gait that is gentler and more agreeable under all conditions. One is compelled to hold the bridle to prevent it from breaking into a trot or a gallop. A bit bigger than those of Europe, and above all more lively, Egyptian donkeys hold their ears to perfection, almost upright and cocked with a certain pride. This comes from the fact that, at an early age, young

donkeys have their ears pierced, which are then pulled together with a string of
horse hair and fixed in place with a second string, in such a way as to make the
ears acquire a vertical position. In addition, these animals have a very smooth
coat; some are brown or black, but the majority are reddish grey.

Champollion's journal of the expedition, based on his letters to his brother and some others in France and Italy, is as rich in observations of contemporary Egyptian life as it is in comment, analysis and sketches concerning ancient Egyptian art and scripts. Everywhere he travelled, he could not help but compare the ancient with the modern, despite the long intervening centuries of Muslim rule. Fascination with the land and affection for its people, even for some of its harsh rulers, dominate his words, but criticism and exasperation are never far from the surface. In fact, of all his writings, the journal probably gives the clearest picture of his personality. Champollion had always been an enthusiast for life; in Egypt he showed himself to be a poet, too. But he never allowed himself to be distracted from the ancient Egyptians and their hieroglyphs for long. After a day spent wandering among the wonders of Cairo's mosques, minarets and arabesques, he remarked to his brother: 'There is enough of the old Egypt, without occupying myself with the new.'

Champollion's interview with Drovetti on the evening of his arrival appeared to go well. Although the consul reiterated what he had said in his 'diverted' letter, he added that the political situation had recently improved somewhat: Muhammad Ali and the British had signed a treaty in Alexandria in early August, agreeing to an evacuation of Egyptian troops from Greece. Drovetti was therefore now certain that Champollion's expedition would receive permission from the pasha to proceed up the Nile to Cairo and beyond, along with official permits and facilities. His own house in Alexandria would be put at Champollion's disposal, and another rented for his travelling companions. After spending one more night aboard the corvette, the expedition fully disembarked on 19 August 1828 and settled down in Alexandria. Champollion found himself staying in the same room as had General Kléber, Napoleon's successor in Egypt and the celebrated victor over the Turks at the battle of Heliopolis in 1800.

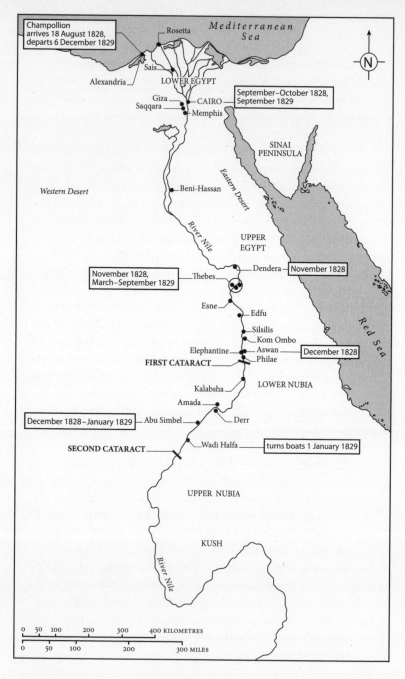

Champollion
arrives 18 August 1828,
departs 6 December 1829

Mediterranean
Sea

Rosetta

Sais

Alexandria

LOWER EGYPT

Giza

Saqqara

CAIRO

Memphis

September–October 1828,
September 1829

SINAI
PENINSULA

Western Desert

Beni-Hassan

Eastern Desert

UPPER
EGYPT

Dendera

November 1828

Thebes

November 1828,
March–September 1829

Esne

Edfu

Silsilis

Kom Ombo

Elephantine

Aswan

FIRST CATARACT

Philae

December 1828

Red Sea

Kalabsha

LOWER NUBIA

Amada

Abu Simbel

Derr

December 1828 – January 1829

SECOND CATARACT

Wadi Halfa

turns boats 1 January 1829

UPPER NUBIA

KUSH

River Nile

| 0 | 50 | 100 | 200 | 300 | 400 KILOMETRES |

| 0 | 50 | 100 | 200 | 300 MILES |

Map of Egypt with the main sites visited by Champollion and the Franco-Tuscan expedition.

The following evening – on his first full day in Alexandria – a restless Champollion was determined to see Cleopatra's Needles. These two obelisks were outside the city proper, where they would remain until one was moved to London and erected in 1878 and the other transferred to New York shortly after. To reach them Champollion had to walk, followed by a large number of dogs, across bare mounds of debris – pottery, glass, marble and other materials mixed with sand – that had covered the remains of ancient Greek and Roman buildings. Some of the high arches of these structures poked up through the debris like the low mouths of caverns, inside which Champollion saw families of peasants dwelling in miserable circumstances – the earliest of his many contacts with the grinding poverty of Egypt under the pasha's rule. A blind old Arab guided by a young half-naked child accosted him: 'Good day, Citizen, give me something, I have not yet had lunch.' Stunned by this Republican greeting, Champollion found some French coins in his pocket and put them into the blind man's hand. The Arab felt them for a moment then called out: 'These are no longer in use, my friend!' So Champollion produced a Turkish piastre. 'I thank you, Citizen!' cried the old Arab. 'At each moment in Alexandria one comes across old souvenirs of our campaign in Egypt,' Champollion mused to his brother in Paris.

One obelisk was still upright, the other long since fallen in the sand. Both were made of pink granite, like those in Rome. Champollion noted:

A quick examination of their three columns of hieroglyphs, inscribed on each of their faces, informed me that these beautiful monoliths were carved, consecrated and erected in front of the temple of the Sun at Heliopolis by Pharaoh Thuthmosis III ... The lateral inscriptions were added afterwards in the reign of Ramesses the Great; and the royal inscription of Ramesses VII ... was carved on the northern and eastern faces between the lateral inscriptions and the tip of the obelisk, but in very small hieroglyphic characters. – So the obelisks of Alexandria go back to pharaonic times, as the beauty of their workmanship alone demonstrates, and were carved in three different periods, but always in the 18th dynasty. It was the first European travellers or the first French to settle in Alexandria who gave these monuments the name Cleopatra's Needles, an appellation as inexact as the name Pompey's Pillar, applied to a monument of the late Roman period.

Champollion was correct about Thuthmosis III and Ramesses the Great, and about the obelisks' lack of connection with Cleopatra: in fact they had been moved from Heliopolis to Alexandria in 10 BC, two decades after her death, during the reign of the Emperor Augustus, to stand in front of a temple to the recently deified Julius Caesar. As for Pompey's Pillar, it was erected by the Emperor Diocletian in AD 297, not by Pompey in the 1st century BC. So both Champollion's analysis and his analogy were sound. Sadly, the hieroglyphs on both obelisks are now so badly eroded by the climate and pollution of London and New York that many are barely legible.

On 24 August 1828, six days after the expedition's arrival, Drovetti presented Champollion, Lenormant and the commander of the corvette to Muhammad Ali Pasha. They talked in French, since the pasha, who was a Macedonian of Albanian parentage, did not know Arabic. Apart from the hookah pipe inlaid with diamonds held in his hands, what struck Champollion most about Muhammad Ali was his simplicity and his vivacious eyes, which contrasted strangely with the flowing white beard that reached his stomach. The pasha came to the point without any excess of Oriental politesse and immediately granted the expedition permission to travel up the Nile as far as the second cataract. Furthermore, he appointed two guards to accompany them to ensure their proper treatment. After some talk about the Egyptian military situation in Greece over a cup of sugarless coffee, the visitors took their leave. Champollion immediately started making plans to depart Alexandria as soon as the permissions were in his hands and the August heat had abated.

But now Drovetti again interfered. No permissions were forthcoming from the pasha for well over a week. Champollion, emboldened by his audience and by his usual courage in the face of opposition, decided that there was now no option but to make an official protest to the French consulate. Through his own research, he had become convinced that Drovetti had all along been hindering him, chiefly for commercial reasons of his own. He therefore informed the consulate that, having come to Egypt on an official research mission for the royal museums in Paris, were he unable to discharge his mission he would be obliged to explain to the king's ministers the reasons why, which appeared to him merely a matter of commercial intrigue. Not only would this failure be an affront to Charles X, it would also damage Muhammad Ali's reputation in Europe for being a guardian of the arts and sciences – especially since the French–Italian mission, unlike those undertaken by previous visitors who had received permits (such as Belzoni and Passalacqua), was not pursuing its own commercial gain. A copy of this letter went to Minister Boghoz, who represented the pasha.

It was a somewhat risky strategy, but the official protest worked, bolstered as it was by public opinion in Alexandria and, more significantly, by the Egyptian government's fear of bad publicity in the French newspapers, which Champollion had shrewdly emphasized as a threat – no doubt aimed mainly at Drovetti. The pasha's permits arrived on 10 September, even including the right to visit locations formerly reserved to the French consul and his Swedish counterpart. The biographer of Drovetti, Ronald Ridley, somehow manages to credit this satisfactory resolution to the 'skills and generosity' of his subject, but it is hard to acquit the French consul of simple greed, in trying to corner the Egyptian antiquities trade, and of short-sightedness, given that he had already sold a collection to the Louvre in 1827 and was unlikely to sell another to the French king if he contrived to infuriate the museum's curator of Egyptian antiquities.

In the end, the pasha did the expedition proud. Apart from the permits and the guards, he provided a large sailing boat of a type known as a *maasch*, one of the largest in the country, which Champollion named *Isis*. A second, much smaller boat, known as a *dahabieh*, big enough for five people to sleep in, was hired by Champollion and Rosellini, named *Athyr* (Hathor), and put under the command of Duchesne instead of the naturalist Professor Raddi, who had temporarily left the expedition to chase butterflies in the Libyan desert. 'So we shall sail under the auspices of the two most jolly goddesses of the Egyptian Pantheon,' Champollion wrote to his brother on 13 September. The total number on board both boats, including the sailors, the pasha's guards, a dragoman interpreter, two Nubian servants and a cook, was thirty people. Drovetti provided some bottles of superior French wine for the *Isis*, but would take his revenge on Champollion by failing to forward his mail from France.

Champollion was determined not to dawdle in the Nile Delta, where he knew from the *Description de l'Égypte* – in so far as it was trustworthy – that little of note remained above ground. His only major stop on the way to Cairo was at the site of ancient Sais, a town mentioned as significant by Herodotus, Plato and Plutarch. But there was not much to be seen, partly because of the destruction of ancient buildings by the locals over many centuries, and also because the site was inundated by the annual floodwaters of the Nile; the waterlogged modern cemetery created a foul stench, strongly suggesting to Champollion one cause of the plague in modern Egypt. (Even so, he continued to drink Nile water, as a matter of pride.) Early on 19 September, when the haze lifted, they caught their first sight of the pyramids at Giza; at first only two were visible, then all three came into view as they sailed nearer to Cairo. Champollion had a drawing made of the magnificent vista. While the boats were briefly moored to adjust their rigging, he also saw his first scarab beetle, brought to him by a sailor. The beetle's habit of rolling a ball of dung along the ground was linked by the ancient Egyptians with Khepri, a creator god associated with the sun god Ra, responsible for rolling the sun through the sky from east to west; Khepri is depicted in the hieroglyphic script as a scarab beetle. In the late afternoon, the party beached their *maasch* and *dahabieh*, along with many other similar boats, on the riverbank at Bulaq, the port of Cairo, and prepared to travel in several convoys of loaded donkeys and camels for some days' stay in the fabled capital.

Despite Cairo's mixed reputation among Europeans, including Napoleon and his savants in 1798–1801, the city appealed strongly to Champollion. The common European criticism that Cairo (and Baghdad) had no wide streets, unlike Paris and London, struck him as stupid, because it did not take account of the Egyptian climate: wide streets in Cairo would have been furnaces for three-quarters of the year. Moreover, he pointedly noted – no doubt thinking of the mud and filth in Paris from which he suffered – that the streets of Cairo were remarkably clean and free from litter.

All over the city, in the stones of old buildings, he saw signs of the ancient past. In the most important room of the old palace of Saladin, the famous 12th-century Ayyubid sultan of Egypt and Syria, Champollion noticed thirty columns of pink granite of Greek or Roman origin. They were topped with Arab capitals whose stone was originally quarried from the ruins of Memphis and still carried traces of hieroglyphs, including a bas-relief of King Nectanebo (the last Egyptian ruler before the arrival of the Persians and the Greeks) making an offering to the gods. 'Thanks to the Thoulounid dynasty, to the Fatimid caliphs, to the Ayyubid sultans, and to the Bahriyya Mamluks, Cairo is still a city of a Thousand and One Nights,' Champollion told his brother, 'although Turkish barbarism has destroyed or allowed to be destroyed in large part the delightful artistic products and civilization of the Arabs.' He gave a subtle example of the latter from an evening concert he attended at the house of the pasha's physician. There the expedition party sat on a great divan while smoking and drinking coffee, and listened to female Arab singers discreetly veiled from male view by a curtain. But the performance was spoiled by the way in which the singers were encouraged to push their art to extremes so as to pander to the prevailing Turkish taste. The husband of the best singer, Nefisseh, loudly applauded and interrupted his wife's singing to encourage her, 'in the tone with which Blue-Beard called his wife to cut off her head'.

Cairo's charms soon proved too enticing for the younger members of the expedition, and by the end of the month its leader was anxious to leave the city for the desert. They sailed on 1 October from Bulaq and the next day stopped to visit ancient stone quarries at the foot of a range of mountains. Champollion, by now thoroughly Arabized in both dress and speech, and with a growing beard, walked the considerable distance to the site wearing a burnous and protected by an umbrella from the strong sun. Under his instructions, the expedition members each explored a different cavern in the mountainside and whistled to him if they came across an inscription or sculpture. Champollion then went and determined how important it was, and either sketched the inscription himself or had a drawing made if the signs were clear enough to the others. The inscriptions were in both hieroglyphic and demotic.

Some contained royal cartouches and dates: one example included the name of Achoris (Hakor), a ruler from the early 4th century BC – one of the earliest pre-Ptolemaic cartouches Champollion had deciphered and published in the *Lettre à M. Dacier*. On the stone ceilings red lines were sometimes visible, accompanied by demotic words consisting of technical instructions written by the ancient quarrymen.

At the site of ancient Memphis, Champollion was overwhelmed by the fallen colossus of Ramesses the Great, sculpted from limestone and clearly identifiable by its cartouches. After detailed study and the making of a sensitive drawing, Champollion concluded that the head of the statue was a faithful copy of the smaller colossus of Ramesses the Great at Turin he had profoundly admired. Harping on a favourite theme, he told his journal: 'Any impartial man may recollect a type of *dread mixed with disgust* that cannot be avoided in Rome, as I felt, in front of the colossal heads of the emperors preserved on the Capitol and elsewhere; would that he might compare this feeling with his experience before the head of an Egyptian colossus.' Curiously enough, the more Champollion discovered of Ramesses the Great – at Thebes, Abu Simbel and other sites – the more he idealized this most vainglorious of pharaohs, celebrated for an imperial ambition worthy of Napoleon Bonaparte.

By comparison with Memphis, the necropolis of the Memphites on the nearby plateau of Saqqara, about 16 kilometres (10 miles) from Giza, was a deep disappointment. Saqqara had been used as a burial site from the beginning of the 1st dynasty (3100 BC) until the late Christian period that followed the end of the Roman Empire – that is, some three-and-a-half millennia. But after this huge span of time, the necropolis had lain abandoned for well over a thousand years, left to the busy attentions of tomb robbers. Champollion's journal again:

We managed to climb the mountain, and, when we got to the plateau at the top, we could form for ourselves an idea of the devastation that people have wreaked over the centuries on the burial places of the Memphites. The vast expanse interrupted by pyramids was riddled with hillocks of sand covered in debris consisting of shards of ancient pottery, wrappings from mummies, shattered bones, the skulls of Egyptians whitened by the desert dew, and other stuff. At every moment one

*encounters under one's feet either the remains of a dried-brick wall or the opening
of a square shaft, dressed in beautifully cut stone but more or less filled up with
the sand that the Arabs have dug away to get at the shafts. All these hillocks are
the result of excavations in search of mummies and antiquities, and the number of
shafts or tombs at Saqqara must be enormous, if you consider that the sand thrown
up in discovering one shaft must itself hide the openings to several other shafts.*

Although Champollion decided to camp in this bleak setting, only
two of the tombs proved fruitful. In one he discovered a series of birds
admirably sculpted on the walls, with their accompanying hieroglyphic
names, five species of gazelle, with their names, and a few domestic
scenes, such as the milking of cows and two cooks showing off their
culinary arts. The other tomb had walls covered with now familiar
scenes from the Book of the Dead, but the vaulted ceiling was of great
interest. It was covered with bas-reliefs representing the twelve hours of
the day and the twelve hours of the night – a division of time apparently
conceived by the Egyptians – in the form of women, each carrying a star
on her head. Daytime was on the left side of the vault, nighttime on the
right. The concept of 'hour' was expressed in the hieroglyphic group

in which Champollion recognized the root of the Coptic word for 'hour'
and its plural, 'hours'. 'The star ★ is the *determinative* of all divisions of
time,' he noted in his journal, and then added: 'Each of these hours has
its own particular name among the ancient Egyptians … I am collecting
them here in the hope of completing this list in some tomb at Thebes.'
The term he had coined, 'determinative', describes a concept integral to
hieroglyphic script that seems to have occurred to Champollion in Egypt,
since it made no appearance in the second edition of his *Précis du système
hiéroglyphique des anciens Égyptiens* (1828). Although he would not have
time to develop this 'grand discovery' (Edward Hincks's description in
1847) fully before his death, the Egyptologist John Ray goes as far as to
call Champollion's concept of the determinative 'probably his greatest
single achievement' as a scholar. We shall return to it in Chapter XVI.

Sketch of the Sphinx by Champollion. Its actual inscription was covered by sand.

And now the expedition proceeded to the pyramids and the Great Sphinx at Giza. Here, a mystery arises. Champollion's journal for 8 October records his impression – familiar to many visitors – that the pyramids are grand from afar, but that as one approaches them they seem to become reduced, until one is close enough to touch them, when the marvel of their construction asserts itself. He also notes his urge to excavate the sand from around the Sphinx in the hope that he would be able to read the inscription of Thuthmosis IV carved on its chest, but that he has been discouraged by a throng of local Arabs who estimate that the task would require forty men working for eight days. Finally, he adds that he has set up his tent more or less alone on the eastern edge of the Giza plateau, because most of the expedition has preferred to sleep in a nearby series of tombs or in a house belonging to Giovanni Caviglia. This eccentric Italian excavator had attempted to enter the middle of the three great pyramids in 1817, the year before Belzoni succeeded in this feat. At this point, however, Champollion's journal simply stops for reasons unknown – and does not resume until 20 October.

As a result, almost nothing is known about Champollion's activities in the two days between his arrival at the Giza pyramids on 8 October and his departure on 11 October. During this interval, according to the memoirs of the expedition member L'Hôte, on 9 October the two commissions, French and Italian, entered the long corridors inside the Great Pyramid, led by an Arab, with just two candles for illumination in the overheated, bat-smelling atmosphere. They felt a mixture of admiration and terror. But there was complete silence about this intriguing visit from the normally loquacious Champollion. Did he accompany them or not? One surprising speculation, mentioned by Hartleben, is that Champollion spent this two-day period with a secret society dedicated to the wisdom of the ancient civilizations, known as the 'Brothers of Luxor', of which Caviglia was an enthusiastic member and to which the recently deceased Salt had also belonged. A modern Egyptologist, Christian Jacq, has woven a charged relationship between Champollion and Caviglia into the plot of an implausible romantic novel based on Champollion's Egyptian journey. Nonetheless, the idea of a relationship between Champollion and the Brothers of Luxor has some slight credibility, given his lifelong devotion to ancient Egypt, and to Thebes (modern Luxor) in particular, and the fact that he is known to have spent time with Caviglia in Florence – not to mention his past membership of secret political societies in Grenoble. But if Champollion really did become one of the mystical Brothers, he never gave so much as a hint of it, even to his own cherished brother.

On 5 November, after a long silence, Jean-François told Jacques-Joseph that he had expected to be in Thebes by 1 November, and every night was dreaming of scenes in the palace of Karnak. However, 'Man proposes, my dear friend, and God disposes.' In fact, the expedition had covered less than half the distance between Cairo and Thebes and become bogged down at Beni-Hassan. For this delay Champollion bluntly blamed Jomard, as he would frequently do throughout the expedition, complaining of the poor quality of the information and drawings in the *Description*. The book's write-up for Beni-Hassan had given Champollion no inkling of the wonders that awaited him there. On the walls of a grotto, using simply a wet sponge to remove a crust of fine desert dust, the expedition had uncovered a fabulous series of murals depicting ordinary life, crafts, the professions, and even, for the first time, the military caste: 'The animals, quadrupeds, birds and fishes are painted there with such subtlety and lifelikeness that the coloured copies I have had taken resemble the coloured engravings of our best natural history books: we shall need the evidence of all fourteen witnesses who saw them to make Europe believe in the faithfulness of our drawings, which are absolutely exact.'

On the evening of 16 November, after several stops en route, they at last reached Dendera, just north of Thebes – the erstwhile location of the notorious zodiac in Paris. This had been cut from the ceiling of the great temple, leaving behind the controversial cartouche for 'Autocrator' that had made Champollion an unwitting champion of the true Catholic faith six years earlier. Here, in the temple itself, a further surprise awaited him.

So tempted was Champollion to see the building, and so bright the moonlight, that the expedition members left the boats after a quick supper and set off across the fields in the dark, singing marches from the latest French and Italian operas, but found nothing after an hour and a half. Then they came across a raggedly impoverished local, 'a walking mummy' (wrote Champollion) who ran away as fast as he could, imagining them to be nomadic Bedouins in their hooded white burnouses, armed with guns, sabres and pistols. The fugitive was captured and proved to be an excellent guide. Reaching the temple, they were thrilled by its moonlit outline, which 'united grace and majesty', and even attempted to read some of the inscriptions by feeble torchlight. Returning to the boats at three o'clock in the morning, they were back again in the temple at seven.

In the bright light of day, they quickly realized why they had been unable to read some of the inscriptions. Many of the intended cartouche inscriptions did not exist. They had not been erased, as often happened in Egypt when a former ruler was censored by a successor: the temple had actually been left unfinished by its patron. 'Don't laugh', Champollion informed his brother – but the famous cartouche for 'Autocrator' was in fact empty of hieroglyphs: the signs must have been added by the artists working for Jomard, in the belief that the Egyptian Commission had forgotten to include the hieroglyphs in the original drawing, made around 1800. (Ironically, Denon's drawings of Dendera in his book of Egyptian travels were accurate in this detail.) 'That is called "offering the rod to be flogged"', Champollion joked about Jomard's mistake. His own

View of the temple of Hathor at Dendera by Dominique Vivant Denon.

vaunted evidence for the age of the zodiac was now plainly a sham, as a consequence of the trust he had placed in the *Description de l'Égypte*. But he quickly concluded from the 'decadent' style and poor quality of the temple carving that its date must still be Greco-Roman, regardless of the (lack of) hieroglyphic evidence. Certainly, the Dendera temple and its zodiac had nothing whatsoever to do with the beginnings of Egyptian civilization, as had once been vociferously proposed.

Much as he admired the architecture of the temple, if not its sculptural decoration, Champollion spent only a day or so at Dendera. Thebes – described in Homer's *Iliad* as 'Thebes of a Hundred Gates', from each of which 200 warriors sallied with horses and chariots – now lay around a bend in the Nile. Late in the morning of 20 November, the wind picked up after a teasing lull and allowed the expedition to sail on to its long-awaited destination. Champollion's fevered dreams of the palace of Karnak and the tombs of the Valley of the Kings were about to assume an astonishing reality.

XIV

IN SEARCH OF RAMESSES

The great temple of Ibsamboul [Abu Simbel] is worth the voyage to Nubia
all by itself: it is a marvel that would stand out as wonderful
even at Thebes. The labour that its excavation must have cost frightens
the imagination … But it is a tough business to visit it …
I undressed almost completely, down to my Arab shirt and long linen
underpants, and pushed myself flat on my stomach through the small
opening in the doorway that, if cleared of sand, would be at least
25 feet in height. I thought I was entering the mouth of a
furnace, and, when I had slid entirely into the temple, I found myself
in an atmosphere heated to 52 degrees: we went through this
astonishing excavation, Rosellini, Ricci, I and one of the
Arabs holding a candle in his hand. The first chamber is supported
by eight pillars against which are backed as many colossal
statues, each 30 feet tall, representing yet again Ramesses the Great.
The walls of this vast chamber are dominated by a series of grand historical
bas-reliefs relating to the conquests of the Pharaoh in Africa.

(letter from Jean-François Champollion to his
brother, Wadi Halfa, New Year's Day 1829)

Almost exactly thirty years before Champollion's expedition, the French army reached Thebes in wearisome pursuit of a force of Mamluk horsemen fleeing south after their defeat by Napoleon at the battle of the Pyramids. As the marching soldiers turned the end of a range of mountains, they suddenly beheld the vast extent of the legendary city's ruins, which could be seen stretching across the River Nile between two containing chains of mountains. According to Denon, who was travelling with the army as a daredevil war artist, the Theban panorama brought the troops to an abrupt halt, and by one spontaneous impulse they grounded

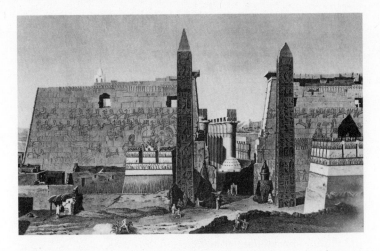

View of the temple of Karnak at Luxor by Dominique Vivant Denon, who visited in 1798.

their arms – as if they felt that, by possessing the remains of the most celebrated ancient city of Egypt, they had completed their conquest of Egyptian territory. Denon himself commented that 'the situation of Thebes is as beautiful as fancy can conceive it', and immediately got down to drawing the ruins.

Champollion's expectations of Thebes in 1828, after two decades of immersion in ancient Egypt, were naturally far higher than those of the French soldiers and even of the aesthete Denon. He would not be disappointed. In four days, between 20 and 23 November, like some hurried modern tourist in Luxor, he made a reconnoitre of the sprawling site and encountered 'marvel after marvel', from the royal tombs in the mountain valleys on the western edge, with their stone sarcophagi and wall paintings 'of astonishing freshness', to the palace of Karnak, 'or rather the city of monuments at Karnak', with its obelisks and gigantic hypostyle hall, on the eastern side. He quickly spotted that the so-called Tomb of Ozymandias – an identification suggested by the ancient Greek historian Diodorus Siculus – on the western riverbank was covered in cartouches of Ramesses the Great and two of his successors, and that the name of the surrounding palace, the Ramesseum, was written on its walls. ('Ozymandias' is now thought to be a Greek corruption of 'User-maat-ra' or 'User-maat-re', part of the throne name of Ramesses the Great, probably meaning 'the justice of Ra is powerful'.) Champollion also came across two inscribed royal lists that caused him to begin revising his dynastic chronologies. But the more he scanned the ancient ruins with the eye of a decipherer, the more he realized how much there was to learn from the hitherto inarticulate mass of colonnades, obelisks and colossi. He would have to scrutinize them one by one.

Champollion promptly decided he would return to Thebes for as many months as the expedition could afford, after first fulfilling the intention he had expressed to Muhammad Ali Pasha back in Alexandria: to follow the course of the Nile via the first cataract of the river at Aswan and Philae – Egypt's frontier in Roman times – into Nubia and beyond Abu Simbel as far as the second cataract, just south of Wadi Halfa. On the day after concluding his tour of Thebes, he told his brother:

I shall take good care to describe nothing; because if I yield, one of two things will happen: either my expressions will convey a mere thousandth part of what one ought to write in speaking of these objects, or if I content myself with a mere outline sketch, even one bleached of colourful language, people will take me for a mere enthusiast, or, to be frank, for a fool. Suffice it to say, for now, that we in Europe are just Lilliputians and that no people, ancient or modern, has conceived the art of architecture on a scale so sublime, massive and awe-inspiring as did the old Egyptians.

The expedition reached Esne on 28 November, where it nearly subsided into disaster. The men disembarked to visit a temple that turned out to have been demolished twelve days previously, to provide stone for the quay at Esne, which was under attack by the swirling floodwaters of the Nile. When the group returned to the riverside, they found that their big boat, the *maasch*, had sprung a leak and filled with water. Luckily, this happened when the *maasch* was anchored in a shallow spot, not sailing in mid-river, where it would have sunk like a stone; still, many provisions were lost. After repairs and refloating of

The campsite of the Franco-Tuscan expedition at Philae, 1828, beneath the Kiosk of Trajan, as sketched by Nestor L'Hôte. Philae's inscriptions disappointed Champollion.

the *maasch*, the expedition continued, stopping at the great temple at Edfu, the quarries of Silsilis and a second great temple at Kom Ombo, before reaching Aswan (ancient Syene) on 4 December.

Here Champollion experienced another disappointment. As soon as the flaming sun had dropped low enough in the sky, he went out to explore two temples on the famous island of Elephantine in the middle of the Nile. However, they, like the temple near Edfu, had simply vanished, leaving only their sites. He had to be satisfied with a ruined doorway in granite dedicated in the late 4th century BC to Khnum, the god of Elephantine, in the name of Alexander (the son of Alexander the Great); a dozen acts of adoration engraved on an old wall in hieroglyphics; and some scattered pharaonic debris used as building material in Roman times.

The boats would not be able to pass the first cataract, so at Aswan the entire expedition left them behind and had its baggage transported, initially by camel and then by small boat, to the island of Philae. Champollion himself was suffering in his feet from a bad attack of the gout that had first started to afflict him in Italy, when he travelled to Rome from Turin. He pictured the pathetic scene to his brother in a letter of 8 December:

As for me, at five in the afternoon I mounted a donkey, and, supported by an Arab Hercules, for I had a rheumatic pain in my left foot, was carried to Philae across quarries of pink granite bristling with the hieroglyphic inscriptions of the ancient pharaohs. Incapable of walking, and having crossed the Nile in a small boat to reach the shore of the sacred island, I was lifted onto the shoulders of four men, supported by six others – for the slope is practically perpendicular – and hoisted to a point almost next to a small modern temple, where a room had been prepared for me within the old Roman buildings, resembling a prison cell, but very clean and protected from evil winds. At six in the morning, supported by my two servants, Muhammad the Barabra [an old term for Nubian] and Suleiman the Arab, I went on a painful visit to the great temple.

The gout disappeared after a few days, leaving Champollion free to examine Philae thoroughly. As he had expected, all the buildings and inscriptions were from the time of the Ptolemies and the Roman Empire – indeed, a gate at Philae carries the latest known hieroglyphic inscription, dated AD 394. Champollion, wedded to the beauty of pharaonic art, was repelled by the 'decadence' of the Greco-Roman art at Philae. But he was pleased to find pharaonic inscriptions while walking among the rocks of the nearby cataract. Strangely, he never mentioned in his journal the Philae obelisk removed ten years previously by Belzoni and Bankes, which had provided him with the all-important cartouche of Cleopatra in Paris in 1822. Perhaps, as a result of his triumphal progress in applying his decipherment to Egyptian monuments, he was in no mood to be reminded of its awkward beginnings.

Events in Paris were on his mind at Philae, after a gap of many months. For it was here, in December, that Champollion at long last received his very first letters from France: one written by his wife on 15 August, and two written by his brother on 25 August and 3 September. The Italian members of the expedition had received mail from Europe long before Philae, and Champollion had more than once complained

The last of the hieroglyphs. This is the latest known hieroglyphic inscription (top), carved by a priest on 24 August AD 394 in the Gate of Hadrian at Philae.

to his brother about his silence. 'I do not know whether some malicious genie is meddling with my correspondence, but I am at a loss to imagine the reasons for its delay,' he told him on 8 November. Although the cause was never proved beyond doubt, it was very likely Drovetti in Alexandria who was responsible for the long interruption.

Today, the Nile Valley in Lower Nubia, between Aswan and Wadi Halfa on the northernmost border of Sudan, is occupied by Lake Nasser. This deep body of water, some 550 kilometres (340 miles) in length, was created by the inauguration of the Aswan High Dam in 1971, which drowned many ancient monuments and the second cataract of the Nile. But in Champollion's day, the great river flowed past numerous important sites of the ancient Egyptians, including Kalabsha, Derr and Abu Simbel. (Some of these sites, such as the island of Philae and the temples at Abu Simbel, were spectacularly salvaged by Unesco in the 1960s and moved to their present positions stone by stone.) Below the first cataract at Aswan, the expedition embarked on a flotilla of boats: a *dahabieh* flying a French flag and a Tuscan flag (the flagship, so to speak); four small boats (two for the French and two for the Tuscans); a kitchen and provisions boat; and a boat for the armed forces (that is, the two guards provided by the pasha, who carried silver-knobbed canes). One of the pasha's governors had also lent the expedition a cannon at Philae, which would be fired in a loud salute on arrival at the second cataract at Wadi Halfa.

The highlight of this Nubian leg of the expedition was of course Abu Simbel, reached on the morning of 26 November. The forgotten temples built by Ramesses the Great and Queen Nefertari had been rediscovered in modern times by the Swiss traveller Johann Ludwig Burckhardt, who stumbled upon them in 1813; the main entrance and part of the four celebrated seated colossi of Ramesses were covered by sand. The site had clearly been abandoned to the desert by at least the 7th century BC, on the evidence of ancient Greek graffiti from this period written at a high level – presumably above the surface of the drifting sands – by Greek mercenaries of Psamtek, an Egyptian ruler of the 26th dynasty. Bankes had first visited Abu Simbel in 1815, but it was Belzoni who cleared the sand in 1817 and was able to open the temple, after which Bankes returned in 1819, removed some more sand and discovered the Greek graffiti. In 1817, a supplement to the *Description de l'Égypte* included drawings of the exterior and interior of Abu Simbel – which were much derided by Champollion for their ugliness and inaccuracy.

View of the temple of Abu Simbel under excavation in 1819 by Linant de Bellefonds. By the time Champollion arrived in 1829, sand had blocked the entrance again.

A decade later, the infernal sand had returned. But, after the minimum of necessary digging and shoring up of the entrance, Champollion was able to enter the great temple, as he dramatically recounted at the head of this chapter. His description continued:

After two and a half hours of admiration, and having seen all the bas-reliefs, the need to breathe a bit of pure air made itself felt, and we had to regain the entrance to the furnace while taking precautions for our exit. I put on two flannel vests, a woollen burnous, and my large coat, in which I wrapped myself up as soon as I emerged into the light; and there, seated beside one of the exterior colossi whose immense calf blocked the wind blowing from the north, I rested for half an hour to allow myself to perspire. Then I went back to the boat, where I sweated for

another hour or two. This experimental visit proved to me that one can spend
two and a half to three hours in the interior of the temple without suffering any
breathing difficulties, only some weakening of the legs and joints; from this
I concluded that on our return journey we would be able to draw the historical
bas-reliefs, by working in squads of four (so as not to use up too much air),
for two hours in the morning and two hours in the evening. That would be our
battle campaign; but the result would be so interesting, the bas-reliefs were so
fine, that I would do everything to have them, as well as the complete inscriptions.
I compare the heat of Ibsamboul [Abu Simbel] to that of a Turkish bath,
and this visit amply confirmed the comparison.

Leaving Abu Simbel on 28 December, two days later they reached Wadi Halfa, which was a mere half an hour's sail from the second cataract of the Nile – the farthest limit of the expedition. At the cataract itself, Champollion discovered the foundations of three buildings bearing some remnants of hieroglyphic inscriptions. Looking past the rocks and rapids of the cataract, he recorded in his journal that there must be more of the ancient Egyptians to be discovered farther up the Nile, as the river headed south into Upper Nubia. (Today, Sudan is the focus of compelling archaeological interest as the location of the ancient kingdom of Kush, centred on Meroe. At one time Kush and its 25th dynasty of pharaohs, such as Taharqo, ruled all Egypt and had their own, as yet undeciphered, writing system based on the Egyptian hieroglyphs.) But Champollion felt no urge to explore further into Africa. There was so much to be studied back in Egypt, at Abu Simbel, Thebes and other sites. In addition, the expedition had practically run out of food in this barren desert land: they were surviving on biscuits brought from Aswan.

Champollion was also beginning to feel homesick. On New Year's Day, he wrote at length to his brother, briefly to his school friend Thévenet, and respectfully to his mentor at the Academy of Inscriptions and Belles-Lettres, Bon-Joseph Dacier. He told Dacier: 'I am proud now, having followed the course of the Nile from its mouth to its second cataract, to have the right to announce to you that there is nothing to modify in our "Letter on the Alphabet of the Hieroglyphs". Our alphabet is good.' It could be applied with equal success, he wrote, to the Egyptian monuments of the pharaohs as to those of the Greek and Roman rulers.

At nine in the morning on 1 January 1829, the cannon was fired and the seven boats lowered their sails, turned around and headed north, moving at last with the river's current, as their sailors seized the oars and sang a song of departure. That evening, at supper, 'The food was delicious, for a Nubian supper: our cook surpassed himself, and two bottles of Saint-Georges wine, despite being deadened by the tropics, lent the meal a certain air of festivity very suitable for the first day of the year.' After the meal, baksheesh was distributed to the servants, the expedition members gathered for coffee on board the *dahabieh* flagship, and they all drank to the success of the expedition with a bottle of liqueur, a ratafia from Grenoble.

Back at Abu Simbel on 3 January, the hard work began of recording the bas-reliefs and inscriptions accurately for the first time. Champollion laboured indefatigably, notwithstanding another disabling attack of gout. On the first afternoon he walked painfully from the *dahabieh*, supported by two servants, half-undressed himself as before, entered the furnace again and, sweating profusely, climbed a ladder by candlelight. After verifying, and where necessary correcting, Rosellini's drawings of the bas-relief inscriptions on the right, he transcribed those on the left, beginning with the great inscription next to a tableau in which Ramesses announces that his enemies are attacking his lines and that his battle chariot is ready. Two hours or so of this effort were all that Champollion could cope with before he had to leave and lie prostrate on his bunk in the boat for a further two hours. For the next three days, he remained on the vessel and transcribed a decree of Ptah – a key deity in the temple – from a tracing brought to him by a Nubian. But Champollion was not satisfied with the man's tracing and had to leave many blanks in his copy. He therefore went back into the temple at night – when the temperature was no cooler – and worked from half past one to four fifteen in the morning, collating six lines of his transcription with the original decree, and then copying fifteen new columns of inscription from a bas-relief, before exhaustion compelled him to retreat. But this time, after sweating again on the boat, he found that his gout had left him.

An inscription commonly seen in these bas-reliefs included the sign of a lion accompanying Ramesses. This raised an interesting issue in Champollion's mind: was the lion purely symbolic, standing for the courage and ferocity of the pharaoh, or did Ramesses take a tame lion to war? Later, at the site of Derr, on his way back to Aswan, Champollion came across similar bas-reliefs created by Ramesses the Great that featured the following inscription. It included the lion sign, but here the hieroglyphs appeared above an image of a lion throwing itself on the Nubian enemies of Ramesses:

Champollion translated the inscription as: 'The lion, servant of His Majesty, tearing to pieces his enemies'. To his brother, he noted: 'This seems to me to demonstrate that the lion really existed and followed Ramesses into battle.'

The thirteen days at Abu Simbel were among the happiest of the whole expedition, not least because they involved very close cooperation between the French and Tuscan commissions in recording the extraordinary art – in contrast to later disagreements over some of their work at Thebes. All of Abu Simbel's historical tableaux got drawn, and Champollion himself took notes on the remainder of the temple's decoration and inscriptions. By 16 January, it was time to leave. The scaffolding of wooden planks that had prevented Ramesses' temple from becoming a tomb for the expedition was removed from the entrance. The sand collapsed, covering the doorway to a depth of some two metres above the cornice. Then the boats entered the current of the Nile, and Champollion watched the great temple recede into the distance. He wrote in his journal: 'I could not help but feel sadness at leaving forever, as it would appear, this beautiful monument, the first temple from which I was moving on and which I would never see again.' But on the other hand, as he had noted when the boats first turned northwards on New Year's Day, 'I felt a keen pleasure at going in this direction, which was bringing me with each passing second closer to Thebes, and even to Paris.'

His lack of contact with Europe, due to the disruption to his mail, was getting on Champollion's nerves, despite his joy in his work. In mid-February, by now at Kom Ombo, well on his way back to Thebes, he scolded his brother at the end of a 27-page letter: 'Remember that I am a thousand leagues from you and that your littlest piece of gossip has the most fabulous piquancy here. The evenings are so long! Always smoking or playing at *bouillotte* [a card game] – one becomes tired of it, and I would get so much pleasure from going back over small packets from Paris!'

Perhaps this is why on 20 January, at Amada, Champollion was delighted to greet a passing English explorer. The former naval captain, Lord Prudhoe – the future fourth duke of Northumberland, and almost the same age as Champollion – was on his way up the Nile with his travelling companion, Major Orlando Felix, intending to explore Abyssinia. Champollion went aboard Prudhoe's boat and talked news and antiquities until midnight. Prudhoe and Felix, a long-time admirer of Champollion's work, were excited to see the expedition's portfolios from Abu Simbel and elsewhere, and for their part gave suggestions of areas in Thebes that would repay meticulous study. 'I bid them adieu with real sorrow,' noted Champollion, 'seeing a man leaving on such a perilous journey who, in possession of an immense fortune, yet had a spirit noble enough to throw himself into a dangerous enterprise, though useful to science.' This was high praise for an Englishman, coming from him.

The expedition arrived back in Thebes on 8 March 1829, three and a half months after its first visit on the way southwards. To begin with, they moored their boats on the east bank of the river next to the palace of Karnak, so as to investigate Luxor more easily. Then, in late March, they moved into a tomb on the other side of Thebes in the Wadi Biban el-Muluk (Arabic for 'gate or court of the kings') – the place now generally known as the Valley of the Kings. It was the obvious thing to do, given the new location of their research and the steadily rising daytime temperatures.

Champollion joked about their novel abode to his brother:

*It is King Ramesses (the fourth of the 19th dynasty) who has offered us
hospitality, for we are all living in his magnificent tomb, the second tomb that
one encounters on entering the Biban el-Muluk. This hypogeum, in a remarkable*

state of preservation, receives enough air and enough light to accommodate us marvellously. We occupy the three first chambers, which cover a length of 65 paces; the walls, 15 to 20 feet in height, and the ceilings are totally covered with painted sculptures, the colours of which have kept almost all of their brilliance. It is truly the habitation of a prince, almost as convenient as a suite of rooms; the floor is entirely covered in mats and reeds.

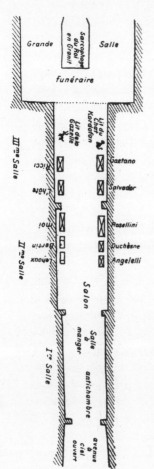

It has sometimes been stated that the Franco-Tuscan expedition stayed in the tomb of Ramesses VI, located directly above the (as yet undiscovered) tomb of Tutankhamun, not in that of Ramesses IV, as stated by Champollion. But the sketch plan of 'their' tomb that he sent to his brother – with its delightful touches showing the 'bed of the cat Kordofan' opposite the 'bed of the gazelle' (two of their pets, which later included Rosellini's sharp-toothed leopard cub) – shows that Champollion was correct in his identification. He was wrong, though, about the dynasty: Ramesses IV is now allotted to the 20th dynasty, not the 19th dynasty of Ramesses II. By chance, Champollion had selected the very tomb of which he had discovered a plan among Drovetti's papyri in Turin; this happy coincidence escaped his notice, however, because the plan in the papyrus was incomplete and the survey of Ramesses IV's tomb in the *Description de l'Égypte* was inaccurate.

Without doubt, if he had had the choice, Champollion would have settled in the tomb of Ramesses the Great, his favourite pharaoh – 'the most celebrated and finest of the princes

Champollion's sketch of the tomb of Ramesses IV in the Valley of the Kings at Thebes. The tomb was the abode of the Franco-Tuscan expedition in 1829.

that old Egypt can count in her long annals,' as he recorded at Thebes. 'I felt a burning desire to locate the tomb.' But when he entered it, he found the tomb was in very poor condition, as he bitterly lamented, because it had been open since antiquity, at least in part, and had also suffered badly from flash flooding. Full of rubble, its paintings badly damaged, the tomb was fit only for snakes and scorpions, not archaeologists. Ramesses the Great, despite the immortality of many of his other monuments, had selected a fragile site for his mortal remains.

It was at this moment that the faraway Young briefly reappeared in Champollion's life, just before his premature death in London in May 1829, aged 55. Champollion-Figeac had written to say that Young had been corresponding with their mutual friend François Arago, in an effort to persuade the French scientist of his priority in the decipherment. Arago profoundly admired Young as a physicist and as a man, but was inclined to support Champollion on this issue. Young's repeated claim had caused a renewed debate in Paris in the second half of 1828, but this was the first the French protagonist had heard about it. From the tomb of Ramesses IV, an exasperated Champollion responded with vigorous sarcasm: 'So the poor Dr Young is incorrigible? Why stir up old matter that is already mummified? Thank M. Arago for the cudgels he has so valiantly taken up for the honour of the *Franco-Pharaonic* alphabet. The Briton can do as he pleases – *it shall be ours*: and all of *old* England will learn from *young* France to spell hieroglyphs by a totally different method from "the Lancaster method".' In other words, Champollion was no Lancaster-style pupil of Young: his alphabet had borrowed nothing from Young's. 'Anyway, let the Doctor discuss further about the alphabet, while I, immersed for six months in the midst of the monuments of Egypt, I am frightened by what I can fluently *read* rather than what I may dare to imagine.' Aware that his correspondence might be seen by others, Champollion did not explain what he meant by this last cryptic remark, although he dropped a hint: 'I have some results (this is *entre nous!*) that are extremely embarrassing under a great many headings and must be hidden under a bushel; my wait for enlightenment has not been in vain, and many things that until now I had only vaguely suspected have here taken on a substance and certainty that is incontestable.'

Champollion had in mind the impact that his latest understanding of Egyptian history, science and religion would have on the expedition's royal supporter, Charles X, the French clergy and the Catholic Church in general. In 1824, the Turin Royal Canon had first suggested to Champollion the existence of pharaonic dynasties predating the biblical Flood, which was confirmed by the king lists he had discovered at Thebes and other sites. This controversial dating – rejected by the Church – was supported by Champollion's discoveries about Egyptian astronomy, which rendered obsolete the then current Egyptian chronology for the period before 1000 BC. Moreover, his reading of papyri and wall paintings showing the Book of the Dead – with its most famous scene, depicting the day of judgment, when the dead person's heart is weighed against the feather of truth in front of Osiris – and other visual and textual evidence of the Egyptian belief in the afterlife suggested to Champollion that the ancient Egyptians had believed in a concept akin to the Holy Trinity and in the immortality of the soul. The pagan idolatry and startling animal deities illustrated by Dubois in gaudy colours in Champollion's *Panthéon égyptien* (1823–25) masked, he now thought, a profound monotheism, as pure as that of Christianity and long predating Jesus Christ. Champollion may not have been at risk of being burnt for heresy in Egypt, but plainly he 'no longer ran the risk of being made a cardinal', as his amused biographer Lacouture observes.

Two centuries later, it is perhaps hard to grasp fully why these results of his decipherment should have made Champollion quite so apprehensive, although we have only to think of Charles Darwin's worries in the 1830s–1850s concerning his theory of evolution to be reminded of the power of biblical creationism in the early part of the 19th century. France in the late 1820s, after the accession to the throne of Charles X, was, as we know, a country in the grip of religious orthodoxy. After the July Revolution of 1830, which ousted Charles X, the religious atmosphere changed, however, and by the time Champollion's brother published the results of the expedition under King Louis-Philippe in 1835–45, well after Champollion's death, ancient Egypt's challenge to the biblical chronology could be publicly discussed. His royally sponsored expedition to Egypt happened to fall within a short period of extreme religious intolerance.

above: 'Cleopatra's Obelisk' in Alexandria, painted by Dominique Vivant Denon in July 1798, soon after the arrival of the French expedition in Egypt.

following pages: The Franco-Tuscan expedition in Thebes, 1829, painted by Giuseppe Angelelli between 1834 and 1836. From left to right: (standing) Salvador Cherubini, Alessandro Ricci, Nestor L'Hôte and the dragoman interpreter; (behind this group, half-hidden) the artist Angelelli; (seated with hand on head) Giuseppe Raddi; (standing) François Lehoux; (reclining at front) Alexandre Duchesne; (standing, draped in white) Ippolito Rosellini, watched by his uncle Gaetano Rosellini; and (seated, with sword) Champollion.

4° Des Insectes tels que l'abeille, le Scarabée &ᶜ;

5° Des Plantes; telles que diverses Espèces de Lotus et de Roseaux &ᶜ;

Mais on n'employait dans les inscriptions moins détaillées peintes
sur les Sarcophages ou les Stèles, que des couleurs totalement conven-
tionnelles pour les images d'êtres appartenant au règne animal
ou au règne végétal.

Ainsi les Quadrupèdes, ou des portions de quadrupèdes, des Reptiles et
des plantes étaient peints en Vert et quelquefois rehaussés de
Bleu.

2⁰ Les ailes et la partie Supérieure du corps des Oiseaux Sont coloriées
en bleu, le reste du corps en vert et les pattes en bleu ou en Rouge:

A page from the manuscript of Champollion's 'Egyptian Grammar', published in 1836.

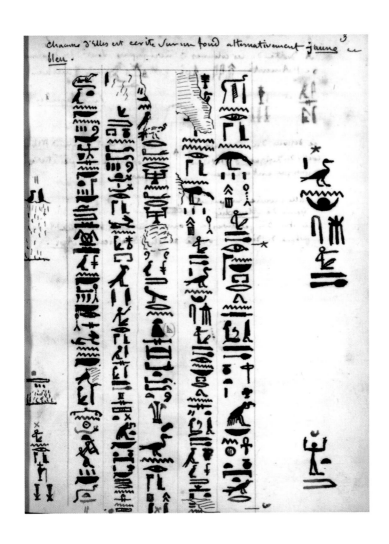

above: A page from one of Champollion's notebooks.
following pages: A bas-relief from Abu Simbel showing Ramesses II in a chariot, published in Champollion's *Monuments de l'Égypte et de la Nubie*.

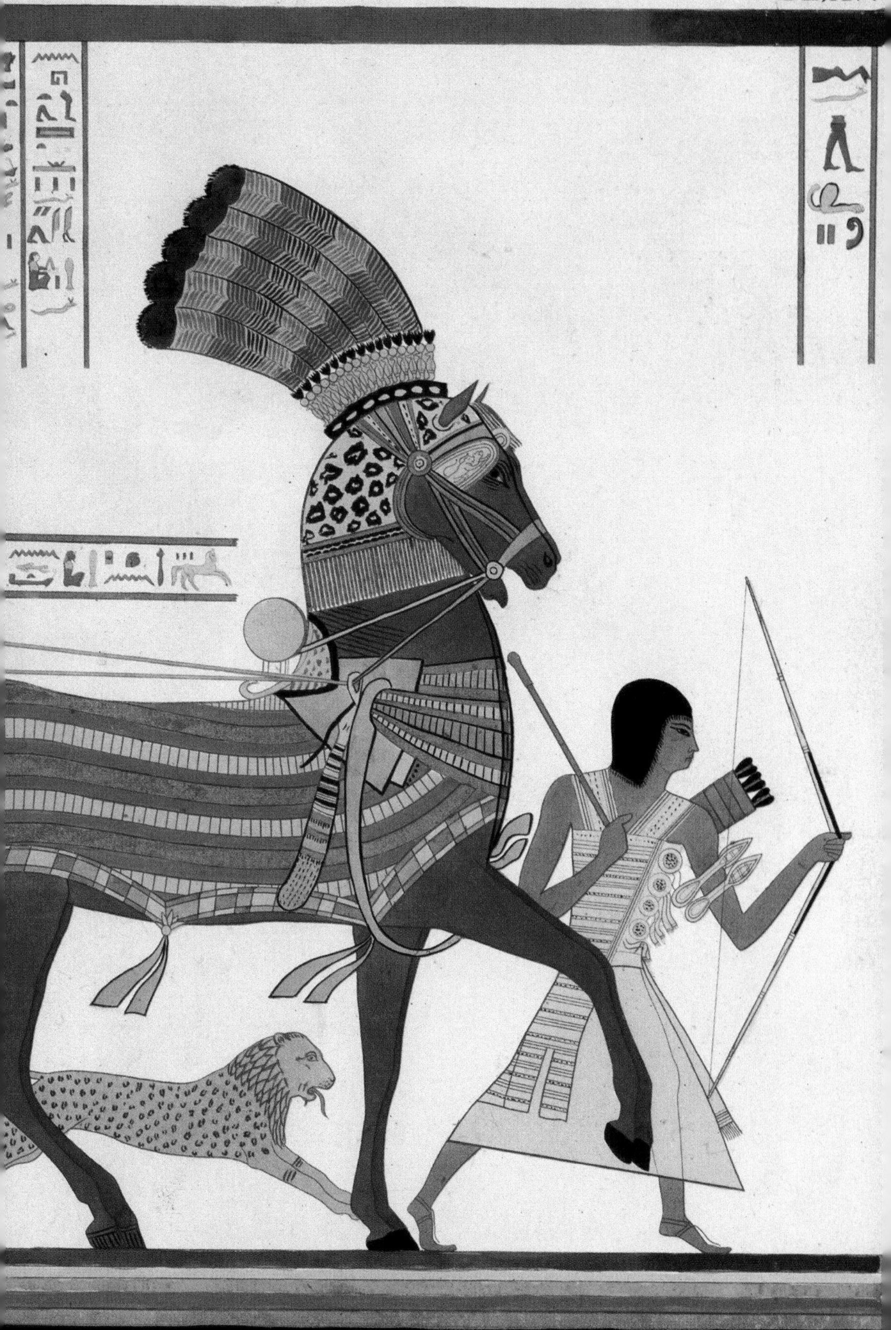

PAROI SUD.

Detail from a portrait of Champollion by Léon Cogniet, 1832 – the year of Champollion's death.

Overawed by his burgeoning understanding of Egyptian thought, derived from the wall paintings and hieroglyphics in the tombs, Champollion drove himself mercilessly for many weeks in the Valley of the Kings. Despite the searing heat of April and May outside the tombs, and the resistance of some exhausted and disgruntled expedition members (notably L'Hôte), the expedition studied as many tombs as possible – some sixteen in all. Riding on a donkey or going on foot, Champollion saw no animals in this valley of death other than a few snakes and lizards, plus flies, foxes, wolves and hyenas attracted only by the presence of the expedition in the tomb and the smells from its kitchen. His health inevitably suffered further from his overwork. Once, he was found by Cherubini unconscious, sprawled on the floor of a tomb among his papers. In fact, he fainted several times in the tombs. He apparently told the young Cherubini, who was very fond of him but annoyed by his lack of care for himself: 'Absolute silence is necessary for me, to hear the voice of the ancestors – the local atmosphere is formidable!'

Writing at length about the Valley of the Kings to his brother in late May 1829, Champollion described the mythology and symbolism represented in a typical tomb belonging to one of the Ramesses. Every tomb begins with a prefatory image, he explained, showing a pale yellow disc, in the middle of which the sun god is depicted with the head of a ram – in other words representing the setting sun, which is entering the underworld and being worshipped by the kneeling king. To the right of the disc (the east) appears the goddess Nephthys, and to the left (the west) the goddess Isis, the paired deities occupying the two limits of the sun god's course across the upper hemisphere. Beside the sun, and within the yellow disc, a large scarab beetle is sculpted, which is a symbol of regeneration or successive rebirths.

Champollion commented:

The general sense of this composition is that the king is deceased. During his lifetime, like the sun on its course from east to west, the king must act as the vivifier, the illuminator of Egypt and the source of all the physical and moral goods required by its inhabitants. The dead pharaoh is therefore naturally compared with the sun setting and descending towards the twilit lower hemisphere, through

*which the sun must pass in order to be born anew in the east and bring light and
life to the upper world (the one that we inhabit), in the same way that the dead
king, too, must be reborn, either to continue his transmigrations, or to inhabit the
celestial world and be absorbed into the bosom of Amun, the Universal Father.*

On the walls of the tomb itself, the twelve hours of the day and the
twelve hours of the night in the sun god's progress through the upper
and the lower hemispheres are portrayed as humans, each with a star
on the head and walking towards the bottom of the tomb as if to mark
the direction of the sun's progress. Daytime and nighttime scenes are
on opposite walls. In both day and night scenes, there are dramatic
encounters, but of different kinds: for example, the daytime triumph
in battle of the sun god over the serpent Apophis, and at night the sun
god's witnessing of the torment of condemned souls – a precursor of
Dante's vision of hell, as Champollion was quick to observe, while dismissing the idea that these torments were scenes of human sacrifice,
as suggested by some earlier travellers. After a long exegesis of these
paired day and night scenes, he summed up:

*This double series of tableaux gives us the Egyptian psychological system in
regard to its two most important and moral aspects – rewards and punishments.
Completely confirmed here is everything that the classical writers have said on
the Egyptian doctrine of the immortality of the soul and the positive goal of human
life. It is certainly a great and happy idea to have symbolized the double destiny
of souls in that most striking of celestial phenomena, the path of the sun through
the two hemispheres, and then to have depicted this imposing and magnificent
spectacle in paint.*

Champollion concluded his long letter about the Valley of the Kings
with a reference to a different kind of immortality: the graffiti scrawled
on the paintings and bas-reliefs in the tombs by visitors over three or four
millennia. The earliest graffiti were by Egyptians, writing in hieratic and
demotic, and the latest by European travellers 'drawn by love of science,
war, commerce, chance or idleness to these solitary tombs'; between them
in time came graffiti written in archaic Greek alphabets, in Latin, from the

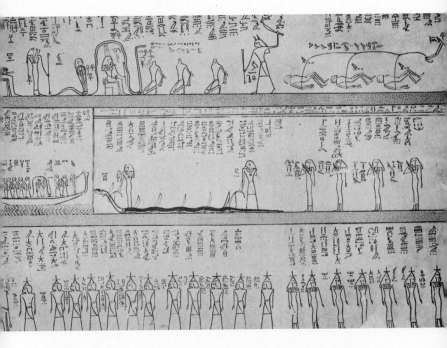

Section from the *Book of the Hidden Chamber*, or the *Amduat*, from the walls of an 18th-dynasty tomb in the Valley of the Kings. The *Amduat* describes the twelve hours of the sun god's nocturnal journey, each denoted by human figures carrying stars. This is the Seventh Hour, when the forces of chaos are checked.

time of the Roman emperors, and in Coptic, from the Christian period. Champollion himself was not immune: the name 'CHAMPOLÉON' is carved on a stone column at Karnak; and in a small tomb at Beni-Hassan, where he came across the words '1800. 3e RÉGIMENT DE DRAGONS' written in faded charcoal, he respectfully retraced the lines with a brush in black ink and added 'J. F. C. RST. 1828' ('Jean-François Champollion *restituit*', i.e. 'restored by J. F. C.'). While no one could really object to the latter, even today, he went much further in the Valley of the Kings. Following in the footsteps of Belzoni, Champollion and Rosellini permitted themselves to cut two life-sized, brightly painted murals from the walls of the tomb of Seti I – one of Seti with Hathor, the other of Seti with Horus – which now reside in Paris and in Florence.

'CHAMPOLÉON' inscribed on a pillar at Karnak in Luxor, presumably in 1829.

The expedition left its tomb and the valley in early June 1829 and, despite the heat, moved into a one-storey mud shack, which they jokingly called their 'chateau'. From this base they spent the rest of that month and all of July working on the monuments of the west bank at Thebes, such as the Ramesseum, the colossi of Memnon (Amenhotep III) and the as yet unidentified mortuary temple of Queen Hatshepsut (whom Champollion almost, but not quite, grasped was a female pharaoh).

It was now that Champollion, following the example of the ancient Romans, began to push for the idea of transporting an obelisk from Egypt to Paris. He had been contemplating this grand proposal ever since Alexandria, when he saw the two obelisks of Cleopatra's Needles, which Muhammad Ali Pasha had promised to the British and the French governments, if they could manage the transport to London and Paris. In fact, soon after arriving in Egypt, Champollion had encouraged his brother to lobby the government in Paris to facilitate the removal of one of the Alexandrian obelisks, and Champollion-Figeac had started a campaign. But it was now obvious to Champollion that the two obelisks of Ramesses the Great at Karnak were superior to those at Alexandria. 'A single column from Karnak is more of a monument on its own than all four facades of the courtyard of the Louvre,' he claimed to his brother in early July. With enough French engineering ingenuity, it should be possible to build a barge and float one of the obelisks down the Nile to Alexandria with the annual flood, he said. Both brothers continued this campaign after Champollion returned to France, as we shall see, but it would take until 1836, four years after Champollion's death, for one of Ramesses' obelisks from Luxor to be erected in the Place de la Concorde in Paris.

At the beginning of August 1829, the expedition crossed the river to Karnak, based itself inside a small temple and continued to work on the east bank throughout the month. However, Champollion was now seriously exhausted – there are no letters to his brother for two months from mid-July – and expedition numbers were depleted as both French and Tuscans departed for various reasons, including illness. With much work unfinished, the remaining members finally sailed from Thebes on 4 September, having spent six months in its ruins.

Returning with the current, the boat made rapid progress, as Champollion relaxed on board, watching the flooded riverbanks and contemplating life 'almost like a monk'; it was his first break from field research since setting out from Alexandria a year earlier. For Rosellini, 'In the midst of tamarinds, mimosas and intertwined willows, this was a brief but delicious voyage that, after the desert's aridity, brought serenity to our souls, thanks to the smiles of nature.' For Champollion,

'The inundation this year is magnificent for those who, like us, travel for the love of it and have no interest in the countryside other than as scenery. It is not the same for the poor and unhappy peasants and cultivators ... It is a distressing scene, which disturbs the heart. This country is not a place for subscription societies, and the government will not demand a penny less in tax, despite such disasters.'

Champollion stopped only at Dendera, to make absolutely sure that the notorious cartouche supposedly containing the title Autocrator *really* was empty of hieroglyphs (it was), and was back in Cairo on 15 September. Here, his main task was to select and bargain for antiquities on behalf of the Louvre, for which the French government, through the sympathetic minister Rochefoucauld, had at the last minute granted the expedition a budget of 10,000 francs. Given Champollion's newly acquired prestige, the antiquities dealers in Cairo were apprehensive that anything he did not want to buy would lose much of its value. He quickly purchased more than a hundred pieces for the museum, several of which were important acquisitions, but stayed as short a time as possible in the city. He was anxious to get away to Alexandria, which he reached a mere five days later, and thence to France.

Drovetti had retired as consul-general earlier in the year, and been replaced by a native-born Frenchman, who treated Champollion with affection. But, to the latter's deep frustration, the French naval transport promised for early October was delayed by two months. Rosellini and his remaining compatriots, tired of waiting, left on a merchant ship for Livorno. Then the three French artists, L'Hôte, Bertin and Lehoux, decided to remain in Egypt to paint portraits and theatre scenery. In the end, only Champollion and Cherubini waited for the French vessel, which finally set off for Toulon on 6 December.

Champollion filled the two months' wait in Alexandria mainly by conversing with, and writing reports for, Muhammad Ali Pasha, the pasha's son and some of his circle. The decipherer and the ruler became quite friendly, partly because of Champollion's closeness to a French physician, Étienne Pariset, who saved the life of the pasha's son during an apoplectic fit during October. On 4 November, a royal holiday in France, Champollion was woken early in the morning by a messenger on

Portrait of Muhammad Ali Pasha, with whom Champollion formed a genuine, if wary, friendship at the end of his expedition to Egypt, encouraged by the pasha's son.

horseback carrying a present from the pasha: a magnificent Persian sabre, richly worked in gold. (Rosellini had earlier received a similar sword.)

Muhammad Ali asked Champollion to write an outline history of ancient Egypt, which he completed at the end of November. Here he placed the building of the pyramids at Saqqara and Giza in the period of the earliest dynasties, though without assigning them a date. But he went further in challenging Catholic religious orthodoxy: he openly supported the idea that Egyptian civilization began 'about 6,000 years before Islam', which meant that it must be at least a millennium older than the date of the Creation in the Bible. At the same time, uninvited by the pasha, he reported on the deplorable destruction of ancient Egyptian monuments, drew up a list of the buildings that had recently been demolished plus a list of existing buildings that must be preserved, and promoted the idea of a Luxor obelisk for France. While his conservation efforts were greeted with some interest, there were obviously limits to his relationship with the pasha. Muhammad Ali liked to hear Champollion speak of Napoleon in Egypt and of Ramesses the Great, a penchant that led to a discussion of whether Champollion could create a map of pharaonic Egypt. Champollion showed the pasha an impressive map of the Nile Delta and the course of the great river, which had been presented to him by one of the Egyptian staff on the boat, the son of a peasant. But when Champollion boldly used this opportunity to put in an impassioned plea for education as a way to improve the miserable lot of the Egyptian peasantry, the autocratic pasha fell silent. Then, avoiding a direct reply, he continued with a smile: 'So was Ramesses really the greatest of the pharaohs?' Muhammad Ali had touched on a sensitive point for Champollion, whose hero, Ramesses II, was certainly no social reformer. The French scholar had to be restrained by the pasha's son from making a furious riposte.

To the very end of his visit, which had lasted almost a year and a half, Egypt remained a source of mingled inspiration and frustration for Champollion. Its autocratic traditions – whether those of Ramesses the Great, Alexander the Great, the Ptolemies or Muhammad Ali – both enthralled and appalled him. Just after his arrival back in France, he enthused in a letter to Dubois, his assistant at the Louvre: 'I have amassed enough work for an entire lifetime.' But he would not be granted a long life to enjoy the fruits of his unique labour.

XV

FIRST PROFESSOR
OF EGYPTOLOGY

If I knew there were still some years ahead of me,
I would not even consider publishing now.

(Jean-François Champollion's frequent comment to Charles
Lenormant about his 'Egyptian Grammar' during 1830–31)

When Champollion returned from his Egyptian expedition to French
soil on 23 December 1829, his 39th birthday, he did not have very long
to live. He himself seems to have sensed this, judging from various
comments he made to his intimates. His last years would be troubled
ones. Not only would his health continue to decline, he would lose his
faithful royalist patron, the duke of Blacas, in the July Revolution of 1830,
and his detractors and enemies in the court, government and academe
would intensify their private and public attacks against his Egyptian
decipherment, his research and himself. Nonetheless, Champollion
was appointed the world's first professor of Egyptology, at the College
of France, and he continued to work as hard and productively as ever,
as long as he was physically able – like the majority of geniuses as they
approach their deaths.

In this respect at least, Champollion resembled his rival Young,
although he never knew this. For several months until his dying day
in 1829, a seriously unwell Young continued to correct the proofs of
his demotic dictionary, philosophically telling his friend Gurney, who
discouraged him from this tiring labour, 'that it was a work which if he
should live it would be a satisfaction to him to have finished, but that if it
were otherwise, which seemed most probable, as he had never witnessed

a complaint which appeared to make more rapid progress' – speaking as a professional physician, that is – 'it would still be a great satisfaction to him never to have spent an idle day in his life.' Champollion's passion for Egyptology would consume him down the last wick of the candle, and, like Young with his demotic dictionary, he would leave the manuscript of his hieroglyphic grammar unfinished.

There had been portents of impending trouble in France during Champollion's Egypt expedition. He knew, for example, that longstanding opposition from the count of Forbin, the director of the Louvre, and others had delayed the government's financial support for the expedition's plans to excavate and acquire objects in Egypt; when the funds were finally granted, they were almost too late to be of use. Then the French vessel sent to collect the expedition from Alexandria had been unaccountably held up for two months. There is no certainty as to why this happened, but it seems likely from the available evidence that the recently appointed minister of state for the navy – none other than Champollion's old sparring partner, the baron of Haussez – contrived the delay to inconvenience the liberal Champollion.

Most obvious of all, the Academy of Inscriptions and Belles-Lettres had failed to elect Champollion for the second time, despite the support of its permanent secretary Dacier and, of course, that of Champollion-Figeac. This second rejection occurred in April 1829, while Champollion (who was entirely unaware that he had been nominated) was in Thebes. Instead of Champollion, the academy elected an expert on French maritime law named Pardessus. Although Jean-Marie Pardessus was fairly distinguished in France as a jurist, Champollion was internationally renowned. The rejection was deliberately humiliating, but Champollion tried to make light of his hurt, wrily punning in a letter to his embarrassed brother that he had been placed 'par-dessous M. Pardessus' ('below Mr Above'), while hoping that Dacier was not too upset by the behaviour of 'his flock'. From now on, he added, a formal recognition by the academy would impress him as much as a bottle of champagne opened for six months would impress a connoisseur of wine. In May 1830, Champollion was at last elected an academician – third time around – but only after the number of seats had been increased by six. Even so, he immediately became a diligent attender at the academy's meetings, delivering several communications about Egypt. The Academy of Inscriptions had been the scene of his greatest triumphs in 1822–23; the institution was of major importance to him.

As soon as Champollion arrived at Toulon on 23 December, he and Cherubini were quarantined in a cold and filthy lazaret for a month – ten days more than was usual for passengers coming from Egypt. The official reason was that their vessel had visited the coast of pestiferous Syria before calling in at Alexandria, but, according to Hartleben (who gave no evidence), the extra quarantine was the decision of the minister Haussez, and was motivated more by spite than any real risk of plague. The enforced stay in the lazaret certainly helped to worsen the health of Champollion, who was already fearful of the French winter after his year-long acclimatization to the heat of Egypt. He was not released from quarantine until 23 January 1830.

The first person he met when he emerged was, strangely enough, Drovetti, the former French consul in Egypt. Although relations had become fraught during their last contact in Alexandria in August 1828, Champollion wanted to cooperate with him in the interests of getting a Luxor obelisk (or even two Luxor obelisks) to Paris. Drovetti had brought to meet Champollion some senior French naval officers who wished to hear his plan for a Nile barge to transport the obelisks. Initially, the officers rejected his proposal, but by the following day they had changed their minds and recommended it to the minister in charge of the navy, who was of course Haussez. Champollion-Figeac then person-ally met the minister in Paris, who told him that he appreciated

Portrait of Thomas Young in Westminster Abbey, London, on a medallion by the sculptor Sir Francis Chantrey.

Champollion's advice and would like to hear more; Jacques-Joseph even encouraged his brother to write directly to Haussez. But, not too surprisingly, nothing came of this. Instead, a common friend of Haussez and Jomard was despatched to Egypt in March 1830, with the consent of Charles X, to undertake the excavation of one of the obelisks. This venture, too, came to nothing, because a few months later Haussez was compelled to flee to England in a fishing boat to avoid certain punishment after the July Revolution. In his memoirs, written much later, Haussez discussed the obelisk but maintained a discreet silence about Champollion and his plan to bring it from Egypt.

The transport of an obelisk from Luxor to Paris eventually occurred in 1833, through the extraordinary efforts of an engineer, Apollinaire LeBas. When the monument was erected in the Place de la Concorde in 1836, the main plaque named only King Louis-Philippe and LeBas. There was no reference to Ramesses the Great, creator of the obelisk (and no translation of his hieroglyphic inscription), nor to Muhammad Ali Pasha, who donated it to France, nor to Jean-François Champollion, who had selected it and done much to persuade Muhammad Ali to part with it. This suited the vision of Louis-Philippe, who did not want the monument to be a celebration of autocracy – whether Egyptian or French – especially as Louis XVI had been executed on the site in 1793, well within the lifetime of the 'Citizen King' and the memories of many of his Parisian subjects. 'His goal was a monument that had no political content, a centerpiece that symbolized, effectively, nothing,' according to a recent history of obelisks: 'The [Luxor] obelisk was perfect. It had no clear associations with any faction. Its presence in France was vaguely due to Napoleon, but only vaguely. It celebrated kingship, but not French kingship.'

After finishing with Drovetti in January 1830, Champollion was by no means anxious to return to the rigours of a Paris winter, or to continue his battles with Forbin, Jomard, Haussez and other confirmed enemies. So he remained in the south, in Montpellier, Narbonne, Carcassonne, Bordeaux and elsewhere. At Aix-en-Provence he at last had a chance to study in detail the Sallier papyri (having only glanced through them on his way to Toulon in July 1828), and at Toulouse he saw his mysterious friend Madame Adèle, while at Villefranche he met his sisters, who made the journey from Figeac to see their beloved brother. However, Jacques-Joseph was soon impatient to see him in Paris, where a new apartment awaited him, chosen for its warmth at Jean-François's specific request. At two o'clock in the morning on 4 March, Champollion arrived back in Paris after an absence of more than a year and a half to greet his wife, Rosine, and daughter, Zoraïde, in the apartment – on the very same calendar day and at almost the same hour as his death there two years later.

In the spring of 1830, the political atmosphere in the capital was becoming febrile. At the end of January, the king's council of ministers had decided to launch an expedition against Algeria, partly in the hope that a military success would strengthen the position of Charles X. The first French victory in Algiers occurred in June, leading to the French colonization of Algeria. But it came too late to save the king and his ministers. On 2 March, Charles X had been obliged to recall the Chamber of Deputies, which resulted in confrontations between the ministers appointed by the king and a majority of liberal opposition deputies supported by a public opinion inflamed against the king's reactionary government. On 18 March, the deputies had voted, with a majority of thirty in favour of the opposition, to compel the king to choose a ministry that enjoyed the support of the chamber. The king had then dissolved the parliament and ruled through the ministers until elections to the chamber in late June produced an overwhelming defeat for his government. The ensuing deadlock provoked some infamous repressive ordinances from the ministers (including Haussez), which were signed into law by the king on 25 July. These ordinances attempted to disenfranchise the electorate and to re-create something close to the absolute monarchy that had existed before 1789, at the very time when, across the Channel, the British monarchy and its ministers were planning to enlarge the electorate through the Reform Bill of 1832. Charles X and his ministers were now swimming against the tide of history; the result was the July Revolution.

Champollion's sympathies naturally lay with the liberal deputies, and he became actively involved with their cause. However, he was not enthusiastic about the July Revolution. In the first place, it displaced one monarch and replaced him with another, Charles X's distant cousin Louis-Philippe, rather than with a republic. At the same time, it removed Blacas (who loyally followed Charles X into exile), about whom Champollion truthfully confessed: 'I owe everything to Blacas.' Moreover, it led to a public assault on the Louvre, including the Egyptian collections, which lost some important objects to looters that were never returned. It also disrupted Champollion's Egyptian research. Although he had received an invitation from Rosellini in late April 1830 to come to Florence with his wife and daughter, Champollion never took this up, feeling that he should remain in Paris at such a turbulent time.

As a consequence of the tense political situation, there had been no official welcome and no honours for Champollion and the other French expedition members – unlike their counterparts in Tuscany. Paris, as L'Hôte remarked, 'was now too tormented by its own contemporary history to wish to give any attention to the history of nations that no longer existed'.

Following Champollion's return, Blacas had proposed to the king and to the minister in charge of public instruction that the decipherer be offered a chair in Egyptian archaeology, but his idea had not been received with enthusiasm. In this disturbed period, Charles X and his court had become receptive to the count of Robiano, a priest who claimed 'to explain Egypt by the Bible' with the help of one of Champollion's most persistent opponents, the scholar Julius Klaproth. One evening at court, Robiano had given a reading of part of a manuscript he had written on the hieroglyphs, from which he had periodically broken off to cast aspersions on Champollion's supposed decipherment, until he himself was unexpectedly interrupted by the late appearance in the room of Blacas, who silenced the priest's malicious commentary with a thunderous look. Even so, the king had agreed to have Robiano's work on the hieroglyphs published at royal expense, just before he (and Blacas) were ousted from power in July.

After the July Revolution, Champollion himself tried to revive Blacas's idea of a professorial chair with the help of friends. He appealed to the French government representative on the expedition, Charles Lenormant, one of his admirers, who was now in the corridors of power, and to Victor Cousin, a philosopher at the Sorbonne who was influential in forming the government's education policy. The eternal de Sacy, Champollion's former teacher, now administrator of the College of France, fell into line. In March 1831, Louis-Philippe ordered the creation of a chair in Egyptian archaeology for Champollion at the College of France.

The new professor's inaugural lecture, postponed from 12 April by bad health, took place on 10 May 1831, in front of a large audience of scholars, diplomats and grandees, including the German polymath Alexander von Humboldt and one of the sons of Louis-Philippe. Hence, no doubt, the diplomatic praise in the lecture for the work of the Egyptian Commission of 1798–1801 – necessary for such an occasion of national celebration, but a shade hypocritical coming from Champollion, given his long-running, devastating criticism of the drawings of inscriptions published by the commission in the *Description de l'Égypte*.

Intended to serve as an introduction to his published Egyptian grammar, Champollion's inaugural lecture is probably most noteworthy for its discussion of the role of Young in the decipherment of the hieroglyphs. Now that Young was safely beyond making a response, Champollion spoke better of his rival's achievement than he had while he was alive. At least, he did so when speaking of Young in general terms, as he introduced his erstwhile rival:

This scholar brought to the comparative examination of the three texts on the monument from Rosetta a methodical spirit eminently trained by the highest theoretical speculations of the physical sciences and mathematics. He recognized through an entirely material comparison, in the surviving portions of the demotic inscription and the hieroglyphic inscription, groups of characters corresponding to words used in the Greek inscription. This work, the result of an approach full of astuteness, at last established some definite notions of the principles peculiar to various branches of the Egyptian writing system and their interconnections; it provided solid proofs for the assertion by the ancient [i.e. classical] writers regarding the use of figurative and symbolic characters in hieroglyphic writing; but the precise nature of this writing, its relationship with the spoken language, the number, essential nature and combinations of its fundamental elements, still remained uncertain in the indefiniteness of hypotheses.

However, when Champollion came to specifics, he would not give up one iota of credit for the decipherment. Thus he failed to mention that it was Young who compared not only the demotic with the Greek, and the hieroglyphic with the Greek, on the Rosetta Stone (as he remarked above), but also the demotic with the hieroglyphic – thereby becoming the first person to detect that demotic was derived from hieroglyphic. He falsely accused Young of believing demotic to be entirely alphabetic in 1816, whereas in fact Young had stated in 1815 (to de Sacy) that demotic was a mixture of conceptual and phonetic signs. He then accused Young, also falsely, of changing his mind in 1819 and rejecting all alphabetic signs in the demotic and hieroglyphic scripts in favour of purely conceptual signs, despite the fact that Young had published two tables in the *Encyclopaedia Britannica* of what he called 'something like a hieroglyphic alphabet' and a 'supposed enchorial alphabet'. Finally, Champollion claimed, outrageously, that Young's analysis of the cartouches of Ptolemy and Berenice was 'defective in principle' and therefore led to 'no results of any kind', since Young had not applied his phonetic readings of signs derived from these two names to other cartouches (such as those of Cleopatra and Alexander). Throughout this fairly brief discussion of Young, Champollion neither made any reference to his own highly defective analysis, published in Grenoble in 1821, which he had suppressed because it was wrong in dismissing phoneticism, nor admitted to the fact that he had changed his own mind about the prevalence of phoneticism in the Egyptian scripts in 1822–23. Thus the hubris of 1822, evident in the *Lettre à M. Dacier*, was still on egregious display a decade later, despite Champollion's by now established position in the intellectual world.

Following his inaugural lecture, Champollion began to give the course proper, with the professed intention of explaining the principles of the ancient Egyptian writing system, in both the hieroglyphic and the hieratic scripts. He lectured on 23 May, and again on 26 May. Then he stopped, because the effort was proving too much. He was already working flat out on his grammar, at the same time as continuing his duties as a curator at the Louvre, campaigning for a Luxor obelisk or two to be brought to Paris, writing articles at the insistence of a Parisian editor, and corresponding with scholars across Europe. Although Champollion would resume giving the course at the College of France in December, he would come nowhere near to completing the lectures as a result of illness.

In July 1831, Rosellini made the journey from Florence, having by now realized that Champollion's travelling days were over. They had not seen each other since Rosellini sailed from Alexandria in October 1829. The two collaborators spent a few weeks working on the prospectus for the joint publication of their expedition results and enjoying each other's company, along with their families and the Cherubinis (in-laws of Rosellini). But, whereas the relationship between Champollion and Rosellini continued *con amore*, unchanged by the vicissitudes and occasional disagreements of the Egyptian expedition, Champollion-Figeac had become cool towards his brother's Italian collaborator. He therefore drew up a detailed contract for the publication, aware that Champollion lacked business sense and that he himself might need to take over the project in due course. In the event, the elder brother was proved right, as so often in practical matters. He knew that his younger brother was determined to concentrate his entire efforts on his Egyptian grammar and leave publication of the expedition drawings until the grammar was done. Rosellini, however, had been under pressure from his patron, the Grand Duke Leopold, since late 1830 and could not afford to delay its appearance for too long. As a result, the joint Franco-Tuscan publication did not get beyond the planning stage. After the death of Champollion, and subsequent disagreements between his brother and Rosellini, the project split into two grand, folio-sized publications: a ten-volume Italian one, *Monumenti dell'Egitto e della Nubia*, published in Florence in 1832–40, edited by Rosellini; and a four-volume French edition, *Monuments de l'Égypte et de la Nubie*, published in Paris in 1835–45, edited by Champollion-Figeac. Although this division was probably an inevitable consequence of Champollion's death, it was a loss to the new science of Egyptology, as we shall see in the next chapter.

In mid-August 1831, Champollion had a private audience with Louis-Philippe to discuss dedicating the expedition volumes to him. The king granted his wish. They also spoke of the Luxor obelisks and their possible placing in Paris. A week later, on 21 August, an exhausted Champollion left Paris to recuperate in his native Figeac and to work uninterruptedly on his grammar. If he had got his way, he would not have returned to the capital for many months.

Looked after by his sisters in the old family house on the Rue de la Boudousquerie – and perhaps also by Madame Adèle – and without the strain of his late father's presence that had bedevilled his previous stay in Figeac, Jean-François was able to work like an obsessive for nearly three months. His health somewhat improved; he coughed less than in Paris. On 20 November, he wrote optimistically to his friend Abbé Gazzera in Turin, asking him to take a holiday at Easter and come to Paris to visit him, and see his grammar, his papers and his museum. But he did not have quite enough time to complete the manuscript. 'Only one month more – and my 500 pages would be finished,' he wrote to Jacques-Joseph. 'But one must resign oneself and be content with what is possible.' His brother wanted him back in Paris, to deal with museum intrigues, impatient Tuscans, questions about the Luxor obelisks, and editorial demands, not to mention the resumption of his course at the College of France in early December. Champollion mournfully told a locally based scholar, the baron of Crazannes, who had participated in the excavations of Roman Uxellodunum back in 1817: 'Death lies in wait for me at Babel.' But at the end of November he obediently boarded a *diligence* and returned to Paris.

He gave his next lecture on 5 December, and began a further one on 9 December – before collapsing unconscious in the hall. It was his last appearance in the College of France. On 13 December, he suffered a stroke that left him partly paralysed and bed-ridden. Thanks to some drastic treatment, he was able to leave his bed after a few days, but was no longer master of his movements and had great difficulty in writing.

On 23 December 1831, his birthday, Champollion suddenly requested to be taken to the room at 28 Rue Mazarine, where he had experienced his breakthrough in September 1822 and which he had not visited since he left for Italy in May 1824. 'It is there that my science was born and we form an inseparable entity,' he said. He remained in the room for a long time, profoundly moved.

In mid-January 1832, while talking about Egyptian astronomy to his friend Jean-Baptiste Biot, he suddenly cried out and had another very serious collapse. This left him almost completely paralysed, but he could still speak. With his brother's help, he continued to work a little more on his grammar. Then he passed the almost finished manuscript to Jacques-Joseph and told him: 'Look after it carefully. I hope that it will be my visiting card to posterity.' (The remark is quoted by Champollion-Figeac in his preface to the published *Grammaire égyptienne*.)

At the end of the month, during a period of slight improvement, Champollion uttered the following tragic words: 'So soon – there are still so many things inside!' As he spoke, he lifted his hand to his forehead. During February he was reduced to silence, his inner torment expressed only by the burning orbs of his eyes. After falling into a semi-coma, he is said to have rallied on the evening of 3 March and received extreme unction, after which his family, including the 8-year-old Zoraïde, heard a long groan in which they believed they could discern his final words: 'And now for the afterlife, on to Egypt, on to Thebes!' He died around four o'clock in the morning the following day.

The cause of Champollion's premature death at the age of 41 was never exactly established, because Champollion-Figeac refused to allow a post-mortem. It was certainly not cholera, which was then ravaging Paris. More likely was a disease contracted in Egypt, perhaps from drinking the infected waters of the Nile. Several Europeans of Champollion's time died prematurely after living in Egypt, including L'Hôte (aged 37), Salt (aged 42), Rosellini (aged 43) and Lenormant (aged 57). What seems virtually certain is that Champollion's death was accelerated by exhaustion brought on by overwork, especially during his travels in Egypt.

His coffin rested at the church of Saint-Roch, where as a student Champollion had learnt Coptic from a priest. Then, on 6 March – which happened to be the holiday of Mardi Gras – it was borne to the famous cemetery of Père Lachaise by its pallbearers, the count of Forbin, Silvestre de Sacy, Alexander von Humboldt and François Arago. The coffin was accompanied by Champollion's family, members of his Egyptian expedition, friends and no doubt some detractors, plus an immense crowd of Parisians, to whom his death had come as a shock. There, Champollion was laid to rest near the grave of Joseph Fourier, who had introduced him to ancient Egypt, in a grave that was in due course marked with an obelisk. Its sandstone carries the simple inscription: 'Champollion le Jeune'.

Of the many contemporary comments on his passing, perhaps the most fitting was that of the writer and diplomat François-René de Chateaubriand, who had known Champollion personally. In a letter to Champollion-Figeac, he wrote: 'The admirable works of your brother, clarified by your own light, will last as long as the monuments that he came to explain to us.' Chateaubriand was, however, ahead of his time in this verdict. It would require several decades of debate before the world of Egyptology would generally accept this assessment of Jean-François Champollion and come to regard him as its true founding father.

Champollion's grave at Père Lachaise cemetery, Paris.

XVI

THE HIEROGLYPHS
AFTER CHAMPOLLION

A man has departed: his corpse is in the ground.
His contemporaries have passed from the land.
But writing will preserve his memory
In the mouth of a person who speaks it.
A book is better than a built house,
Better than the tombs constructed in the West.
It is more beautiful than a well-built villa,
More beautiful than a stela in a temple.

(lines from a 19th-dynasty Egyptian papyrus,
exhorting the reader to become a scribe, *c.* 1190 BC)

Founders of a new field of science, such as Galileo Galilei, Isaac Newton, Charles Darwin, Louis Pasteur, Albert Einstein and Francis Crick, have tended to lead long lives, lasting into their late sixties or beyond, during which they published prolifically and defended their original and controversial works against criticism, in the process acquiring both faithful supporters and persistent critics. Champollion's early demise in March 1832 left both his own reputation and that of the nascent field of Egyptology in an uncertain state: he had hardly any truly knowledgeable supporters, even in France, yet plenty of critics and many personal detractors, such as Jomard, Klaproth and Seyffarth, who did not let up in their attacks. Few of Champollion's discoveries had been published since the appearance of the second edition of his *Précis du système hiéroglyphique des anciens Égyptiens* in 1828; indeed, a large part of what he discovered in Egypt in 1828–29 would remain buried in his papers for decades after his death, to be appreciated only by later generations. Moreover, some of Champollion's thinking about the hieroglyphic writing system was inchoate or erroneous, as he himself perceived; without doubt, he would have developed, corrected and refined it, had he survived for another decade or two. Furthermore, he left behind no pupil whom he had systematically trained – not even the excellent Rosellini in Florence, and definitely not his devoted brother, Champollion-Figeac, for all the latter's years of immersion in the world of ancient Egyptian studies. Thus, in 1832, there was a real possibility that Champollion's system of decipherment would be still-born, never to be understood widely and applied by others.

Champollion's old teacher de Sacy could see this. When in August 1833 de Sacy – now permanent secretary of the Academy of Inscriptions after the death of Dacier – delivered a eulogy for Champollion, he extravagantly praised the character of the deceased and paid tribute to the 'genius' of Champollion's work, but expressed concern for its future. De Sacy's hope, he said, was that the decipherment, rather than being interred with Champollion, would give birth to worthy scholars, who would cultivate the field that he had cleared through their judicious weeding, pruning and planting. Ever the cautious scholar himself, he remarked:

We do not wish to say that there will be nothing to modify in the numerous applications of his system made by Champollion; nor do we pretend to assert that he could never be mistaken in his readings or in his interpretations of some signs or of some words. That will be for those who enter into the same career and follow up what he has done in good faith and with his habitual sincerity; and of course it will not be among those who attach themselves to his best discoveries and bring to fruition that which jealous Time deprived him of, that his memory will find its detractors.

Yet being himself a former detractor, never completely reformed, de Sacy could not help but enter the following reservation about Champollion's work, with a rhetorical flourish at the tomb paintings in the Valley of the Kings: 'The debate continues, as if the death of the decipherer was nothing more than the temporary crossing of the kingdom of the underworld, in anticipation of the rebirth of the sun.'

De Sacy was in a good position to make such an astute judgment. Some months before the eulogy, he had sat on an official commission appointed by the French government to consider whether it should buy Champollion's papers for the nation, at the urging of Champollion-Figeac. De Sacy had been flabbergasted at the extent of Champollion's research, and by its characteristic leaps of intuition, which he simultaneously envied and disapproved of. In April 1833, at the commission's recommendation, the government had finally agreed to pay 50,000 francs for the papers and a pension of 3,000 francs to Champollion's widow and young daughter, who had been left without financial support. Publication of the papers would remain under the control of Champollion's elder brother, but the papers themselves would be deposited in the National Library in Paris, where Champollion-Figeac, conveniently enough, was now curator of manuscripts. Today, Champollion's enormous mass of drawings and notes comprises 88 volumes in the library.

As editor of his late brother's work, Champollion-Figeac started with the simplest task: the publication of Champollion's letters written during his Egyptian expedition in 1828–29, which appeared in 1833. (Bowdlerized of sensitive passages, the letters reappeared in a second edition in 1868, the year after Champollion-Figeac's death, with the permission of Champollion's daughter, Zoraïde Chéronnet-Champollion.) Then, in 1835, having rejected joint publication with Rosellini of the expedition's drawings and notes, Champollion-Figeac began to publish the four folio volumes of the *Monuments de l'Égypte et de la Nubie*, which continued to appear until 1845. He abandoned the scheme outlined by Champollion and Rosellini in their prospectus of 1831, following their last meeting in Paris: to group the plates by theme, and include joint notes by Champollion and Rosellini. Instead, Champollion-Figeac organized the plates by locality, beginning with the monuments of the second cataract of the Nile and concluding with those of the delta, which were reproduced with field notes exactly as written by Champollion. The published result was certainly elephantine and magnificent, but was not considered of great scholarly value to Egyptologists, either then or now.

After the first volume of *Monuments de l'Égypte et de la Nubie* came the publication in 1836 of Champollion's almost completed deathbed project, his Egyptian grammar. Entitled *Grammaire égyptienne, ou Principes généraux de la langue sacrée égyptienne appliquée à la représentation de la langue parlée* ('Egyptian Grammar or General Principles of the Egyptian Sacred Language as Applied to the Representation of the Spoken Language'), it was published exactly as it stood in the manuscript, and dedicated by Champollion-Figeac to de Sacy. Then followed the much more challenging, far-from-complete manuscript of Champollion's Egyptian hieroglyphic dictionary, *Dictionnaire égyptien en écriture hiéroglyphique*, which Champollion-Figeac published in parts in 1841–43. Finally, he attempted to publish Champollion's notebooks in the form of *Notices descriptives*, in which the Egyptian monuments were described from the point of view of a student of the inscriptions. But, after criticism from experts, Champollion-Figeac abandoned this plan in 1848, and the project lapsed until it was taken up by the Egyptologist Gaston Maspero and published in 1870–89, half a century or so after Champollion's death.

Champollion-Figeac faced severe editorial difficulties. The gravest of these involved theft. Immediately after Champollion had died, some of his manuscripts were found to be missing, most obviously the first thirty-eight pages of the hieroglyphic dictionary and their accompanying drawings, dealing with the Egyptian calendar, that Champollion had made public in the form of a lecture at the Academy of Inscriptions in 1831. Champollion-Figeac's suspicions focused on a young Italian scholar of Oriental languages called Francesco Salvolini, a graduate of Bologna University, who had been strongly recommended to Champollion as a student by his old friend at Turin, the Abbé Gazzera. During the last year of Champollion's life, Salvolini enjoyed his teacher's trust and had access to all of his manuscripts. After 1832, he published some of this previously unseen research under his own name, but naturally denied any plagiarism when challenged and even went as far as to support public appeals by de Sacy and Champollion-Figeac for the return of the missing manuscripts. Although the scandal became public in Salvolini's lifetime, his villainy was proved only after his premature death in Paris in 1838, when his family in Italy wished to sell his papers through a French artist friend of Salvolini. The friend, acting in good faith, happened to

Title page of the artistic record of Champollion's expedition to Egypt, published by his brother in 1835–45.

ask Lenormant, Champollion's expedition member in Egypt, for advice on the manuscripts, and Lenormant immediately recognized Champollion's handwriting. The stolen manuscripts were returned to Champollion-Figeac, who commented on their disappearance in the preface to the published dictionary, without naming the deceased Salvolini:

In the month of March 1832, my brother left us. Soon after this I realized that, as a result of disastrous advice and deadly passions, most of the sheets and most of the cards of the Dictionary had been removed. Against all expectation, 329 sheets and a very large number of cards were recovered in 1840, and this restitution authorizes me to think I possess almost all of the two autograph compilations of the Dictionary.

Further editorial difficulties for Champollion-Figeac arose from his brother's own work. The *Grammar* set out Champollion's theory and classification of hieroglyphic signs, with their values and their equivalents in hieratic; in addition, it showed how the different parts of speech, including verb conjugations and noun declensions, were represented in hieroglyphic signs, with illustrative phrases taken from the monuments. 'But though complete in design and marvellously rich in material, inconsistencies in detail and one or two notes for unfilled headings show how far it was from satisfying the author's ideals when the pen fell from his skilful hand and his teeming brain could no longer find expression,' wrote the Egyptologist Francis Llewellyn Griffith in 1922, on the centenary of Champollion's *Lettre à M. Dacier*.

With the unfinished *Dictionary*, on the other hand, the intractable problem for Champollion had been how to arrange the hieroglyphic words – a similar problem to that still faced by makers of Chinese character dictionaries. A purely phonetic classification of the words – such as that used in a French dictionary, based on the French alphabet – was obviously a non-starter for the Egyptian hieroglyphs. Broadly speaking, therefore, the issue was whether the hieroglyphs should be classified according to the initial sign of a word (which might be a phonetic sign, a conceptual sign, or a sign that could be both phonetic and conceptual, depending on context) or, alternatively, according to the word's meaning (for example, as part of a group of words all associated with the general meaning 'water').

Since there were no ancient Egyptian dictionaries available to Champollion to guide his decision, and no evidence about dictionary word order in the works of classical writers on the Egyptian scripts, he decided to favour neither a classification based on the initial sign nor one based on meaning, but instead a classification of his own devising. He chose a modification of the order used in Coptic vocabularies, on the grounds that the Copts must have used a word order based on one created by their ancient Egyptian ancestors. Champollion called his method a 'natural classification', because he grouped his hieroglyphic words into sections based on figures of men, parts of the human body, animals, birds, fish, reptiles, vegetables, plants, and so on. To quote Champollion-Figeac's preface to the *Dictionary*:

In the general order of the divisions, the characters are placed according to the order of merit of the object that they represent; heaven before the stars, which appear therein; man before all other animated creatures; the products of the divine creation before the products of human invention; plants before objects of art and fantastic emblems. Finally, the whole before the parts, and these even in a certain order or relative pre-eminence, which is regulated by the customs or opinions of the world.

Such an arrangement does not sound easy to use; nor was it – especially for new students of the hieroglyphs. This drawback, combined with the fact that many of the translations were inevitably tentative and conjectural, meant that Champollion's dictionary was not a success. In fact, key Egyptologists who followed Champollion in the 19th century, such as Karl Richard Lepsius, Edward Hincks, Samuel Birch, Peter le Page Renouf, Ernest A. Wallis Budge and Francis Llewellyn Griffith, rejected Champollion's dictionary as a working tool, while admiring it as a fine monument to its author's research and learning, which might be quarried by the already knowledgeable researcher. The problem of how best to arrange Egyptian hieroglyphic dictionaries for easy access remains tricky to this day, because of the script's complexity.

Another weakness in both the *Grammar* and the *Dictionary* arose from Champollion's employment of Coptic. Ever since he had been a student in Paris in 1807, as we know, Champollion had been convinced that Coptic was by far the most important clue to the language of the ancient Egyptians. The phonetic transcripts of hieroglyphic groups in these two reference works were therefore written in the Coptic alphabet, which suggested that they were intended to represent Coptic words.

But this overlooked two major difficulties with Coptic. First, Champollion oversimplified the connection between the ancient Egyptian language and the Coptic language. 'In reality Coptic is a remote derivative from ancient Egyptian, like French from Latin; in some cases, therefore, Champollion's provisional transcripts produced good Coptic words, while mostly they were more or less meaningless or impossible, and in transcribing phrases either Coptic syntax was hopelessly violated or the order of hieroglyphic words had to be inverted,' observed Griffith: 'This was all very baffling and misleading.' Second, the Coptic script, being written in a form of the Greek alphabet, imposed the sounds of the Greek alphabet onto written Egyptian, which was inappropriate, especially for the earlier stages of the hieroglyphs (which of course predated Greek). A more satisfactory basis for the sounds represented by the hieroglyphs, ignored by Champollion, would probably have been the signs used to write the Semitic languages of the Middle East, notably Hebrew and Arabic – a connection first suggested by Hincks in the 1840s and subsequently accepted by most Egyptologists during the 19th century.

Other serious weaknesses in Champollion's decipherment concerned his classification of hieroglyphic signs into classes and his choice of phonetic hieroglyphic signs. 'In addition to the defects which exist in his classifications, Champollion committed many errors in respect to particular characters: he placed some in wrong classes with respect to their powers; he marked some that were in use in early times as not being so; and he omitted marking many that were certainly not in use till the low [late] epoch, if, indeed, they were ever in use at all,' wrote Hincks in an important critique of 1847. He continued: 'His alphabet was thus in every point of view defective; and though highly creditable to him as a first attempt, is quite unworthy of the present state of hieroglyphical knowledge, and unfit to be even made the basis of a more perfect arrangement.' Indeed, the sounds in the current model of the hieroglyphic alphabet, as we shall see, are based not on the vowels and consonants of Coptic, both of which are written in the Coptic script, but to a considerable extent on the Semitic languages, in which consonants, but not vowels, are written.

There were at least four important defects in Champollion's analysis of the sign system. First, in his hieroglyphic alphabet of 1822 (page 163) there were far too many homophones – that is, too many different signs with the same phonetic value. To put this in another way, his system implied a confusingly large number of ways to spell a particular word in the Egyptian language. Second, Champollion had not understood that there were phonetic signs that could represent two or even three consonants rather than the single consonant given in his hieroglyphic alphabet. One example, already mentioned, is the biconsonantal sign ⋔, which stands for *ms* in the cartouche for Ramesses. Third, he was not fully aware of what is now known as a 'phonetic complement'. This is a uniconsonantal sign, or signs, added to a hieroglyphic word to emphasize or confirm its pronunciation. (The addition of 'm' to the interjection 'Hm' to make 'Hmm' is a sort of phonetic complement.) Fourth, although Champollion had understood the existence of the unpronounced signs known as determinatives – such as the already mentioned star sign added to a word as the determinative of all divisions of time (year, day, hour, and so on) – he had constrained the determinative's grammatical function too narrowly. We shall show some details of all this a little later.

The scholar who made good these omissions and launched Champollion's decipherment as a working tool was Karl Richard Lepsius, a German. Along with the somewhat older Champollion and Rosellini, Lepsius is generally regarded by Egyptologists as one of the founding trinity of their discipline. (Some, such as Leclant, would add the name of Young.) In 1873, Lepsius told Renouf: 'I was, for a certain period, when Champollion and Rosellini had departed from this life, pretty much the only one representing Egyptian philology, a thin thread of the living tradition. Now, how numerous a new generation; a broad basis is already established.'

Born in 1810, Lepsius studied Greek and Roman archaeology at three universities in Germany, completed a doctorate, and in 1833 switched to studying Egyptian in Paris, using Champollion's newly published *Grammar* to learn the language. He also lived in Italy in the 1830s, where he enjoyed close contact with Rosellini. In 1842–45, at the behest of Frederick William IV of Prussia, Lepsius led an expedition to Egypt on the model of Napoleon Bonaparte's expedition, which yielded a twelve-volume work called *Denkmäler aus Aegypten und Aethiopien* ('Monuments from Egypt and Ethiopia'). Published in 1849–59, it is still a useful source for Egyptologists. In 1865, Lepsius was appointed director of the Egyptian Museum in Berlin. The following year, he returned to Egypt to record the monuments of the eastern delta and Suez region, where he discovered an important stone inscription. The so-called Canopus Decree of Ptolemy III, dated 238 BC, was comparable with the Rosetta Stone (a slightly later decree of Ptolemy V, dated 196 BC), since the newly discovered stela also carried equivalent inscriptions in hieroglyphic, demotic and Greek. Lepsius translated the hieroglyphic portion of the Canopus Decree using Champollion's system and showed that it matched with the Greek. The discovery of the Canopus Decree effectively laid to rest any remaining doubts about the basic correctness of Champollion's work: 'only now did Champollion's decipherment become certainty, not hypothesis,' writes the present-day Egyptologist Richard Parkinson in *Cracking Codes: The Rosetta Stone and Decipherment*.

Lepsius' most significant publication, from the point of view of Champollion's decipherment, was his hundred-page *Lettre à M. le Professeur H. Rosellini sur l'alphabet hiéroglyphique*, published in Rome in 1837, the year after Champollion's posthumous *Grammar*. This densely referenced essay, bristling with examples, was the next landmark in ancient Egyptian philology, following Young's *Encyclopaedia Britannica* article, 'Egypt' (1819), and Champollion's *Lettre à M. Dacier* (1822) and *Précis du système hiéroglyphique des anciens Égyptiens* (1824).

Lepsius' letter analysed the hieroglyphs into sections entitled 'hieroglyphic alphabet', 'ideographic signs', 'phonetic signs' and, lastly, 'intermediate signs'; this latter group he subdivided into 'initial signs of special phonetic value', 'initial signs of limited phonetic value', 'ideographic signs taking the second place in a phonetic group', 'determinative signs' and 'determinative grammatical signs'. His general approach was indicated in his introduction to the hieroglyphic alphabet:

One of the greatest embarrassments for those of us who wish to familiarize ourselves with the discoveries of Champollion is undoubtedly the curious mixture of signs of a totally different nature that comprise one and the same alphabet. One asks oneself how it was possible to keep one's bearings in a script that embraced at one and the same time images, symbols and phonetic signs ...? One finds it even more strange that the same sign can sometimes change its meaning, and one is terrified by a purely phonetic alphabet of more than 200 letters, representing between 16 and 20 articulations of the spoken language ...

I think that one can answer this objection in a manner worthy of science, by making clear, through a reasoned analysis, that the set of these signs, though diverse, is not at all an arbitrary and confusing assemblage, nor is it the premeditated choice of an inventor who could not imagine a simpler way, but that it is in fact an organism, that is to say a whole, motivated by both reality and necessity, as with any organism that develops itself over time, according to internal and immutable laws. One needs only to break down an organism, to anatomize it while researching the relationships between all its details, to convince oneself of its existence and at the same time to understand that it is possible for us to comprehend an organism.

Though replete with respect for Champollion's achievement, Lepsius' letter of 1837 discreetly modified the founder's system as set out in his *Grammar*, by correcting the four defects mentioned earlier and making other improvements, such as emphasizing the fact that the ancient Egyptians did not write vowels – another point on which Champollion had not been entirely correct. For instance, Lepsius reduced Champollion's gallimaufry of more than two hundred 'phonetic hieroglyphs' in the version of his hieroglyphic alphabet published in the *Grammar* to a mere thirty or so letters that Lepsius chose to call a 'general phonetic alphabet'. And he introduced the concept of the 'phonetic complement' and the idea of biconsonantal and triconsonantal hieroglyphs, without actually using these modern terms.

The so-called 'hieroglyphic alphabet', being a construct of modern Egyptologists rather than a historic formulation devised by ancient Egyptians, changed again after Lepsius' *Lettre à M. le Professeur H. Rosellini*. In its modern version, learned by all beginners in Egyptology, it comprises twenty-four uniconsonantal signs – six fewer than Lepsius' version. It was formulated in the 1870s by another German Egyptologist, Heinrich Brugsch, while he was compiling his own hieroglyphic and demotic dictionary, which appeared in seven volumes in 1867–82. For the order of the twenty-four letters, Brugsch created an entirely artificial arrangement that groups similar-sounding consonants together and omits vowels; and for the sounds of the letters he adopted Semitic parallels, as suggested by Hincks, rather than the Coptic parallels favoured by Champollion. John Ray, a present-day Egyptologist, does his best to explain this fairly complex, and not entirely satisfactory, situation:

[The] hieroglyphic signs for the vulture (nowadays transliterated and normally pronounced as a short a), *the outstretched arm* ⌐ *and the reed-leaf* ⟨ *are not vowels, as the use of Coptic and our general habit of convenience would suggest, but are consonants, and are the exact equivalents of Semitic aleph, 'ayin and yod. Similarly, Coptic hides most of the differences between the various aspirates of Egyptian; thanks to the use of Arabic equivalents, Hincks was able to restore these, and other, missing sounds. The beginner, confronted with four kinds of Egyptian*

h *and three of* s, *together with a host of unfamiliar diacriticals, should at least be told who is to blame for this state of affairs.*

To use modern terminology, then, the hieroglyphs comprise a fairly small set of phonetic signs, representing one, two or three consonants. These are combined with hundreds of *logograms* – that is, conceptual or symbolic signs, sometimes known as ideograms, that represent whole words (from the Greek *logos*, meaning 'word'). Many of the hieroglyphic signs function both phonetically and logographically, depending on context. The boundaries are not hard and fast: hieroglyphs do not maintain caste distinctions. Moreover, with the pictograms the picture does not necessarily convey the sign's meaning. A particular pictogram may act as a logogram in one phrase and a phonetic sign in another. To repeat a comment made by Champollion in his *Précis du système hiéroglyphique des anciens Égyptiens*: 'Hieroglyphic writing is a complex system, a script all at once figurative, symbolic, and phonetic, in one and the same text, in one and the same sentence, and, I might even venture,

vulture, ꜣ (glottal stop)	horned viper, f	sieve?, ḫ	basket, k
reed-leaf, i	owl, m	animal's belly, ẖ	pot stand?, g
arm, ʿ (a)	water, n	door bolt, s	loaf of bread, t
quail chick, w	mouth, r	folded cloth, ś	tethering rope, ṯ
leg, b	reed hut, h	pool of water, š	hand, d
mat, p	twisted flax, ḥ	hill, ḳ	swimming serpent, ḏ

The 'hieroglyphic alphabet', devised by Egyptologists in the late 19th century and used today.

in one and the same word.' This ambiguity may cause headaches for decipherers and Egyptologists, but it is also part of the fascination of reading the hieroglyphic script.

To give one of the simpler examples, the 'child' pictogram 𓀔 can act either as a determinative (i.e. a logogram) for 'child' or as a biconsonantal phonetic sign for *nn*. A second, somewhat more complex, example is 𓇏, the 'sedge plant', the heraldic plant of Upper Egypt:

𓇓𓏏   *sw.t*   sedge plant

Here, 𓇏 is a logogram, with a phonetic complement ⌓ and a determinative |, which indicates that 𓇏 is functioning as a logogram.

Now compare:

𓇳𓈖𓇓   *Ḥnsw*   moon god

Here, 𓇏 is a biconsonantal sign representing *sw*, and the first two signs are uniconsonantal signs (as found in the hieroglyphic alphabet).

Coptic	name	phonetic value
Ⲁ	alpha	*a*
Ⲃ	vita	*v (b)*
Ⲅ	gamma	*g*
Ⲇ	delta	*d*
Ⲉ	epsilon	*e*
Ⲍ	zita	*z*
Ⲏ	ita	*i, e*
Ⲑ	tita	*t*
Ⲓ	iota	*i*
Ⲕ	kappa	*k*
Ⲗ	laula	*l*
Ⲙ	mi	*m*
Ⲛ	ni	*n*
Ⲝ	xi	*x*
Ⲟ	omicron	*o*
Ⲡ	pi	*p*
Ⲣ	ro	*r*
Ⲥ	sima	*s*
Ⲧ	tau	*t*
Ⲩ	ypsilon	*y, u*
Ⲫ	phi	*ph*
Ⲭ	khi	*ch, kh*
Ⲯ	psi	*ps*
Ⲱ	omega	*o*
Ⲩ	shei	*s*
ϥ	fai	*f*
Ϩ	hori	*h*
Ϫ	djandja	*g*
Ϭ	chima	*c*
Ϯ	ti	*ti*

Finally, compare:

𓇓𓏏𓈖   *n-sw.t*   king of Upper Egypt

Here, 𓇏 is both a logogram and a phonetic sign. It has been moved to the beginning of the word as a sign of respect for the royal emblem: relying only on the sign order, we would expect to read the word *sw-t-n*, rather than *n-sw.t*.

With these caveats, hieroglyphs may be classified as follows: (a) uniconsonantal signs; (b) biconsonantal signs; (c) triconsonantal signs; (d) phonetic complements; and (e) logograms, including determinatives.

As already remarked, there are some twenty-four uniconsonantal signs (depending on how variants are counted), some of which appear in the cartouches of Alexander, Cleopatra, Ptolemy and Ramesses, as discovered by Young and Champollion. The uniconsonantal signs are often referred to as an 'alphabet', despite their not including true vowels and despite the fact that their usage is not distinct from that of other kinds of hieroglyphic phonetic sign. It is instructive to compare the hieroglyphic 'alphabet' with the thirty signs that make up the Coptic alphabet, a true alphabet. In its standard (Sahidic) form, the Coptic alphabet, as mentioned earlier, consists of the twenty-four letters of the Greek alphabet plus six signs borrowed from demotic, which represent Coptic sounds not symbolized in the Greek alphabet. Vowels are represented, and no letter is pictographic, unlike in the hieroglyphic alphabet.

Here are some of the biconsonantal and triconsonantal hieroglyphs:

biconsonantal signs

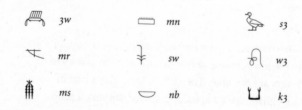

triconsonantal signs

'nḫ		ḥtp		ḫpr	
w3ḥ		nfr		sm'	

'Phonetic complementing', as already explained, means the addition of a uniconsonantal sign to a word to emphasize or confirm its pronunciation. There is no equivalent in written English, though we might imagine the addition of a special vowel sign (similar to that found in the International Phonetic Alphabet) to 'bow', so as to distinguish 'bow [and arrow]' from 'bow [one's head]'. With hieroglyphic, the usual phonetic complement is a single sign reiterating the final consonant of the main sign. Some examples are as follows:

3w	wr	nḏm
w3	b3	ḫpr
w3ḫ	mn	

But it is common to add two or even three phonetic complements:

b3	nfr	ḥtp
'nḫ	ḫpr	

'Determinatives' are logograms added to the end of phonetic signs to indicate a word's meaning and to discriminate in cases where two or more meanings are possible. The cartouche is also a sort of determinative (as, in English, is the capital letter used to mark a proper name). Many determinatives are clearly pictographic, as shown here:

lady, mistress

to go forth

old man

to be stood on one's head

to plough

The 'striking man' determinative shown in the last word is used, too, in the words for 'education' and 'taxes'! It determines words that involve forceful activity or action of some kind.

An exquisite example of determinatives is provided by the word *wn*, which consists of a biconsonantal sign ∿∿∿ and a phonetic complement, which may be combined with the following six determinatives to give six quite different meanings:

open
determinative: door

hurry
determinative: running legs

mistake
determinative: evil bird

become bald
determinative: lock of hair

Hermopolis
determinative: crossed roads

light
determinative: sun with rays

Sometimes more than one determinative is used:

cut open
determinatives: knife, force

fugitives
determinatives: legs, man, plural

The cartouche of Tutankhamun shown on page 279, from the upper part of an inlaid box found in his tomb almost exactly a hundred years after the publication of the *Lettre à M. Dacier*, demonstrates the above fundamentals of hieroglyphic writing in its combination of logograms with consonantal signs. We can read the cartouche from the top, with the help of the hieroglyphic 'alphabet'.

The single reed is a uniconsonantal sign with the value *i* (a vowel in English but a weak consonant in Egyptian).

The game board with playing pieces is a biconsonantal sign with the value *mn*.

Water is a uniconsonantal sign with the value *n*. Functioning (as here) as a phonetic complement, it reinforces the sound of *n* in *mn*.

These three signs are therefore read *imn*, which is normally pronounced *imen* or, more commonly, *amon* or *amun*. (Vowels are of course mostly absent in hieroglyphic spelling.) Amun was the god of Thebes, and regarded as the king of the gods during the New Kingdom, when Tutankhamun ruled (1333–1323 BC). Out of respect, Amun's name is placed first.

The half-circle is a uniconsonantal sign with the value *t*. It appears twice in the cartouche.

The quail chick is a uniconsonantal sign with the value *w*, a weak consonant similar to the vowel *u*.

This is the triconsonantal 'ankh' sign meaning 'life' or 'living' (which later became the 'handled' or 'eyed' cross, *crux ansata*, of the Coptic Church).

These four signs therefore read *tutankh*.

The shepherd's crook is a logogram meaning 'ruler'.

The column is a logogram for Heliopolis, a city near Cairo.

This is the heraldic sedge plant of Upper Egypt. Here it is a logogram for Upper Egypt.

'Heliopolis of Upper Egypt' is another name for the city of Thebes. So the complete cartouche reads: 'Tutankhamun, Ruler of Thebes'.

Egyptian hieroglyphic inscriptions have been described as 'boasting made permanent'. But at their finest they also exert a mysterious charm exceeding that of all other ancient scripts. The skilful integration of hieroglyphs with the objects they adorn is a quintessential feature of Egyptian writing. Another of the objects belonging to Tutankhamun is a wooden mirror case covered in gold and shaped in the form of an 'ankh'. The 'ankh' in this case is a hieroglyph with the dual meanings of 'life' and 'mirror', and also a symbol of life itself. Here is a typical ancient Egyptian ambiguity to delight both the mind and the heart of Jean-François Champollion.

Cartouche of the pharaoh Tutankhamun from an inlaid box found in his tomb in the Valley of the Kings, c. 1327 BC.

POSTSCRIPT:
GENIUSES AND POLYMATHS

A century ago, in 1906, the first – and still the most comprehensive – of Champollion's biographers, Hermine Hartleben, concluded her account with an impassioned defence of her subject against the old charge that he had plagiarized ideas from his English rival Thomas Young. Hartleben's voluminous text ran to almost 1,200 pages in the original German, yet even as late as her penultimate paragraph she felt compelled to pursue her battle with the nefarious Young. First, Hartleben quoted a polemic against Young from a lecture by the British Egyptologist Renouf, given ten years earlier at London's Society of Biblical Archaeology (*not* at the Royal Society, Young's wholly scientific former home, as Hartleben stated). 'Two undeniable facts remain after all that has been written: Champollion learnt nothing whatever from Young, nor did anyone else,' claimed an exasperated Renouf, as previously noted. Then, no doubt intentionally echoing Renouf's view, Hartleben thundered: 'One thing is sure: no intrigue, no attack will be able to inflict lasting injury on the master and on the system of decipherment that he created. His oeuvre is solid, built on rock, his honour is without blemish, his glory illuminates all countries and his disciples proclaim their filiation with ever-increasing pride.'

Ever since 1822, feelings have been excited by the stand-off between Champollion and Young. They go deeper than hoary Anglo-French antagonism and chauvinism, or the clash between Enlightenment and Romantic ideals. In the 21st century no biographer of either Champollion or Young – indeed, no one interested in Egyptology – can be indifferent to their two-centuries-old rivalry. Having written a biography of Young, I find my sympathies acutely divided. As must be plain to the reader, I salute Champollion for his self-confidence, his fanaticism for a single cause, his courage, his sense of humour and his *joie de vivre*. Young attracts me for his modesty, his wide-ranging interests, his honesty, his analytical powers and his love of moderation.

However, there is a deeper issue at stake here than simply the extremely different personalities of two extraordinary individuals, and their behaviour towards each other. The relationship between Champollion and Young has resonance beyond the 19th century and is relevant to today's intellectual world, with its propensity towards specialization and its reverence for genius.

Champollion was a specialist who sacrificed himself, literally, to the study of ancient Egypt. Young, by contrast, was of course a polymath, almost equally gifted in his studies of languages and literature, of the physical sciences and of medicine, the last of which became his profession. Champollion fits easily into the general expectation of tortured genius; Young appears more like an even-tempered all-rounder.

We have no difficulty in comprehending and respecting Champollion's dedication to a single field of study. Regarding Young's versatility, however, there is a difference of opinion. Some specialists admire and advocate it; others suspect and disparage it. In an age of narrow, and sometimes narrow-minded, specialization in academe and in the professions, unthinkable in Young's time, polymathy probably disturbs us more than it did 19th-century scholars. We are made uneasy by those who effortlessly bridge several disciplines. It is only too natural to regard them as dilettantes, or even to try to dismiss them as charlatans.

As for genius, our awe of it means that many prefer to believe more in inexplicable flashes of inspiration than in the less glamorous path of step-by-step preparatory labour. With Champollion, there is the evidence of an archetypal eureka moment, in Paris in September 1822, when he cried out to his brother: 'Je tiens mon affaire!' – and then collapsed on the floor. In his writings, Champollion generally gave the impression that his key insights came almost exclusively out of his own mind, arising from his indubitably passionate devotion to ancient Egypt. He pictured himself in the *Lettre à M. Dacier* as a scholar who solved the riddle of ancient Egypt's hieroglyphic writing single-handedly. The fact that Young was known primarily for his work in fields far removed from Egyptian studies, such as physics, and that he published his pioneering work on Egypt anonymously helped to make Champollion's solitary self-image readily believable to most observers.

In my view, the single most fascinating aspect of the story of how Egyptian hieroglyphic was deciphered is that both a polymath and a specialist were required to crack the code. Young's myriad-mindedness provided some initial insights in 1814–19 – but then his versatility obstructed him from making further progress. Champollion's single-mindedness hindered him from arriving at these insights in the same period – but once he got started his tunnel vision allowed him to begin to perceive the system behind the signs. Both Young's breadth of interests and Champollion's narrowness of focus were essential for the revolutionary breakthrough that Champollion, alone, announced in 1822–23.

NOTES AND REFERENCES

Since this book is not intended to be a full biography, only occasional notes are given, citing full references for the quotations in the text. The translations from sources in French are my own, except for the quotations from a few books and articles published in English translation, which are listed in the Bibliography.

PROLOGUE: EGYPTOMANIA

10 'singular combination' Quoted in Reeves and Wilkinson: 59. For a discussion of the influential Egyptian Hall in Piccadilly, see Curl: 260–64. It was demolished in 1905, and in 2011 its supposed statues of Isis and Osiris were languishing incongruously on either side of a lift shaft in the underground car park of the Museum of London.

11 'The first person I met' Quoted in *A New Description of Sir John Soane's Museum*: 48–49.

12 'It is the first time that hieroglyphics' Belzoni: 205–6. Young's discussion of Psammis, Psammuthis and Psammetichus appears in Young, *Miscellaneous Works*, vol. 3: 154.

14 'one of the most fascinating books' Carter and Mace, vol. 1: 68.

I HIEROGLYPHIC 'DELIRIUM' BEFORE CHAMPOLLION

16 'hieroglyphic writing, hitherto regarded' Champollion, *Précis* (1824): 249.

16 'tourists' Ray, *Reflections of Osiris*: 5–6.

18 'not built up from syllables' Quoted in Horapollo: 101.

19 'puerile' Young, *Miscellaneous Works*, vol. 3: 267.

19 'When they wish to indicate' Horapollo: 63.

20 'sometimes called the last' *Encyclopaedia Britannica*, 15th edn: entry for 'Kircher, Athanasius'.

20 'the last man who knew' Subtitle of the book by Findlen. For a discussion

of Kircher and Coptic, see Chapter 12 of Hamilton; Champollion's opinion of Kircher appears on page 218.

20 'The protection of Osiris' Quoted in Pope: 31–32.

22 'The peculiar nature' Young, *Miscellaneous Works*, vol. 3: 269.

23 '*notae phoneticae*' Pope: 58.

23 'Every relic of antiquity' Denon, vol. 2: 241–42.

24 'There appears no doubt' Quoted in Downs: 81.

24 'Taken from the French army' Leclant: 748. Downs discusses the conflicting accounts of the British acquisition of the Rosetta Stone.

27 'This decree' Quoted in Andrews: 28.

28 '[They] proceeded upon' Young, *Miscellaneous Works*, vol. 3: 270.

II A REVOLUTIONARY CHILDHOOD

31 'No genius' Quoted in Lacouture: 38.

35 'Those who had most grounds' Ballard: 18.

37 'Outbursts, renunciations' Lacouture: 53.

37 'volcanic temperament' Hartleben: 43.

38 'Wicked stick!' Quoted in Hartleben: 43.

38 'Fortunately, I was given' Quoted in Hartleben: 44.

38 'his first work of decipherment' Hartleben: 44.

39 'We can feel the yawns' Ballard: 212.

40 'If I have any regret' Quoted in Lacouture: 59.

41 'particular genius' Quoted in Hartleben: 49. For a discussion of the education

of geniuses, see my *Sudden Genius?*, especially Chapter 17.

41 'He has plenty of taste' Quoted in Lacouture: 50.

41 'very dear brother' Quoted in Lacouture: 51.

41 'Since you have confessed' Quoted in Lacouture: 52.

42 'Our house is no longer' Quoted in Hartleben: 50.

42 'I was, by turns' Quoted in Faure: 773.

III RELUCTANT SCHOOLBOY

43 'The deputy head' Quoted in Lacouture: 81–82.

43 'I am always' Champollion, *Lettres de Champollion le Jeune*, vol. 2: 183.

44 'All that is base ... a subtlety' Quoted in Lacouture: 69.

45 'pompous, cunning and venal' Lacouture: 67.

45 'His ordinary work' Quoted in Lacouture: 73.

46 'I take care to look for' Quoted in Lacouture: 73–74.

48 'chronology from Adam' Quoted in Hartleben: 58.

48 'It is without doubt rather singular' Quoted in Hartleben: 60.

49 'There is, every day, a period' Quoted in Lacouture: 77.

50 'Being too young to judge' Quoted in Hartleben: 63.

50 'Send me a little money' Quoted in Hartleben: 64.

51 'whom I have loved with my heart' Quoted in Lacouture: 85.

52 'the young J.-F. Champollion' Quoted in Hartleben: 68–69.

52 'I beg you to be so kind' Quoted in Hartleben: 66.

53 'what is known as a switchback' Lacouture: 79.

54 'In naming you' Quoted in Dewachter: 25.

IV EGYPT ENCOUNTERED

55 'I wish to make' Quoted in Lacouture: 91.

55 'No, Monsieur' Quoted in Lacouture: 92.

55 'in the autumn of 1802' Hartleben: 55.

56 'But on entering ... attain this goal.' Ibid: 55–56.

57 'He invited the boy' Buchwald and Josefowicz: 186.

58 'a fiery colt' Quoted in Buchwald and Josefowicz: 186. Fourier's English biographer, John Herivel, makes no reference to Fourier's anecdotal encounter with the boy Champollion in 1802.

58 'There is no reason that' Quoted in Lacouture: 90.

61 'the symbolic signs' Quoted in Hartleben: 71.

62 'a little treatise' Quoted in Lacouture: 93.

62 'Would you have the kindness' Quoted in Lacouture: 93.

V PARIS AND THE ROSETTA STONE

64 'You think to terrify me' Quoted in Lacouture: 124.

65 'The air of Paris' Quoted in Lacouture: 117.

65 'Here I look like a sans-culotte' Quoted in Hartleben: 95.

65 'the caverns of Ali Baba' Lacouture: 102.

66 'I think there are few' Sir William Gell in Young, *Miscellaneous Works*, vol. 3: 431–32. Gell does not name his 'very learned friend'.

66 'On Mondays' Quoted in Lacouture: 114.

68 'the most perfect' Quoted in Dewachter: 31.

69 'He began to make his salaam' Quoted in Hartleben: 81.

70 'As for M. de Sacy' Quoted in Dewachter: 29.

71 'Jomard considered him' Solé and Valbelle: 56.

72 'I do not have a great respect' Quoted in Hartleben: 117.

72 'He was a virulent polemicist' Lacouture: 125.

73 'You have read a line and a half' Quoted in Lacouture: 124.

73 'I am afraid that our efforts ... Greek text.' Quoted in Solé and Valbelle: 57.

74 'I have read a line and a half' Quoted in Lacouture: 123.

74 'The Etruscans occupy me' Quoted in Lacouture: 123.

VI TEENAGE PROFESSOR

76 'The natural tendency of the human mind' Quoted in Hartleben: 108.

76 'the cradle of his thought process' Lacouture: 145.

78 '*intellectuel engagé*' Ibid: 140.

78 'The double object of education … love themselves…' Quoted in Lacouture: 143.

78 'Sophocles and Euripides' Quoted in Hartleben: 108.

79 'One can see that our pedagogue' Faure: 147.

79 'I do not think he ought to attach himself' Quoted in Hartleben: 112.

80 'with ardour' Quoted in Hartleben: 112.

80 'The result of all that we have said' Quoted in Lacouture: 157.

81 'if these hieroglyphs did not have' Quoted in Solé and Valbelle: 59.

81 'abbreviated symbols' Quoted in Lacouture: 155.

84 'the ape-head lid is slightly blackened' Adkins and Adkins: 103.

84 'In the bain-marie' Quoted in Hartleben: 121.

85 'I am always working' Quoted in Lacouture: 161.

85 'In the hieroglyphs, there are two sorts' Quoted in Solé and Valbelle: 60.

85 'It is my conviction' Quoted in Lacouture: 161.

86 'The first step to be taken' Quoted in Solé and Valbelle: 61.

88 'a terrible pleasure' Quoted in Lacouture: 64.

88 'above all in the least well-lit streets' Hartleben: 136.

88 'I do not recognize you' Quoted in Lacouture: 165.

VII THE RACE BEGINS

89 'M. Silvestre de Sacy, my former professor' Quoted in Young, *Miscellaneous Works*, vol. 3: 66.

90 'In France we hardly know' Faure: 192.

91 'was to light what Joseph Fourier was' Lacouture: 267. Like Lacouture, the Egyptologist Christian Jacq stereotypes Young's English background and character in his novel *Champollion the Egyptian*, supplying Young with a non-existent aristocratic niece, 'Lady Ophelia Redgrave', who travels to Egypt and shadows Champollion as a spy and would-be lover.

91 'passed through life' Ibid: 273.

93 'fortunately for our subject' Ray, 'The name of the first'.

93 'could not bear' Gurney: 46.

93 'for employing some poor Italian' Quoted in Peacock: 451.

94 'your Society' Quoted in Young, *Miscellaneous Works*, vol. 3: 63.

95 'conjectural translation' Young, *Miscellaneous Works*, vol. 3: 16.

95 'in which he asserted' Ibid: 264.

95 'my Egyptian researches began' Ibid: 264.

96 'those who have not been in the habit' Ibid: 612.

98 'It is impossible to form' Peacock: 281.

99 'striking resemblance' Young, *Miscellaneous Works*, vol. 3: 54.

99 'I discovered, at length' Ibid: 275.

100 'I am not surprised that' Ibid: 53.

100 'it seemed natural to suppose' Ibid: 133.

101 'it is impossible that all the characters' Ibid: 55–56.

VIII NAPOLEON AND CHAMPOLLION

103 'There is no law of succession' Quoted in Hartleben: 142.

103 'I certainly have more confidence' Quoted in Young, *Miscellaneous Works*, vol. 3: 17.

103 'That is how men are' Quoted in Hartleben: 131.

104 'If I might venture to advise you' Quoted in Young, *Miscellaneous Works*, vol. 3: 51. This notorious advice by de Sacy is not referred to by Solé and Valbelle in their account of the hieroglyphic decipherment – presumably because it would not reflect well on either de Sacy or Champollion.

104 'I do not intend to speak further' Quoted in Young, *Miscellaneous Works*, vol. 3: 59.

105 'Long live the Emperor' J. J. Champollion-Figeac, *Fourier et Napoléon*: 205. Champollion himself never wrote about his personal encounter with Napoleon, even in his letters.

106 'In a career conducted' Lacouture: 173.

106 'It's a good sign' J. J. Champollion-Figeac, *Fourier et Napoléon*: 216–17.

106 'He got up, came towards me' Ibid: 217–18.

107 'This word made a visible impression' Ibid: 229.

107 'They had been working on that' Ibid: 230.

107 'Bring it all to Paris' Ibid: 232.

108 'balance sheet of advantages' Ibid: 310–11.

108 'The prevailing atmosphere' Price: 83.

109 '1. The certainty of a solid' Quoted in Lacouture: 188.

110 'M. Blanc has always said' Ibid.

110 'dangerous men ... knowledge' Quoted in Lacouture: 190.

110 'where the name of Bonaparte' Quoted in Lacouture: 191.

111 'Messieurs Champollion are both remarkable' Quoted in Lacouture: 193.

IX EXILE AND REVOLT

113 'Perhaps one day, the capture' Quoted in Aimé Champollion-Figeac: 53. For a discussion of this incident, see Faure: 406.

114 'I have not a single letter' Quoted in Lacouture: 198.

115 'One finds scarcely four or five people' Quoted in Lacouture: 202.

115 'I am a *Dauphinois*' Quoted in Lacouture: 201.

115 'foolishly sleepy' Quoted in Faure: 282.

116 'not a single danger' Quoted in Lacouture: 196–97.

117 'several inhabitants' Quoted in Lacouture: 211.

118 'As for the Rabbi' Quoted in Lacouture: 213.

118 'Provided he eats' Quoted in Lacouture: 215.

119 'It will not be enough for them' Quoted in Lacouture: 216.

119 'The departure of my brother has' Quoted in Faure: 295.

120 'It gives me as much credit' Quoted in Lacouture: 216.

121 'he certainly has picked out' Quoted in Peacock: 264.

121 'my ex-cabinet' Quoted in Lacouture: 217.

123 'I would rather be the first' Quoted in Faure: 343.

123 'During this period of reflection' Solé and Valbelle: 76.

125 'The square block and the semicircle' Young, *Miscellaneous Works*, vol. 3: 156–57.

126 'In all he was able to equate' Andrews: 15. For a sign-by-sign critical assessment of Young's vocabulary, see Sottas's preface to the centenary edition of the *Lettre à M. Dacier*: 12–15.

126 'mixed up with many false conclusions' Griffith: 65.

128 'I have the satisfaction' Belzoni: 205.

137 'The Englishman knows' Champollion, *Champollion inconnu*: 65. Unfortunately, no date is given for Champollion's letter to his brother.

137 'is no more than a simple modification' Quoted in Solé and Valbelle: 76. Strange to say, given the history of Champollion's 1821 publication, even the British Library's copy has gone missing, despite an exhaustive search by the curator in charge of early printed books in French during the research for my book.

138 'striking resemblance' Quoted in Young, *Miscellaneous Works*, vol. 3: 54.

138 'imitations of the hieroglyphics' Ibid: 54.

138 'disastrous' Hartleben: 186.

140 'I would like to give myself up' Quoted in Hartleben: 179.

141 'Pitiless fate has arrested me' Quoted in Hartleben: 192.

X BREAKTHROUGH

142 'Hieroglyphic writing is a complex system' Champollion, *Précis* (1824): 327.

144 'I hope it is not too rash' Champollion, *Lettre à M. Dacier*: 1; Champollion, *Précis* (1828): 41.

145 'Today Champollion *le jeune*' Aimé Champollion-Figeac: 78.

146 'Had he been candid enough' Hincks, 'An attempt to ascertain': 134.

146 'No one could learn anything' Renouf, 'Young and Champollion': 196. Renouf, unlike his more distinguished and original friend Edward Hincks, was consistently dismissive of Young's contribution to the hieroglyphic decipherment from the beginning of his Egyptological career in the 1850s. However, he was provoked into writing his 1896 polemic, 'Young and Champollion', not by Young's own writings but by the strong support for Young against Champollion of the controversial and prolific Egyptologist E. A. Wallis Budge in an essay on the Rosetta Stone that Budge published in 1893 in his anthology *The Mummy*. Renouf's polemic attacks, and even quotes from, Budge's essay, without ever naming Budge. His long-standing personal contempt for Budge, arising from his dealings with him as a colleague at the British Museum (where Renouf was keeper of Oriental antiquities from 1886 until his forced retirement in 1891), and his *ad hominem* motive for writing 'Young and Champollion', are explicit in Renouf's bitter last letter before his death in 1897, written to a fellow scholar Karl F. Piehl. Here Renouf calls Budge a 'despicable scoundrel who has dared to repeat the ancient calumnies against Champollion', and lists the reasons why Budge should be regarded as a charlatan and a plagiarist in his Egyptological work. (See *The Letters of Peter le Page Renouf*, vol. 4: 375–76.) Although Renouf scored a number of palpable hits against Young in his polemic, he was himself guilty of distorting the historical evidence in order to acquit Champollion of plagiarism, partly as a result of his animus against Budge and also because he apparently suffered from a specialist's prejudice against a polymath. Nonetheless, anyone interested in the debate over Young versus Champollion should carefully read Renouf's essay and make up his or her own mind on the basis of the evidence Renouf actually presents rather than his concealed personal motives.

146 'Two undeniable facts' Ibid: 208.

146 'Even if one allows that Champollion' Parkinson, *Rosetta Stone*: 44.

147 'M. *le docteur* Young has done in England' Champollion, *Lettre à M. Dacier*: 16.

147 'I must say that in the same period' Champollion, *Précis* (1824): 17.

147 'in 1821' Ibid: 21.

147 'a little after my arrival in Paris' Quoted by Sottas in his preface to Champollion, *Lettre à M. Dacier*: 47. Sottas's 1922 preface is the most balanced appraisal of Young versus Champollion written by a Frenchman.

148 'I recognize that he was the first' Champollion, *Précis* (1824): 7–8 (translated in Parkinson, *Cracking Codes*: 40).

149 'something like a hieroglyphic alphabet' Young, *Miscellaneous Works*, vol. 3: 182.

150 'as I had not leisure' Ibid: 296. The brief publication of the Philae obelisk by Bankes is entitled *Geometrical Elevation of an Obelisk … from the island of Philae, together with the pedestal … first discovered there by W. J. Bankes … in 1815: at whose suggestion & expense, both have been since removed … for the purpose of being erected at Kingston Hall in Dorsetshire* (London: John Murray, 1821). There is a copy in the British Library.

155 '*Le Zodiaque de Paris*' For a detailed discussion of the Dendera Zodiac, see Buchwald and Josefowicz.

159 'Je tiens mon affaire!' Quoted in Aimé Champollion-Figeac: 57. Another version of the story has 'Je tiens l'affaire!'.

159 'Fresnel, a young mathematician' Quoted in Peacock: 321–22.

161 'I did certainly expect' Young, *Miscellaneous Works*, vol. 3: 292.

161 'The hieroglyphical text of the inscription of Rosetta' Quoted in Young, *Miscellaneous Works*, vol. 3: 292–93.

162 'This course of investigation' Young, *Miscellaneous Works*, vol. 3: 293–94.

164 'I shall never consent to recognize' Quoted in Young, *Miscellaneous Works*, vol. 3: 256.

164 'Nothing can exceed' Footnote in Young, *Miscellaneous Works*, vol. 3: 255. Although Leitch excoriates Champollion in parts of his edition of Young's papers, he also praises him highly for his later work and does not appear to have been motivated by anything other than his respect for Young's work.

164 '[that] the further he advances' Young, *Miscellaneous Works*, vol. 3: 299.

165 'to *nothing*' Champollion, *Précis* (1824): 38.

165 'I wish he would have the decency' Quoted in Young, *Miscellaneous Works*, vol. 3: 462.

166 'the phonetic writing existed in Egypt' Champollion, *Lettre à M. Dacier*: 41–42.

166 'tradition' Hartleben (1906): 400. Among scholars of the hieroglyphic decipherment, Hartleben's 'tradition' is followed by, for example, Solé and Valbelle in *The Rosetta Stone* and by Parkinson in *Cracking Codes*, but not by Sottas in his preface to the centenary edition of the *Lettre à M. Dacier* or by Pope in *The Story of Decipherment*. Indeed, Sottas specifically notes (page 48) that Hartleben's date, 21 Dec. 1821, and her other dates from this crucial period of Champollion's life, 1821–22, must be treated with caution in the absence of reliable documentary evidence. Champollion's letter of 9 Jan. 1823 to Young about his latest discoveries of the names of pharaohs appears in Young, *Miscellaneous Works*, vol. 3: 249–51.

167 'The fourteen partially damaged lines' Champollion, *Précis* (1824): 266–67.

167 'The publication of his letter to Dacier' Hartleben: 241.

168 'King Louis XVIII to M. Champollion' Quoted in Hartleben: 243.

XI AN EGYPTIAN RENAISSANCE

169 'On entering this room' Champollion, *Lettres de Champollion le Jeune*, vol. 1: 84–85.

169 'For me, the road to Memphis' Quoted by Hartleben in her introduction to Champollion, *Lettres de Champollion le Jeune*, vol. 1: vi.

171 'M. Champollion, who, in speaking to me' Quoted in Young, *Miscellaneous Works*, vol. 3: 391.

171 'the daughter of her father' Quoted in Hartleben: 270.

171 'marked out on the hillsides' Quoted in Hartleben: 271.

173 'the struggle of a Pygmy' Quoted by Hartleben in Champollion, *Lettres de Champollion le Jeune*, vol. 1: 13.

175 'You are, without doubt' Champollion, *Lettres de Champollion le Jeune*, vol. 1: 20–21.

176 'In these remains, so fragile' Ibid: 85–86.

177 'The most important papyrus' Ibid: 87.

177 'I confess that' Ibid: 90.

178 'beautiful yellow costume' Ibid: 114–15.

180 'It is better to be the first' Quoted in Lacouture: 346.

180 'we are wretches, in France' Champollion, *Lettres de Champollion le Jeune*, vol. 1: 184.

180 'He gave me news' Ibid: 186.

181 'the first lively city' Ibid: 194.

181 'From a certain distance' Ibid: 198–99.

182 'a beautiful, great and good service' Quoted in Champollion, *Lettres de Champollion le Jeune*, vol. 1: 227.

182 'two ladies would not agree' Quoted in Hartleben: 309.

182 'the only city in Italy' Champollion, *Lettres de Champollion le Jeune*, vol. 1: 235.

184 'I was no sooner taken into his friendship' Quoted by Franco Serino in Rosellini: 9.

184 'excellent heart and well-furnished head' Champollion, *Lettres de Champollion le Jeune*, vol. 1: 308.

XII CURATOR AT THE LOUVRE

187 'Collections of Egyptian monuments' Quoted in Lacouture: 387.

189 'It is the pomp, then, of the Egyptians' Denon, vol. 2: 63.

189 'in spite of Paris and her pomp' Champollion, *Lettres de Champollion le Jeune*, vol. 1: 408–9.

190 'I have a magnificent' Ibid: 411–12.

191 'the brother of your Stuffed King' Ibid: 421.

191 'it includes Egyptian jewels' Ibid: 421.

192 'Egyptian antiquities in Egyptian rooms' Quoted in Hartleben: 353.

201 'Contrary to all the received wisdom' Hartleben: 373.

202 'colonie Grenobloise' Quoted in Hartleben: 351.

202 'like true sisters' Hartleben: 351.

202 'as a beautiful gift' Ibid: 351.

203 'You write that from time to time' Quoted in Young, *Miscellaneous Works*, vol. 3: 423–24.

203 'has shown me far more attention' Quoted in Robinson, *The Last Man Who Knew Everything*: 230.

203 'kindness and liberality' Young, *Miscellaneous Works*, vol. 3: 469.

204 '30 years ago' 'Advertisement' in Young, *Rudiments of an Egyptian Dictionary*: vii.

204 'Young was the first person' Ray, 'The name of the first'.

204 'I am leaving on a voyage' Champollion, *Lettres de Champollion le Jeune*, vol. 2: 7.

XIII TO EGYPT, AT LAST

205 'The dog in Egypt' Champollion, *Lettres de Champollion le Jeune*, vol. 2: 26–27.

206 'the new knowledge acquired' Quoted in Lacouture: 396.

207 'Between 1810 and 1828' Usick: 101.

209 'There reigns in Egypt' Champollion, *Lettres de Champollion le Jeune*, vol. 2: 1–2.

210 'It is the hand of Amun' Ibid: 41.

210 'types of odes or litanies' Ibid: 11–12.

211 'The rediscovery of ancient Egyptian literature' Parkinson, *The Tale of Sinuhe*: 2. 'The Teaching of King Amenemhat' is discussed and translated on pages 203–11 of Parkinson's book.

212 'Preceded by two janissaries' Champollion, *Lettres de Champollion le Jeune*, vol. 2: 21.

213 'There is enough of the old Egypt' Ibid: 86. The complete text of Champollion's Egyptian journal, annotated by the Egyptologist Diane Harlé, with historical illustrations by expedition artists and others, and contemporary photographs by Hervé Champollion, appears in the magnificent *L'Égypte de Jean-François Champollion: Lettres & journaux de voyage (1828–29)*.

215 'Good day, Citizen' Ibid: 27.

215 'A quick examination' Ibid: 27–28.

217 'skills and generosity' Ridley: 157.

217 'So we shall sail under the auspices' Champollion, *Lettres de Champollion le Jeune*, vol. 2: 47.

219 'Thanks to the Thoulounid dynasty' Ibid: 85.

219 'in the tone with which Blue-Beard' Ibid: 78.

220 'Any impartial man' Ibid: 103.

220 'We managed to climb the mountain' Ibid: 107.

221 'The star is the *determinative*' Ibid: 117.

221 'grand discovery' Hincks, 'An attempt to ascertain': 134.

221 'probably his greatest single achievement' Ray, *Rosetta Stone*: 90.

223 'Man proposes' Champollion, *Lettres de Champollion le Jeune*, vol. 2: 130.

223 'The animals, quadrupeds, birds and fishes' Ibid: 132.

224 'a walking mummy' Ibid: 152.

224 'united grace and majesty' Ibid: 153.

224 'Don't laugh' Ibid: 154.

XIV IN SEARCH OF RAMESSES

226 'The great temple of Ibsamboul' Champollion, *Lettres de Champollion le Jeune*, vol. 2: 177.

227 'the situation of Thebes' Denon, vol. 1: 215.

227 'marvel after marvel … the old Egyptians' Champollion, *Lettres de Champollion le Jeune*, vol. 2: 158–61.

230 'As for me, at five in the afternoon' Ibid: 171.

231 'I do not know whether there is some malicious genie' Ibid: 140.

233 'After two and a half hours of admiration' Ibid: 177–78.

234 'I am proud now' Ibid: 181.

235 'The food was delicious' Ibid: 188.

236 'This seems to me to demonstrate' Ibid: 221.

236 'I could not help but feel' Ibid: 201.

236 'I felt a keen pleasure' Ibid: 188.

237 'Remember that I am a thousand leagues' Ibid: 243.

237 'I bid them adieu' Ibid: 208.

238 'It is King Ramesses' Ibid: 246.
239 'the most celebrated and finest' Ibid: 308.
239 'I felt a burning desire' Ibid: 303.
239 'So the poor Dr Young' Ibid: 249–50.
240 'no longer ran the risk' Lacouture: 429.
241 'Absolute silence is necessary' Champollion, *Lettres de Champollion le Jeune*, vol. 2: 398.
242 'The general sense of this composition' Ibid: 285.
242 'This double series of tableaux' Ibid: 291.
243 'drawn by love of science' Ibid: 307. Champollion's and Rosellini's 'vandalism' of the tomb of Seti I is discussed in Thompson: 360.
245 'A single column' Ibid: 387.
246 'almost like a monk' Ibid: 403.
246 'In the midst of tamarinds' Quoted in Lacouture: 442.
246 'The inundation this year' Champollions, *Lettres de Champollion le Jeune*, vol. 2: 403–4.
248 'about 6000 years' Ibid: 429.
248 'So was Ramesses really the greatest' Ibid: 422. For a discussion of Muhammad Ali, see Mansel, 'The man who remade Alexandria'.
248 'I have amassed' Ibid: 456.

XV FIRST PROFESSOR OF EGYPTOLOGY

249 'If I knew there were still some years' Quoted in Hartleben: 573.
249 'that it was a work which if he should live' Quoted in Robinson, *The Last Man Who Knew Everything*: 235.
250 'par-dessous M. Pardessus' Champollion, *Lettres de Champollion le Jeune*, vol. 2: 406.
252 'His goal was a monument' Curran et al: 251. For a thorough discussion of Champollion's publicly unacknowledged role in the transfer of the Luxor obelisk to Paris, see the Epilogue, 'L'absent de l'obélisque', by Jean Vidal, in Lacouture: 473–92.
254 'I owe everything to Blacas' Quoted in Hartleben: 553.

254 'was now too tormented' Quoted in Hartleben: 522. My account of French political developments in 1830 is based on Price, and also Mansel.
254 'to explain Egypt by the Bible' Quoted in Hartleben: 537.
255 'This scholar brought to the comparative examination' Quoted in Faure: 786.
256 'something like a hieroglyphic alphabet' Young, *Miscellaneous Works*, vol. 3: 182.
256 'supposed enchorial alphabet' Ibid: 183–84.
256 'defective in principle' Quoted in Solé and Valbelle: 153. A translated extract from Champollion's inaugural lecture appears as Appendix 4 in Solé and Valbelle: 147–55.
258 'Only one month more' Quoted in Hartleben: 577.
258 'Death lies in wait for me' Quoted in Lacouture: 464.
258 'It is there that my science was born' Quoted in Hartleben: 583.
259 'Look after it carefully' Quoted in preface to Champollion, *Grammaire égyptienne*: iv.
259 'So soon – there are still' Quoted in Hartleben: 585.
259 'And now for the afterlife' Quoted in Lacouture: 468.
260 'The admirable works of your brother' Quoted in Aimé Champollion-Figeac, *Les Deux Champollion*: 106.

XVI THE HIEROGLYPHS AFTER CHAMPOLLION

261 'A man has departed' An alternative recent translation of this well-known hieratic papyrus (Chester Beatty IV, verso 3.7–11, in the British Museum) appears in Parkinson, *Voices from Ancient Egypt*: 150.
262 'We do not wish to say' Quoted in Dewachter: 131.
262 'The debate continues' Quoted in Lacouture: 470.
265 'In the month of March 1832' Preface to Champollion, *Dictionnaire égyptien*: iii.
265 'But though complete in design' Griffith: 65.

266 'In the general order of the divisions'
Quoted in introduction to Budge: xxxi. A
well-known current dictionary is Raymond
O. Faulkner's *A Concise Dictionary of Middle
Egyptian* (Oxford: Griffith Institute,
1976), which uses an arrangement based
on the hieroglyphic 'alphabet'. But this
dictionary is useful only to already-
trained Egyptologists. It has therefore
been supplemented by David Shennum's
*English–Egyptian Index of Faulkner's
Concise Dictionary of Middle Egyptian*
(Malibu, Calif.: Undena Publications,
1977), which permits the user to find all
the hieroglyphic equivalents of an English
word, listed by their page number in
Faulkner's dictionary.

267 'In reality Coptic is a' Griffith: 65.

268 'In addition to the defects' Hincks,
'An attempt to ascertain': 135–36.

269 'I was, for a certain period' Quoted
in Renouf, *Letters*, vol. 4: 117.

269 'only now did Champollion's
decipherment' Parkinson, *Cracking
Codes*: 42.

270 'One of the greatest embarrassments'
Lepsius: 21–22.

271 'phonetic hieroglyphs' This table appears
in Champollion, *Grammaire égyptienne*:
35–46.

271 'general phonetic alphabet' Lepsius: 42.

271 'hieroglyphic signs for the vulture' Ray,
'Edward Hincks and the progress of
Egyptology', in Cathcart (ed.), *Edward
Hincks Bicentenary Lectures*: 60.

272 'Hieroglyphic writing is a complex
system' Champollion, *Précis* (1824): 327.

POSTSCRIPT: POLYMATHS AND
GENIUSES

280 'Two undeniable facts remain' Renouf,
'Young and Champollion': 208.

280 'one thing is sure' Hartleben: 604.

BIBLIOGRAPHY

Very little of Champollion's writings has been translated into English – not even the *Lettre à M. Dacier*. This is not surprising, since the original papers and books are of interest primarily to professional Egyptologists and historians of Egyptology. The obvious exceptions are the letters and journal relating to his Egyptian expedition of 1828–29, which were published in 1833. Extracts from these appear in *Egyptian Diaries* (2001) and give a vivid picture of Champollion's personality, although the translation is not entirely accurate.

As for memoirs and biographies of Champollion, none has been published in English. The closest to a biography is *The Keys of Egypt: The Race to Read the Hieroglyphs* by Lesley and Roy Adkins, published in 2000. As its title implies, this book concentrates on Champollion's decipherment, the meaning of the hieroglyphs and the development of Egyptology; however, the authors display limited understanding of writing systems and provide no references for their many quotations from French sources. Even in French, no biography of Champollion appeared until the 20th century. The first ever biography was published in German in 1906 by Hermine Hartleben, a schoolteacher who worked in Egypt; it was not translated into French until as late as 1984, in an abridged version. Hartleben's work is inevitably out of date, but as a labour of love it remains a valuable historical source if read with scepticism. The biography by the political journalist and biographer Jean Lacouture, published in 1988, is much better written than Hartleben's book; it is excellent on Champollion's life and personality, but weak on the details of the decipherment and the development of Egyptology. A biography by Alain Faure, a historian of Dauphiné who was born in the region, was published in 2004 and is strongest on Champollion's life in Grenoble. Strangely, these three works contain hardly a hieroglyph in the text (not a single one in the cases of Hartleben and Lacouture). For an account of Champollion in French by an Egyptologist, which also includes some hieroglyphs, one may turn to Michel Dewachter's very brief but attractively illustrated book published in 1990, which features a useful section of original documents.

Books for the non-specialist on ancient Egypt as a whole, including the hieroglyphs, are too numerous to comment on individually. Some of the best appear in the bibliography below. It is, however, worth singling out a well-researched and well-cast six-part television series produced by the BBC in 2005: entitled *Egypt: Rediscovering a Lost World*, it is currently available on DVD. Two of its episodes, 'The Mystery of the Rosetta Stone' and 'The Secrets of the Hieroglyphs', dramatize Champollion's life and work.

SELECTED BOOKS BY JEAN-FRANÇOIS CHAMPOLLION:

Panthéon égyptien: Collection des personnages mythologiques de l'ancienne Égypte, Paris: Firmin-Didot, 1823–25

Précis du système hiéroglyphique des anciens Égyptiens, Paris: Treuttel & Würtz, 1824; 2nd edn Paris: Imprimerie Royale, 1828

Monuments de l'Égypte et de la Nubie d'après les dessins exécutés sur les lieux sous la direction de Champollion le jeune et les descriptions autographes qu'il a laissées (ed. J.-J. Champollion-Figeac), 4 vols, Paris: Firmin-Didot, 1835–45

Grammaire égyptienne, ou Principes généraux de la langue sacrée égyptienne appliquée à la représentation de la langue parlée (ed. J.-J. Champollion-Figeac), Paris: Firmin-Didot, 1836

Dictionnaire égyptien en écriture hiéroglyphique (ed. J.-J. Champollion-Figeac), Paris: Firmin-Didot, 1841–43

Champollion inconnu: Lettres inédites (ed. L. de la Brière), Paris: Plon, 1897

Lettres de Champollion le Jeune (ed. H. Hartleben): vol. 1: *Lettres écrites d'Italie*; vol. 2: *Lettres et journaux écrits pendant le voyage d'Égypte*, Paris: Ernest Leroux, 1909

Lettre à M. Dacier, relative à l'alphabet des hiéroglyphes phonétiques, centenary edn, Paris: Firmin-Didot, 1922 (preface by Henri Sottas)

Lettres à Zelmire (ed. Edda Bresciani), Paris: Éditions l'Asiathèque, 1978 (preface by Jean Leclant)

Lettres à son frère 1804–1818 (ed. Pierre Vaillant), Paris: Éditions l'Asiathèque, 1984

L'Égypte de Jean-François Champollion: Lettres & journaux de voyage (1828–1829), Suresnes: Image/Magie, 1989 (preface by Christiane Ziegler, photographs by Hervé Champollion)

Egyptian Diaries: How One Man Solved the Mysteries of the Nile, London: Gibson Square Books, 2001 (reissued as *The Code-Breaker's Secret Diaries*, London: Gibson Square Books, 2009, with a preface by Joyce Tyldesley)

BOOKS AND ARTICLES BY OTHERS

Adkins, Lesley, and Adkins, Roy, *The Keys of Egypt: The Race to Read the Hieroglyphs*, London: HarperCollins, 2000

Andrews, Carol, *The Rosetta Stone*, London: British Museum Publications, 1981

Baines, John, *Visual and Written Culture in Ancient Egypt*, Oxford: Oxford University Press, 2007

Ballard, Richard, *The Unseen Terror: The French Revolution in the Provinces*, London: I.B. Tauris, 2010

Bednarski, Andrew, *Holding Egypt: Tracing the Reception of the 'Description de l'Égypte' in Nineteenth-Century Great Britain*, London: Golden House, 2005

Belzoni, Giovanni, *Belzoni's Travels: Narrative of the Operations and Recent Discoveries in Egypt and Nubia* (ed. Alberto Siliotti), London: British Museum Press, 2001

Buchwald, Jed Z., and Josefowicz, Diane Greco, *The Zodiac of Paris: How an Improbable Controversy over an Ancient Egyptian Artifact Provoked a Modern Debate between Religion and Science*, Princeton, N.J.: Princeton University Press, 2010

Budge, E. A. Wallis, *An Egyptian Hieroglyphic Dictionary*, 2 vols, London: John Murray, 1920

Burleigh, Nina, *Mirage: Napoleon's Scientists and the Unveiling of Egypt*, New York: HarperCollins, 2007

Carter, Howard, and Mace, A. C., *The Tomb of Tut.Ankh.Amen*, London: Cassell, 1923

Cathcart, Kevin J. (ed.), *The Edward Hincks Bicentenary Lectures*, Dublin: University College Dublin, Department of Near Eastern Languages, 1994

Champollion-Figeac, Aimé, *Les Deux Champollion: leur vie et leurs oeuvres, leur correspondance archéologique relative au Dauphiné et à l'Égypte*, Grenoble: Xavier Drevet, 1887

Champollion-Figeac, Jacques-Joseph, *Fourier et Napoléon: L'Égypte et les cent jours*, Paris: Firmin-Didot, 1844

Clayton, Peter A., *The Rediscovery of Ancient Egypt: Artists and Travellers in the 19th Century*, London and New York: Thames & Hudson, 1982

Collier, Mark, and Manley, Bill, *How to Read Egyptian Hieroglyphs: A Step-by-Step Guide to Teach Yourself*, London: British Museum Press, 1998

Curl, James Stevens, *The Egyptian Revival: Ancient Egypt as the Inspiration for Design Motifs in the West*, London: Routledge, 2005

Curran, Brian A., et al., *Obelisk: A History*, Cambridge, Mass.: MIT Press, 2009

Davies, W. V., *Egyptian Hieroglyphs*, London: British Museum Publications, 1987

Denon, Dominique Vivant, *Travels in Upper and Lower Egypt, during the Campaigns of General Bonaparte*, 2 vols, 2nd edn, London: J. Cundee, 1803

Description de l'Égypte, Cologne: Taschen, 2007

Dewachter, Michel, *Champollion: Un scribe pour l'Égypte*, Paris: Gallimard, 1990

Downs, Jonathan, *Discovery at Rosetta: The Stone that Unlocked the Mysteries of Ancient Egypt*, London: Constable & Robinson, 2008

El-Daly, Okasha, *Egyptology: The Missing Millennium: Ancient Egypt in Medieval Arabic Writings*, London: UCL Press, 2005

Faure, Alain, *Champollion: Le savant dechiffré*, Paris: Fayard, 2004

Findlen, Paula (ed.), *Athanasius Kircher: The Last Man Who Knew Everything*, London: Routledge, 2004

Griffith, Francis Llewellyn, 'The centenary of Egyptology', *Times Literary Supplement*, 2 Feb. 1922, 65–66 (republished as 'The decipherment of the hieroglyphs', *Journal of Egyptian Archaeology*, 37 (1951), 38–46

[Gurney, Hudson], 'Memoir [of Young]', in Young, *Rudiments of an Egyptian Dictionary*, 5–47

Hamilton, Alastair, *The Copts and the West 1439–1822: The European Discovery of the Egyptian Church*, Oxford: Oxford University Press, 2006

Hartleben, Hermine, *Champollion: Sa vie et son oeuvre 1790–1832*, Paris: Pygmalion/ Gérard Watelet, 1984 (abridged translation of Hartleben's two-volume biography *Champollion: Sein Leben und Sein Werk*, Berlin: Weidmannsche Buchhandlung, 1906)

Herivel, John, *Joseph Fourier: The Man and the Physicist*, Oxford: Clarendon Press, 1975

Hincks, Edward, 'An attempt to ascertain the number, names, and powers, of the letters of the hieroglyphic, or ancient Egyptian alphabet; grounded on the establishment of a new principle in the use of phonetic characters', *Transactions of the Royal Irish Academy*, 21 (1847), 132–232

——, *The Correspondence of Edward Hincks* (ed. Kevin J. Cathcart), 3 vols, Dublin: University College Dublin Press, 2007–9

[Horapollo], *The Hieroglyphs of Horapollo* (trans. George Boas), Princeton, N.J.: Princeton University Press, 1993

Iversen, Erik, *The Myth of Egypt and Its Hieroglyphs*, Princeton, N.J.: Princeton University Press, 1993

Jacq, Christian, *Champollion the Egyptian* (trans. Geraldine le Roy), London: Pocket Books, 2003

Lacouture, Jean, *Champollion: Une vie de lumières*, Paris: Grasset, 1988

Leclant, Jean, 'Aux sources de l'Égyptologie Européenne: Champollion, Young, Rosellini, Lepsius', *Comptes-rendus des* séances de l'Académie des Inscriptions et Belles-Lettres, 135 (1991), 743–62

Lepsius, Karl Richard, Lettre à M. le Professeur H. Rosellini sur l'alphabet hiéroglyphique, Rome, 1837

Mansel, Philip, Paris between Empires, 1814–1852, London: John Murray, 2001

——, 'The man who remade Alexandria', History Today, Dec. 2010, 26–32

Memoires d'Egypte: Hommage de l'Europe à Champollion, Strasbourg: La Nuée Bleue, 1990

A New Description of Sir John Soane's Museum, 11th rev. edn, London: Trustees of Sir John Soane's Museum, 2007

Parkinson, Richard B., Voices from Ancient Egypt: An Anthology of Middle Kingdom Writings, London: British Museum Press, 1991

——, The Tale of Sinuhe and Other Ancient Egyptian Poems 1940–1640 BC, Oxford: Oxford University Press, 1998

——, Cracking Codes: The Rosetta Stone and Decipherment, London: British Museum Press, 1999

——, The Rosetta Stone, London: British Museum Press, 2005

Peacock, George, Life of Thomas Young, M.D., F.R.S., London: John Murray, 1855

Pope, Maurice, The Story of Decipherment: From Egyptian Hieroglyphs to Maya Script, rev. edn, London and New York: Thames & Hudson, 1999

Price, Munro, The Perilous Crown: France between Revolutions, London: Pan, 2008

Ray, John, 'The name of the first: Thomas Young and the decipherment of Egyptian writing' (unpublished lecture)

——, Reflections of Osiris: Lives from Ancient Egypt, London: Profile, 2001

——, The Rosetta Stone and the Rebirth of Ancient Egypt, London: Profile, 2007

Reeves, Nicholas, and Wilkinson, Richard H., The Complete Valley of the Kings: Tombs and Treasures of Egypt's Greatest Pharaohs, London and New York: Thames & Hudson, 1996

Renouf, Peter le Page, 'Young and Champollion', Proceedings of the Society of Biblical Archaeology, 19 (1897), 188–209

——, The Letters of Peter le Page Renouf (ed. Kevin J. Cathcart), 4 vols, Dublin: University College Dublin Press, 2002–4

Ridley, Ronald T., Napoleon's Proconsul in Egypt: The Life and Times of Bernardino Drovetti, London: Rubicon Press, 1998

Robinson, Andrew, The Man Who Deciphered Linear B: The Story of Michael Ventris, London and New York: Thames & Hudson, 2002

——, The Last Man Who Knew Everything: Thomas Young, The Anonymous Polymath Who Proved Newton Wrong, Explained How We See, Cured the Sick, and Deciphered the Rosetta Stone, among Other Feats of Genius, Oxford: Oneworld, 2007

——, Lost Languages: The Enigma of the World's Undeciphered Scripts, rev. edn, London and New York: Thames & Hudson, 2009

——, Sudden Genius? The Gradual Path to Creative Breakthroughs, Oxford: Oxford University Press, 2010

Rosellini, Ippolito, The Monuments of Egypt and Nubia, Cairo: American University in Cairo Press, 2003

Shaw, Ian, and Nicholson, Paul, The British Museum Dictionary of Ancient Egypt, 2nd edn, London: British Museum Press, 2008

Solé, Robert, and Valbelle, Dominique, The Rosetta Stone: The Story of the Decoding of Hieroglyphics (trans. Steven Rendall), London: Profile, 2001

Taylor, John H. (ed.), Journey Through the Afterlife: Ancient Egyptian Book of the Dead, London: British Museum Press, 2010

Thompson, Jason, Edward William Lane 1801–1876: The Life of the Pioneering Egyptologist and Orientalist, London: Haus, 2010

Usick, Patricia, Adventures in Egypt and Nubia: The Travels of William John Bankes (1786–1855), London: British Museum Press, 2002

Wilkinson, Richard H., Reading Egyptian Art: A Hieroglyphic Guide to Ancient Egyptian Painting and Sculpture, London and New York: Thames & Hudson, 1992

Young, Thomas, Rudiments of an Egyptian Dictionary in the Ancient Enchorial Character, London: J. and A. Arch, 1831

——, Miscellaneous Works of the Late Thomas Young, M.D., F.R.S., vol. 3 (ed. John Leitch), Bristol: Thoemmes Press, 2003 (reprinted from the 1855 edn)

LIST OF ILLUSTRATIONS

INDEX

Page numbers in *italics* refer
to illustrations

INDEX